J. S. WOOLEY

Generously supported by a gift in honor of The Randel Family

J. S. Wooley

ADIRONDACK PHOTOGRAPHER

Edited by Richard Timberlake *and* Philip Terrie

With a Foreword by Robert Bogdan

SYRACUSE UNIVERSITY PRESS

First Edition 2018
18 19 20 21 22 23 6 5 4 3 2 1

∞ The paper used in this publication meets the minimum requirements of the American National Standard for Information Sciences—Permanence of Paper for Printed Library Materials, ANSI Z39.48-1992.

For a listing of books published and distributed by Syracuse University Press, visit www.SyracuseUniversityPress.syr.edu.

ISBN: 978-0-8156-1096-0 (hardcover)

Library of Congress Cataloging-in-Publication Data

Names: Timberlake, Richard, editor. | Terrie, Philip G., editor. | Wooley, Jesse Sumner, 1895–1930. Photographs. Selections.

Title: J.S. Wooley, Adirondack photographer / edited by Richard Timberlake and Philip Terrie ; with a foreword by Robert Bogdan.

Description: Syracuse, New York : Syracuse University Press, 2018. | Includes bibliographical references and index.

Identifiers: LCCN 2018009365 | ISBN 9780815610960 (hardcover : alk. paper)

Subjects: LCSH: Wooley, Jesse Sumner, 1895-1930. | Photographers—United States—Biography. | Adirondack Mountains Region (N.Y.)—Pictorial works.

Classification: LCC TR140.W3935 J36 2018 | DDC 770.92 [B]—dc23 LC record available at https://lccn.loc.gov/2018009365

Manufactured in the United States of America

For Matt Finley

Contents

Foreword

ROBERT BOGDAN

THE COLLABORATORS who are responsible for this book deserve a big thank you. Their vigilant work explores a gifted and prolific but little known upstate New York photographer, Jessie Wooley. However, the book is about more than just Wooley. The authors direct us to a missing chapter in the history of photography, the work of talented early twentieth-century professional town photographers.

Professional town photographers were commercial picture takers who had studios in minor population centers across the United States and focused their photography business on serving clients in their immediate vicinity. Some found that staying within such narrow geographic confines did not match their vocational goals. To compensate, in addition to photographing their own towns, they took to the road, traveling around their regions.

Although most town photographers were not as successful, skilled, or broadly traveled as Wooley, Wooley was one of these gifted town picture takers. Such photographers settled in every state, and each state had a few particularly noteworthy commercial town photographers. A few stand out: Edward Beebe and Louis Pesha in Michigan, Fredrick Marchant and Ellsworth Eddy in North Carolina, Solomon Butcher in Nebraska, Nelson Calkins in Pennsylvania, John Dedrick in Kansas, Walther Horne in Texas, John Inbody in Indiana, Arthur Kingsbury in Wisconsin, Ole Leeland in South Dakota, Frank Matsura in Washington, Ben Russell in Oklahoma, and Walter Oxley in Minnesota.[1] New York State was especially blessed with, in addition to Wooley, William Mandeville of Lowville, William Kollecker of Saranac Lake, Henry Beach of Remsen, and Herbert Myer of Jordan, to name just a few.[2]

Note that all the photographers listed above were men. Although there were a few female town photographers, the field was dominated by men. Some of the well-known photographers had wives and other female assistants who were active in the business; some took the images attributed to their male collaborators. Their contribution is not yet documented.

Historians of photography have not given the work of town photographers the attention it deserves. Their work, if celebrated at all, is noted only by amateur historians working in the specific regions where the photographers worked. These photographers' legacy is a rich and detailed visual record of aspects of town and rural life as well as of the surrounding landscape. They lived in the places they shot, so they knew the nooks and crannies of the geographical and social landscape and had an intimate knowledge of the people they photographed. They were there in all seasons, at all events, and when others might say nothing was happening, during the routines of everyday life. Before the phrase "documentary photography" was used to describe the work of certain elite photographers, town photographers were doing documentary work as insiders.

Wooley and many of the other village photographers came to their trade at the end of the nineteenth century. The most common photographic formats then were the CDV, cabinet card, and stereo card. By the turn of the century these forms, images mounted on stiff cardboard and uniform in size, had outlived their appeal. Wooley started his career producing these forms, but he and other town photographers realized that they would not sustain their businesses. At the same time, with the development of new technology and cameras that amateurs could easily use, photography was becoming popular among the masses. "You push the button, we do the rest," a Kodak sales slogan, captured the photography industry's appeal to ordinary people. With so many common people taking their own pictures, town photographers' trade was further undermined.

To counter these trends and help town photographers remain in business, many commercial town photographers embraced two emerging forms of photography: photo postcards and panoramic photographs. Postcards became wildly popular. The first commercially produced photographic postcard stock (i.e., photo paper with one side designated for an address that could be sent through the mail) appeared at the end of the nineteenth century. This format dominated amateur as well as commercial photography by 1907. With their studio clientele in decline, commercial photographers produced high-quality photo postcards of local vistas to sell wholesale to local resorts, local stores, and other retail businesses. They also sold them retail in their own shops. Additionally, by taking advantage of the postcard craze, they could print studio portraits on the popular and inexpensive postcard stock. The postcard studio portrait lured customers to their premises because portraits were inexpensive and in vogue.

Another format local commercial photographers embraced was the panoramic photograph, pictures that were significantly longer than they were tall. Cameras that produced this type of picture also became popular with commercial photographers early in the twentieth century. Panoramic cameras were especially effective in taking expansive scenes and pictures of large groups. The Cirkut camera that came on the market in 1904 was one such panoramic camera. It took unusually large, disproportionally long photographs. Although the photos produced by the camera were popularly called "yard long photos," the camera was capable of turning out exposures much longer than thirty-six inches. Wooley employed a Cirkut camera in his commercial work mainly to take pictures of large gatherings of people at special events. This was lucrative because each of the large number of subjects in each picture was a potential buyer. Wooly also embraced cameras that took smaller panoramic photographs. Customers favored scenery shots over group images. These smaller panoramic photos were easy to produce and they could be sold as part of the photographer's regular stock in their shop and at other stores. Some small panoramic photos were printed on special postcard stock that was produced to accommodate the long shape.

Although photo postcards and panoramic pictures helped to keep town photographers in the business of picture taking, the proliferation of amateur photographers required commercial photographers to embrace other forms of commerce to be viable. They gravitated to becoming proprietors of stores that catered to the amateur. They sold cameras and photography supplies and offered developing and finishing photographic services. Wooley remained a photographer, but he also ran a successful photography store and more.

Many town photographers, like Wooley, were talented technicians who took pictures that met the high technical standards of the times, which contributed to the quality of visual documentation available. Wooley was proud to embrace the new technology. As a dealer in Kodak products, he regularly received information on the latest products from Kodak. His openness to new technology was also apparent outside of his photography. He was one of the first in his town to have an automobile.

Wooley was a town photographer who defined himself as an artist. This can be seen in his advertisements, where he describes himself as an artist. He had strong aesthetic sensibilities, what is commonly called "a good eye." He produced pictures that were both moving and beautiful, the kind of work we attribute to people given the honorary title of "artist." He and other town photographers might have seen themselves as artists, but that title was coveted by elite photographers in urban circles who were fighting to have their work appreciated as an art form on par with paintings and sculpture.

Although Wooley was just one of many superb village photographers operating in the United States, other aspects of his life and work set him apart from the crowd. Because of the public nature of what they did, most village photographers were well known in their communities. Wooley was more prominent than most. He was an accomplished entrepreneur. His business in Ballston Spa was centrally located. In addition to being a photography studio, it was the town's exclusive seller of Kodak cameras and accessories. He and his staff processed and printed film and offered other popular nonphotographic merchandise such as Victrolas, cylinder and gramophone records (Caruso was Wooley's favorite performer), fountain pens, and art supplies.

Wooley's visibility was enhanced by his civic activities. While other photographers might be respected business people, Wooley was a community leader. Throughout his professional life Wooley held offices in the Baptist church, including trustee and deacon. Later in life he was given the title of Honorary Deacon in recognition of his lifetime service to the church. He served as president of the Ballston Spa Chamber of Commerce and during WWI he worked for the Red Cross. His work with the church led him to be engaged as the photographer for Silver Bay, a Christian youth and missionary conference and training center. From 1908 until 1923 he was the official resident summer photographer.

His position in the community was improved by his marriage to Susan Arnold Wooley. Although Wooley came from a family of poor farmers, Susan's family was prominent in the community. She was attractive and fashion conscious. Wooley adopted his wife's dress style and the couple was strikingly handsome. They were regulars at community affairs.

What also made Wooley somewhat special in the category of village photographer is the intensity with which he practiced his trade. He loved to take pictures and seldom was without his camera. He tried different approaches to taking pictures, and he kept up with the latest equipment and often incorporated photographic innovation into his work. He mastered particular forms of photography that other village photographers might have overlooked. As the illustrations in this book show, he crafted his pictures using various formats in ways that maximize their strengths. This is particularly striking in his panoramic views. He used the broad scope of the panoramic format to create the moods of the expansive landscapes he captured.

Unlike most local photographers, Wooley traveled far from his town's geographic area. Although the majority of his photographs are of eastern New York State in the areas around Ballston Spa and Lake George, he traveled to Chicago for the 1893 Columbian World's Fair, to the West to the national parks, to Florida, and abroad. He captured all of these sojourns with his camera and gave lantern slideshow lectures in and around Ballston Spa. Although his travel might lead one to cast him as cosmopolitan, his photographs and notes suggest that he processed his travel through the eyes of a town photographer in a strange land. For example, his photos and commentary about poor, rural African Americans reinforce racial stereotypes. The quality of his photographs transcended the ordinary, but he remained a local. Wooley's photographic travel record provides important documentation of faraway places, but his best work came from the environs in which he was most comfortable. His longtime association with Silver Bay, a location that he embraced, produced some of his most beautiful views of the Lake George area.

What I have said about Wooley and his work is covered with in-depth elaboration in the pages that follow. The different authors bring their special expertise to bear on the various aspects of Wooley's life and work, covering his biography, the aesthetics of his images, camera technology, the history of the Adirondack region, and the larger historical context in which Wooley operated.

In 1912, Jess Wooley was at Silver Bay photographing the scenery including young Christians lined up by the shore wearing period swimsuits that covered most of their bodies. Fifteen miles down Lake George, near his summer home at Bolton Landing, Alfred Stieglitz was taking pictures too.[3] Cloud formations over the lake were a favorite subject of Stieglitz, as well as pictures of his partner, Georgia O'Keeffe, frolicking nude in the water. An intellectual from New York City, Stieglitz was an ardent advocate and leader of the "photography is art" movement. He issued limited editions of his work and displayed them in New York galleries. Stieglitz is now considered one of the most influential and important photographers in the history of the practice. During the same period, Wooley was making photo postcards and panoramic photographs on demand and selling them at his stores. He remains unknown and unimportant outside of the confines of the Ballston Spa/Lake George area. Juxtaposing Wooley's and Stieglitz's Adirondack photography provides an extreme illustration of a great disparity between those who produced photos within the framework of the world of art photography and town photographers.

The written history of photography is dominated by the lives and work of photographers like Stieglitz who operated out of America's urban centers, especially New York City. It was there in the early twentieth century that photography became defined as an art form and those at the center of that movement came to define which photographers were important. Town photographers operated in a different world, a world not honored or even recognized by photography's emerging elite. This book about Wooley not only presents the work of a talented and prolific but relatively unknown photographer, but also calls to us to seek out others like him so that we can better understand the range of photographic work of the period and broaden our history of the enterprise.

Acknowledgments

THIS BOOK, which has been a long time coming, is truly a collaborative effort, beginning with the authors of these chapters, each of whom thanks the others for amiable and cooperative interaction.

Gardner Finley, former historian of the Town of Bolton on Lake George, collected antiques, along with a substantial number of Wooley photographs, negatives, and glass slides. This was part of lifelong interest in the history of his family, involving both Ballston Spa, in Saratoga County, and Silver Bay, on Lake George. After Gardner Finley's death in 2002, his son Matt reviewed the extensive collection in his father's house with a friend, Henry Caldwell, owner of the Black Bass Antiques shop in Bolton Landing. Henry and Matt quickly identified the Wooley collection as something extraordinary, but work and other obligations kept Wooley on the back burner. After Matt sold the house to his childhood friend Kathy Conover and her husband Ron, Kathy, who became an admirer of Wooley's photography and an early advocate of this project, examined the Wooley materials and discussed their value with Matt, who agreed that they should be made into a book. Kathy was working in Henry's shop at the time and promoted the photos to interested visitors. That is where Lance DeMuro, a collector and lifelong resident of Lake George, first discovered the Wooley negatives while visiting Black Bass Antiques. He contacted Richard Timberlake, a photographer who was immediately impressed with the quality of Wooley's work. Richard began the process of proofing and cataloging the collection. He and Matt began discussing the possibility of a book focusing on Wooley's Lake George panoramas in 2011; Phil Terrie was brought on board in 2012, Caroline Welsh and Jamie Young joined the team in 2013, and we have all spent quite a few years organizing, researching, and presenting our various takes on Wooley and his work. Along the way we have acquired many debts to a variety of individuals who helped to advance this project.

Hoping that we are not omitting anyone, we express our thanks to the following: Frank Goodyear at the National Portrait Gallery; Jerry Pepper and Laura Rice at Adirondack Experience: The Museum on Blue Mountain Lake (formerly known as the Adirondack Museum); Kathleen Coleman, Carolyn McGraw-Walker, Joy Houle, and Jeanne Obermayer at the Brookside Museum of the Saratoga County Historical Society; Steven Hersh and Eduardo Rabel at the University of Miami; the Bowling Green State University Interlibrary Loan Department; librarians at Cornell University and Ithaca College; Henry Caldwell at Black Bass Antiques; Todd DeGarmo at the Crandall Library; Tony Hall at the *Lake George Mirror*; Harriet Brown; Ted Comstock; Bruce Ronda; John Cromie; Charles Hogan; Caroline Verner; Steve Milanowski, who spent endless hours in the darkroom; Lee Hayes for his technical and reproduction abilities; Kathy Conover; Ron Conover; Lance DeMuro; William Preston Gates; Denise Jordan Finley; Kam Hoopes; Elizabeth Schultheiss; and David Martucci. Special thanks are due to

Robert Bogdan, who blazed the trail and shared his extensive and invaluable Wooley files.

Most of all, this project is immeasurably indebted to Matt Finley, to whom this book is dedicated. Matt has committed significant personal resources and energy to pushing this book to publication.

J. S. WOOLEY

Seeing through the Lens

Photographing Adirondack Life and Landscape

CAROLINE M. WELSH

PHOTOGRAPHY, the taking and making of photographs, has a rich history in the Adirondacks. This overview of that history provides a regional context for the life and work of Jesse Sumner Wooley, a successful entrepreneur and photographer, who flourished from the 1880s through the 1930s.

Noted curator and historian of photography John Szarkowski cogently distinguished the difference between photography and painting:

> The invention of photography provided a radically new picture-making process—a process based not on synthesis but on selection. The difference was a basic one. Paintings were made—constructed from a storehouse of traditional schemes and skills and attitudes—but photographs, as the man on the street put it, were taken.[1]

Even more than art, photographs documented and promoted the Adirondack region of upstate New York for a national and international audience. For more than 150 years, the Adirondack Mountains have been known as a wilderness preserve, a destination for tourists, a paradise for sportsmen, a home for generations, a bountiful lode of natural resources, a laboratory for evolving ecological and environmental thought, and a place of inspiration for artists, poets, writers, philosophers, and historians.

Photographs lured people by the thousands to the Adirondacks and conversely brought the place, in published and unpublished form, to even greater numbers elsewhere. From the 1870s on, the camera captured a physically exact and highly detailed record of Adirondack culture and landscape. Cameras documented everyday life and people at work and play on a scale unprecedented in a place that made such activities challenging by its remoteness. And, for the first time, photographs made the ordinary seem important. While making a fine art painting required training and expertise, taking a photograph could be done by amateurs as well as professionals.

From the 1830s through the 1870s, discoveries in natural science and new knowledge about the natural world stimulated interconnections, begun in the Renaissance, between art, literature, and science, especially among those who adhered to the philosophy of British artist, poet-theoretician, and social and art critic John Ruskin (1819–1900). Ruskin believed that art must be an exact reflection of the details seen in nature and he saw that photographs could record the minute details he valued.[2] With the advent of photography, painters vied with photographers to make the most literal transcriptions of nature, focusing on scientific precision and meticulous rendering of natural details. There is evidence that a number of landscape artists studied photography and in fact relied on photography to supplement their memories of scenes in nature, to depict three-dimensional space, and to create impressions of natural phenomena.[3] From the 1850s to the present, the photographers' low-angle or eye-level perspective captured mountain views, scenes of lakes, streams, and bogs, forest interiors, flora, and fauna, and aspects of geology, geography, and topography, along with views of human activity *in* nature. Among these photographs were works of art that captured nature's textures, colors, and forms and the poetic qualities of light and atmosphere in carefully constructed compositions using traditional pictorial conventions employed by painters,[4] as well as invaluable documents of everyday life and people.

The Beginnings

French scenic artist Louis-Jacques-Mandé Daguerre (1787–1851), along with French father-and-son duo Joseph and Isidore Niepce, was the inventor of the first practical process to capture and create a lasting image, known as a photograph, in 1839.[5] Daguerre successfully recorded an image on a light-sensitive silver-plated copper plate directly in the camera and called the process daguerreotyping. The daguerreotype was a one-of-a-kind positive image and could not be replicated. At the same time, Englishman William Henry Fox Talbot also pioneered a form of photography called callotype that used paper negatives. Talbot's work caught the attention of the young Queen Victoria, who ultimately collected 20,000 photographs chronicling her family as well as historic, artistic, and cultural advancements and events during her reign.[6]

By the end of the 1850s, daguerreotyping was largely replaced by the collodion wet-plate process invented simultaneously in ca. 1850 by Frederic Scott Archer in England and Gustave Le Gray in France. This was a complex and cumbersome process requiring photographic material to be coated, sensitized, exposed, and developed within fifteen minutes, making shooting in the field very difficult. During the 1880s the wet-plate process was supplanted by gelatin dry plates—glass plates that were coated with a photographic emulsion of silver halides suspended in gelatin. This method greatly reduced exposure times and allowed more time for development.[7]

Portrait photography has existed for nearly as long as the camera. Daguerreotype portraiture swept the United States in the 1840s and became a burgeoning business, capturing likenesses without the more expensive services of an artist. However, the lengthy exposure times, five to twelve minutes, often resulted in frozen expressions and less flattering demeanors than those the painter could produce. Nonetheless, the relatively low cost of daguerreotypes and shorter sitting times for the subject led to a general rise in the popularity of photographic portraiture over the painted version in the mid-1800s.[8] Elaborately bound albums were introduced in 1860 to collect photographs of family, friends, celebrities, and events and soon became fixtures in Victorian homes. Portrait photographs documented the economic and social status of the sitter and recorded people as they wanted to be remembered for posterity.[9] Before 1860, the vast majority of all photographs were portraits made in a professional photographer's studio or in the portable stage sets used by itinerant portrait photographers.

The daguerreotype and wet-plate methodologies were overtaken by the dry-plate process in the 1880s. Improvements in equipment and techniques resulted in the more durable and less expensive tintype and carte de visite portraits. Jesse Wooley was among many photographers who launched and conducted thriving businesses at the time of this transition from wet-plate to dry-plate. Wooley chronicled friends, notables, and neighbors in portrait photography in Ballston Spa. Producing albums was also a lucrative aspect of his business.

The earliest Adirondack photograph is likely a daguerreotype portrait of Richard Keese and his wife Lydia Hurlbut Keese, made between 1844 and 1852. Keese, elected to Congress in 1826, was the son of the founder of Keeseville, a town in the northeastern Adirondacks near Elizabethtown. The well-dressed couple exemplifies the growing middle class of the mid-nineteenth century whose affluence was a catalyst for an expanding market in portrait photography. Cityscapes, street scenes, and landscape views prompted travel to see the sites and preserved visual details that often escaped verbal documentation. Daguerre's technology was outmoded by the mid-1850s, although its use lingered into the 1860s in rural areas.

The first known landscape photographs of the Adirondacks were made in 1859 by William James Stillman (1828–1901). Stillman was a Boston artist, founder and first editor of the popular mid-century art journal *The Crayon*, and member of the acclaimed Philosophers' Camp at Follensby Pond, near Tupper Lake, in 1858. That year Stillman summered in the Adirondacks with nine friends, including philosopher Ralph Waldo Emerson, poet James Russell Lowell, and naturalist/scientist Louis Agassiz. They traveled down the Raquette River from Tupper Lake and camped at a spot on secluded Follensby Pond that they called "Camp Maples." Now called the Philosophers'

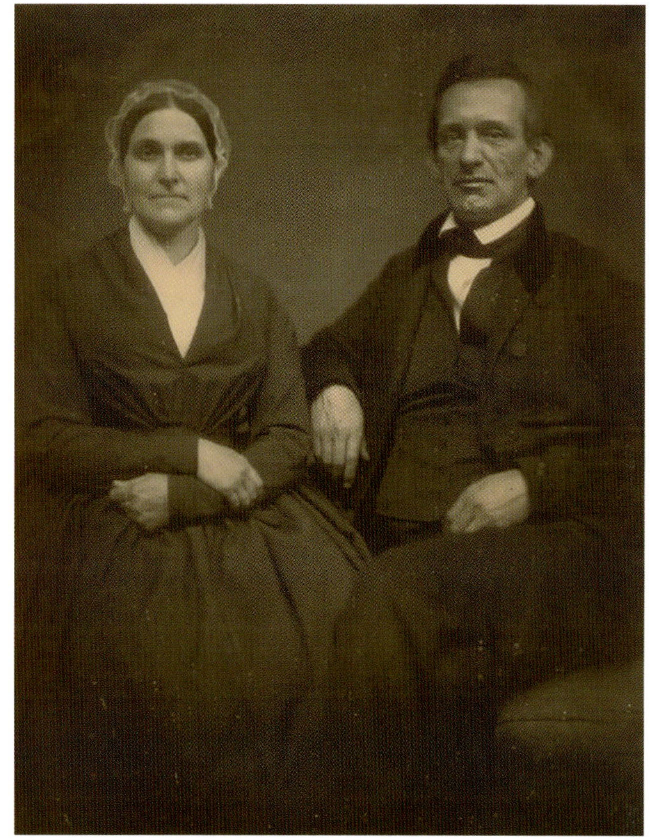

1. *Daguerreotype Portrait of Richard and Lydia Keese.* Courtesy of the Adirondack Experience: The Museum on Blue Mountain Lake, New York, P050882.

Camp, it was one of the most famous gatherings of American intellectuals in the nineteenth century.[10]

Stillman created "still life" photographs of quiet woodland scenes that emphasized the organic details of trees and plants in the same vein as his highly detailed, painted views. Both interpretations adhered to John Ruskin's tenets for capturing the exact details of nature.[11] Stillman's photographs were made from collodion wet-plate glass negatives placed in the back of a wooden box camera without a mechanical lens. The photographer made an image by removing the lens cap and replacing it after the desired exposure had occurred. The negatives were developed in small portable darkrooms that were difficult to manage in the field. The process was able to record microscopically fine detail, a capability Stillman put to good use. Stillman's Adirondack photographs were published in a limited portfolio called *Photographic Studies Part I. The Forest. Adirondac Woods.* His images synthesized the contemporary alliance of aesthetics and scientific knowledge of the species he observed.[12] The viewpoints and subjects made the photographs radical for their time in their introduction of a new way to document nature.[13] They are also noteworthy because they are among the earliest visual records of the forest interior in the Adirondacks. Landscape photography advanced, and became profitable, after the glass dry-plate process made it possible to produce multiple high-resolution prints.[14]

Verplanck Colvin (1847–1920)—lawyer, author, illustrator, and engineer—was named superintendent of the Adirondack Survey, a topographical survey project he had envisioned, in 1872. In 1878, to aid the accuracy and precision of his surveyors and topographers, he organized a photographic division for the Survey.

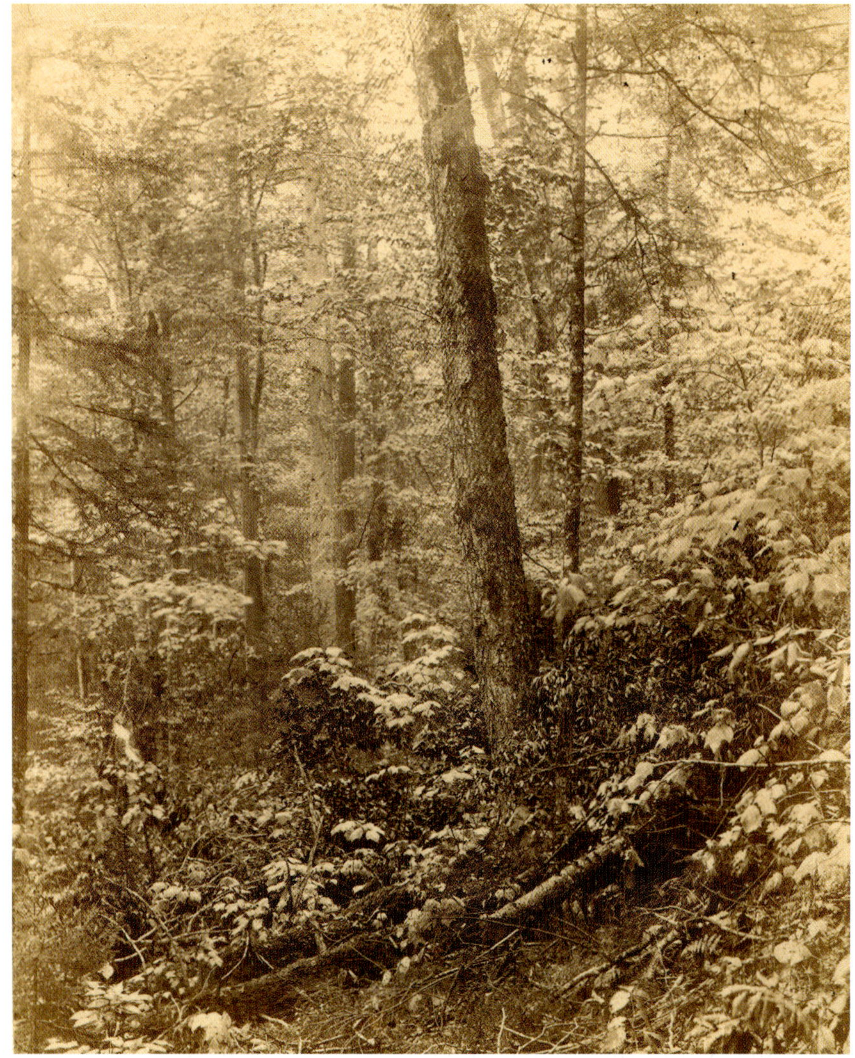

2. *Adirondack Forest*, 1859, William James Stillman. Courtesy of the Adirondack Experience: The Museum on Blue Mountain Lake, New York, P030512.

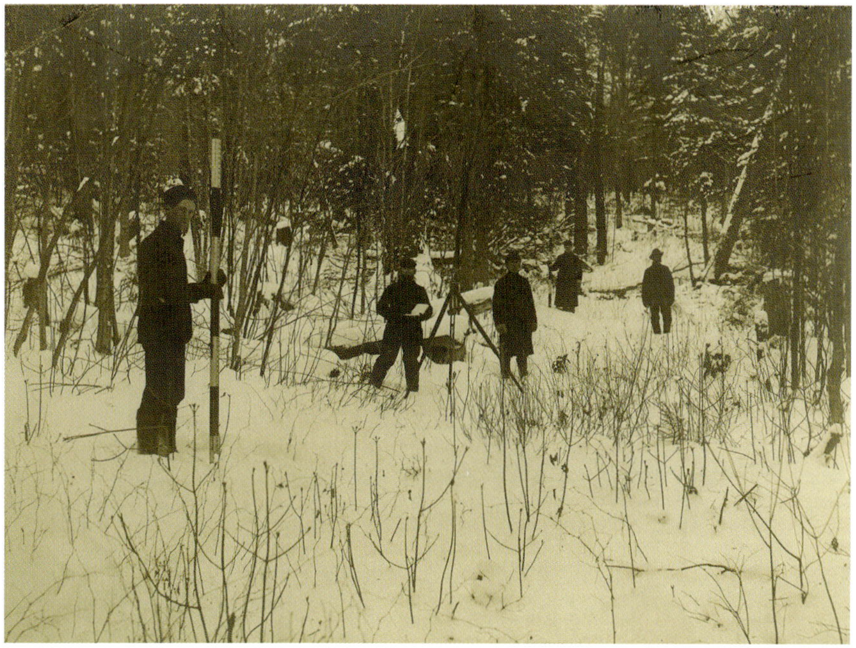

3. *Survey Team 1890*, Verplanck Colvin. Courtesy of the Adirondack Experience: The Museum on Blue Mountain Lake, New York, P011682.

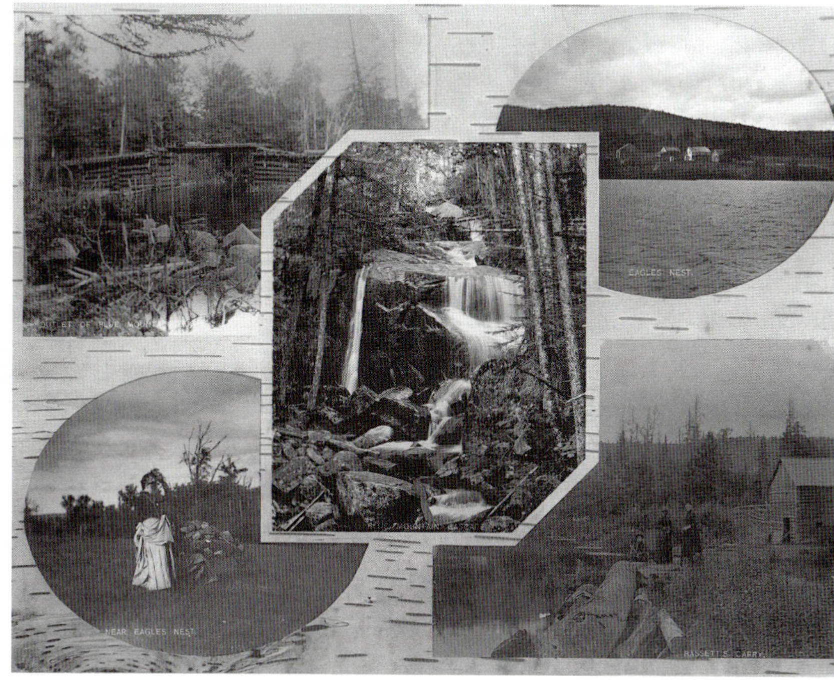

4. *Picturesque Views near Blue Mountain Lake, Adirondacks, N.Y.*, Edward Bierstadt. Courtesy of the Adirondack Experience: The Museum on Blue Mountain Lake, New York, 1965.084.0076.

Adirondack photographer Seneca Ray Stoddard (1843–1917) was one of the Survey photographers, producing around 200 panoramas of the views from Adirondack mountaintops. Colvin printed photographs on albumen paper, an innovation introduced by a German company that was the largest manufacturer of ready-coated photographic papers. Interestingly, his published Survey Reports were illustrated with lithographic drawings based on his and others' photographs because the halftone reproduction process was not yet technologically viable.

Photographs Lure Vacationers

Photographs played a major role in bringing the Adirondacks to the parlors of thousands and encouraging thousands to travel there. Reproductions of paintings in the forms of engravings or lithographs and then photographs illustrated a host of promotional tracts, guidebooks, and articles crafted to lure visitors.

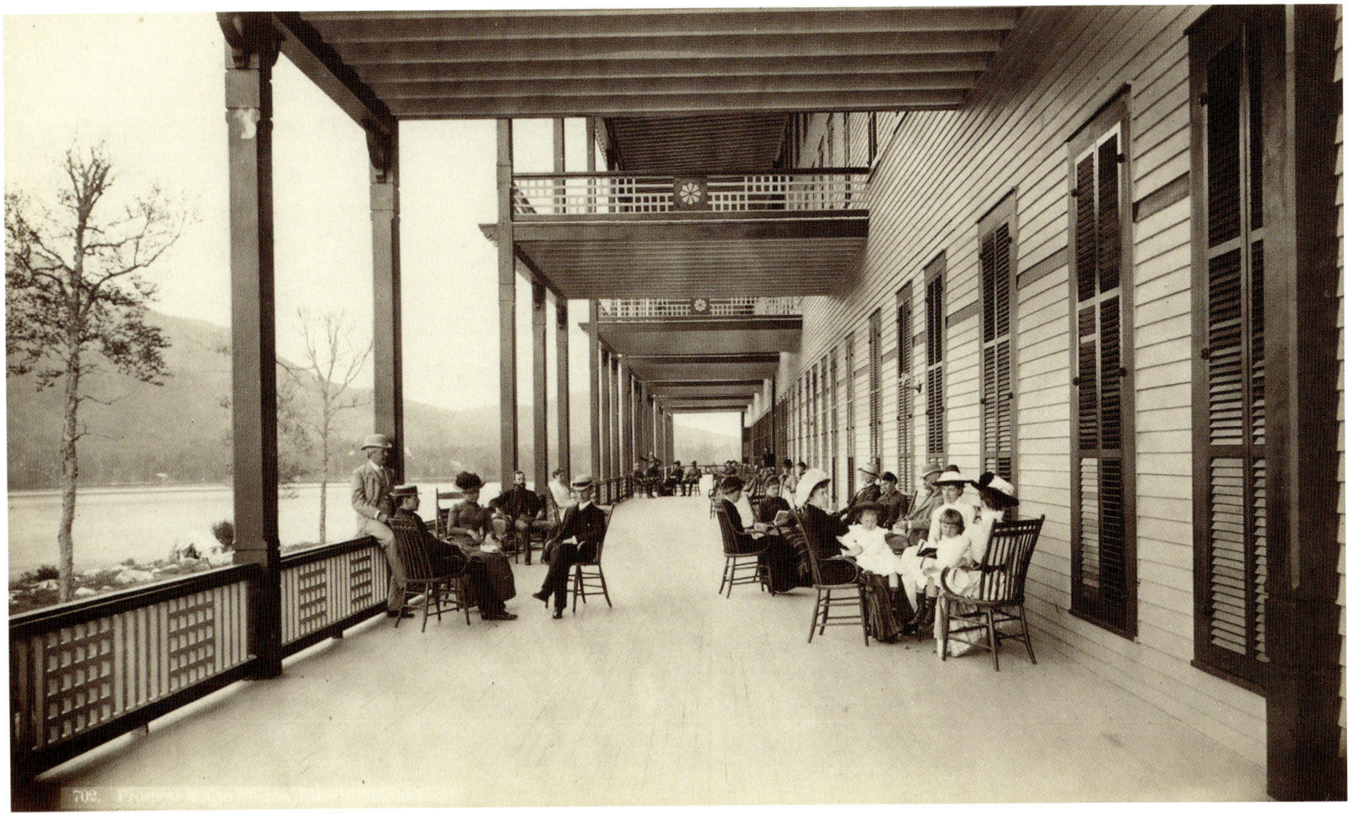

5. *Prospect House Piazza, Blue Mountain Lake*, Seneca Ray Stoddard. Courtesy of the Adirondack Experience: The Museum on Blue Mountain Lake, New York, P001282.

Edward Bierstadt (1824–1906), whose brothers Albert and Charles were noted western landscape artists and photographers of Niagara Falls, came to the central Adirondacks in the 1880s, documenting landmarks and scenery through mass-produced artotypes that he published as bound or boxed sets.

Artotypes, invented and patented by Bierstadt, transferred photographic images to light-sensitive printing plates, a methodology that paved the way for offset lithography. In 1885, William West Durant hired him to take photographs for a brochure called "The Adirondacks, Artotype Views Among the Mountains and Lakes of the North Woods" to promote the charms of Blue Mountain Lake and Raquette Lake as vacation destinations and to encourage land sales.[15]

An eager public purchased the brochures at Adirondack hotels or at his Manhattan studio. Bierstadt's work is probably the single

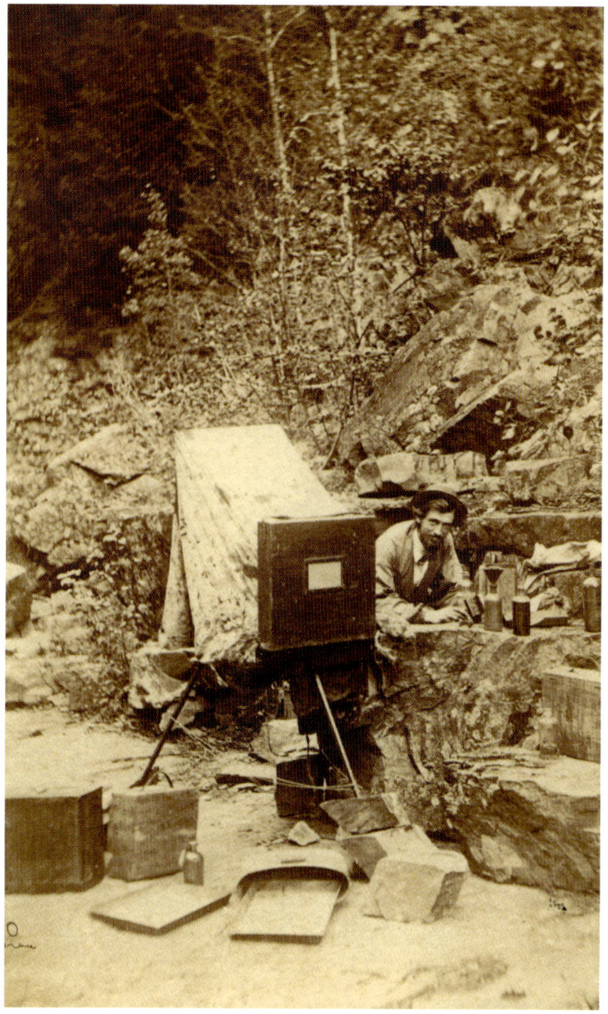

6. *Seneca Ray Stoddard with His Portable Darkroom Equipment, Ausable Chasm.* Courtesy of the Adirondack Experience: The Museum on Blue Mountain Lake, New York, P029497.

most important group of photographs of the central Adirondacks, documenting the region from North Creek to Long Lake, Tahawus, Mount Marcy, and Saranac Lake.

The most significant photographic work is likely that of Stoddard, the most prolific photographer of the Adirondacks between the late 1860s and the early 1900s. Stoddard began his working life in 1862 as an ornamental and sign painter in Troy, NY. He was a classically trained artist who brought a painter's sensibility to his images. A savvy promoter and salesman, he soon capitalized on the demand for images of Adirondack scenery by taking hundreds of Adirondack views, which he advertised and sold in hotels, on steamboats, and in other tourist spots. A few years later, he was working in Glens Falls as a photographer, although he still listed his occupation as "landscape painter."

Stoddard made thousands of photographs on albumenized paper in many formats, from oversize to cabinet cards to stereo views. His scenes enabled people to see as well as imagine what the Adirondacks looked like during the heyday of nineteenth-century tourism. He spent most of his adult life promoting the Adirondacks in print and through images. With guidebooks, paintings, maps, souvenir booklets, magic lantern lectures, travelogues, magazines, and, most particularly, photographs, Stoddard made a career from the burgeoning tourist trade that followed the Civil War. He was also an early and vocal supporter of the late nineteenth-century movement to preserve the natural character of the Adirondacks and to protect it from the wanton exploitation of its natural resources. His passionate magic lantern slide lecture, "The Adirondacks Illustrated," was instrumental in promoting state efforts to protect the northern forests.

Early in his career, Jesse Wooley collaborated several times with Stoddard and made similar career choices especially in the development

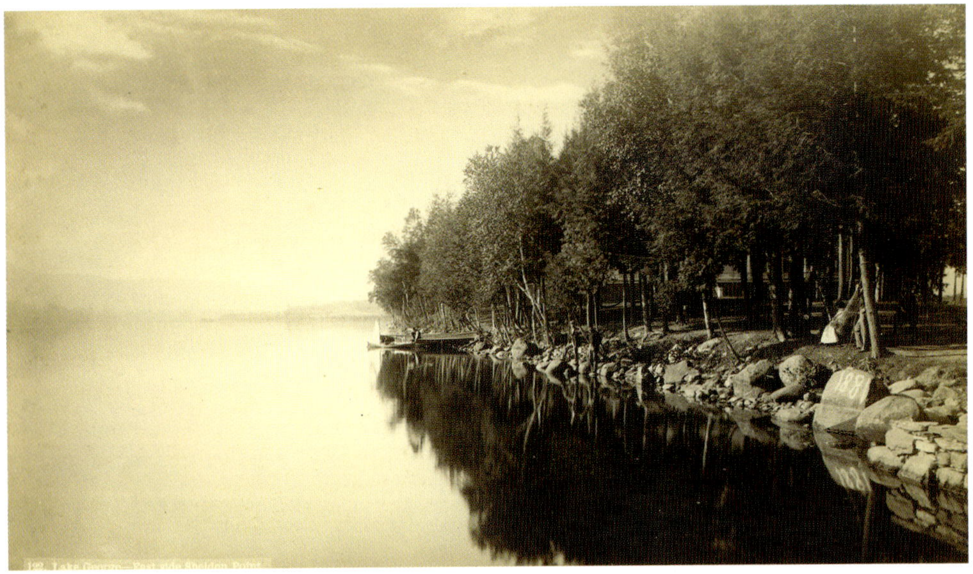

7. *Lake George—East Side Sheldon Point*, Seneca Ray Stoddard. Courtesy of the Adirondack Experience: The Museum on Blue Mountain Lake, New York, P027689.

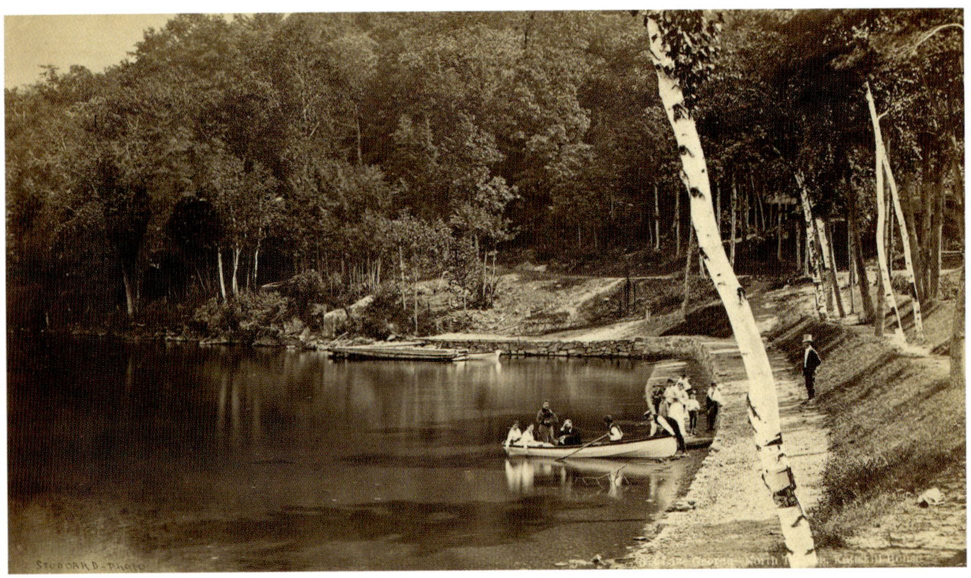

8. *Lake George, North Terrace, Kattskill House*, Seneca Ray Stoddard. Courtesy of the Adirondack Experience: The Museum on Blue Mountain Lake, New York, P027739.

and presentation of illustrated travelogues. Stoddard was twenty-four years Wooley's senior.

Landscape Photography

Like landscape painting, landscape photography evolved in Europe before coming to the United States.[16] A true landscape photograph is defined as a view or scene of nature as the primary subject expressing ideological meanings assigned to it by cultural assumptions.[17] American appreciation of nature as a work of art in the mid-1800s and the rise of American landscape painting were essential to the development and expansion of landscape photography. The use of original landscape photographs to illustrate books and the publication of large-format books devoted entirely to landscape photographs catapulted viewing the medium to a national pastime by 1875.[18]

Seneca Ray Stoddard's greatest achievement as a photographer was his landscape and scenic work. Stoddard imbued his photographs with light and composed his views with a painterly eye. The sky and atmospheric light are as much the subjects of his photographs as are the still waters and the sharply delineated landscape and objects below. Unlike most of his contemporaries, who concentrated on studio portrait work, Stoddard focused most of his images on the outdoors, and as a result he is one of the pioneers in the field of American landscape photography. Stoddard's landscape photographs are outstanding both in execution and choice of subject. A contemporary critic noted the following in the *Philadelphia Photographer* in 1876:

> In looking over some of the beautiful views of European scenery, by some of the best artists, we have often sighed for such work by American artists, and now we have it from MR. STODDARD. The stereos are perfect gems of photography, but the larger views captivate us most. They seem to be filled with the feeling and expression of the true artist. For choice of subjects, arrangement, and balance of lines, depth and beauty of perspective, well-chosen and effective foregrounds, and clearly defined yet subdued distance, which with dainty skies give a charming sense of real atmosphere, we have rarely seen these views excelled.[19]

Stoddard incorporated the conventions of landscape painters who focused first on the details of nature and then shifted to the expressive elements found in vistas and light as Americans grew to see the landscape more as the embodiment of their national and cultural values than as scientific information. His landscape photographs reveal both the detail and the view and, as such, celebrate nature in unique works of art. Like Stoddard, Wooley had the ability to compose pure landscape views with the expressive effects found in paintings. This capacity enabled him to sustain his creativity and meet the needs of his many markets.

After 1860, Americans discovered the grandeur of previously unknown parts of their native land through stunning photographs taken of the American West by professional photographers, who often accompanied government or railroad surveys and exploratory expeditions between 1860 and 1885. Timothy O'Sullivan, A. J. Russell, and William Henry Jackson, among others, worked under this patronage; Eadweard Muybridge and Carleton E. Watkins were important photographers who worked as artists on their own. Together they introduced to Eastern galleries and drawing rooms such magnificent sites as the Grand Canyon, the waterfalls of Yosemite, the geysers of Yellowstone, and the Rocky and Grand Teton Mountains, as well as records of people, towns, and ways of life, especially of American Indians. Knowledge of these works prompted Adirondack photographers to capture the scenic beauty of their landscape. Unlike the mountains of the American West, which soar dramatically upward out of a flat, high plane, the Adirondacks are clusters of ancient rounded mountains covered by trees and punctuated by lakes and mountain cascades.

William Henry Jackson (1843–1942), painter, explorer, and photographer renowned for his 80,000 photographs of the American West, was born in the Adirondack hamlet of Keeseville in April 1843. His father, George Hallock Jackson, was a blacksmith and carriage-maker who moved frequently in pursuit of work. George also experimented with cameras; young William recorded that "I got the feel of a camera almost before I could walk. . . . I can't help but believe that this childhood experience helped direct my life."[20] After serving with the 12th Vermont Infantry in the Civil War, Jackson traveled west, working as a geological survey photographer and explorer and finally settling in Denver, where he opened a photography business. From 1881 to 1892 he supplemented his income with commissions from several railroad companies, including the New York Central, to document their routes and lands and to promote their scenic attributes for tourists. In 1894 he embarked on a seventeen-month, around-the-world trip as the official photographer for the World Transportation Company. Like Stoddard and Wooley, Jackson combined talent with entrepreneurship to build his career and legacy as a pioneer landscape photographer and artist as well as an explorer and storyteller. His Adirondack work includes several images of Lake George scenery and tourist activities.

Twentieth-century photographers of world renown also made the Adirondack landscape their subject. Alfred Stieglitz (1864–1946) had a long connection to the Adirondacks through his family summer home at Lake George.[21] There he entertained American modernists

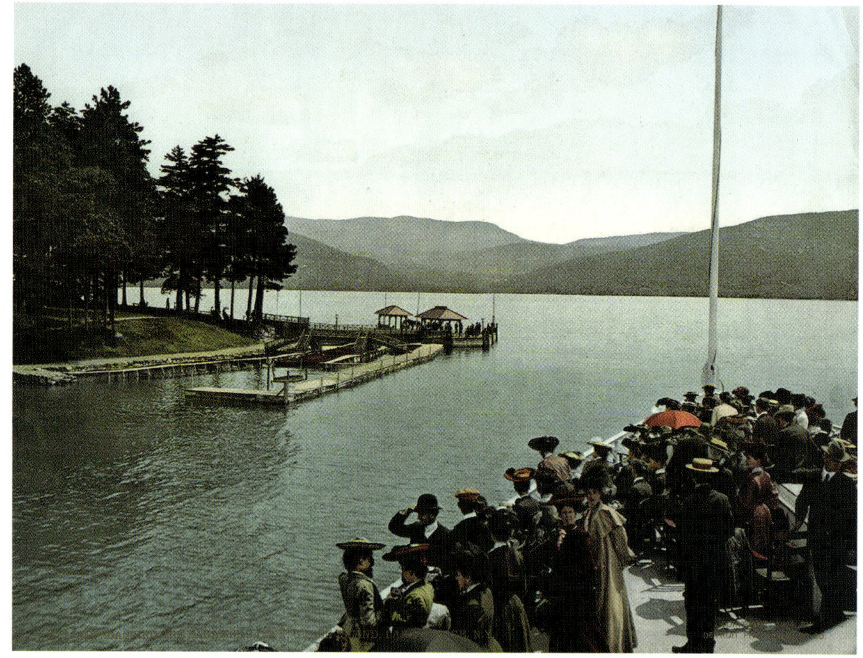

9. *Approaching the Sagamore Dock, Green Island, Lake George N.Y.*, 1904, William Henry Jackson. Courtesy of the Adirondack Experience: The Museum on Blue Mountain Lake, New York, P011425.

and photographed the buildings on his farm, his family, servants, and friends, and the landscape and objects of everyday life. In the late teens he began experimenting with subject matter, theorizing that photographs did not have to be about something. For fifteen years, beginning in 1922, he produced hundreds of 4-by-5-inch images of clouds, sky, and sun above Lake George. He called these pictures "Equivalents" because his intent was to visualize his thoughts and feelings, not the actuality of the subject, and to suspend reality to achieve spiritual awareness of the vastness of the cosmos.

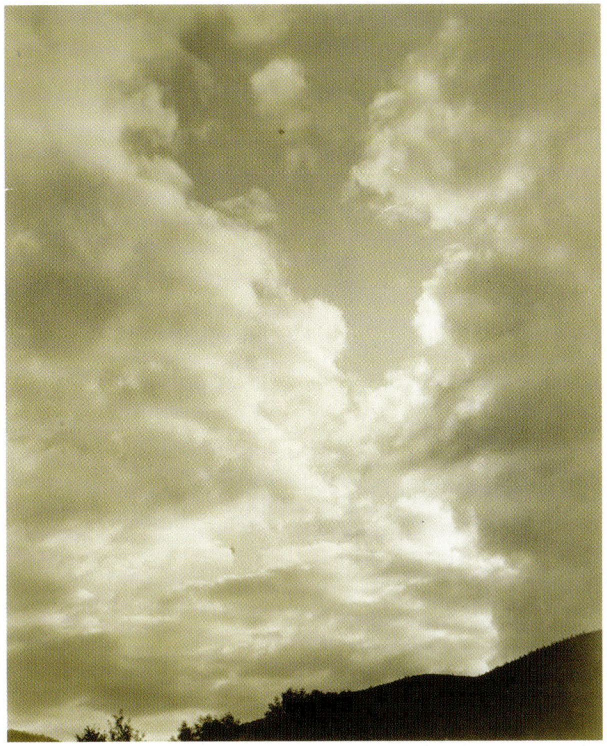

10. *Music—A Sequence of Ten Cloud Photographs, No. 11*, Alfred Stieglitz. Courtesy of the Adirondack Experience: The Museum on Blue Mountain Lake, New York, P061449.

Stieglitz said of his work, "I wanted to photograph clouds to find out what I had learned in forty years about photography. Through clouds to put down my philosophy of life—to show that my photographs were not due to subject matter— . . ."[22] Through their focus on the essential aspects of existence, these works referenced the beliefs of transcendentalists Ralph Waldo Emerson and Henry David Thoreau without the religiosity.[23] Duncan Phillips called the photographs "miracles of sensitized individual perception and interpretation while remaining true to the medium's . . . concern with objective truth." The artist called them "my most profound life experiences."[24]

Landscape photographs were made in various formats, including formal photographs, wide-format or panorama photographs, and more commercially oriented stereographs and postcards. Wooley and his contemporaries recorded the beauty of their natural world in all formats in a marvelous diversity of subjects from the mundane to the sublime. Many of these images were made to be picturesque mementos for vacationers. But the photographers also made certain aesthetic choices in the views that they selected to capture on film and as such elevated some of their images to subjective renderings of moments in time or compositions with pictorial conventions similar to paintings.

Austrian Joseph Puchberger introduced panorama or wide-format photography in 1843. Some of the most famous panoramas documented the American Civil War in the 1860s and the American West in the 1870s and 1880s. George Eastman's improvements in the manufacture of rolling flexible film in the late 1880s revolutionized the technique; a hundred years later, a group of art photographers revived the format in color film and ultimately digital format.[25] Wooley began to use wide-format photography while he was resident photographer for the Silver Bay Association between 1908 and 1923. He produced landscape photographs that captured the scenic beauty as well as effects of light and weather, patterns in clouds and on the water, and sunrises and sunsets on Lake George and its natural environs. He also produced hundreds of panoramas, recording tourist and resident activities, recreation, architecture around the lake and on the west shore's "Millionaire's Row" between Lake George

Village and Bolton Landing, steamboats and hotels, and the myriad events and activities at the YMCA at Silver Bay Association. Wooley's panoramas are considered to be his finest work. Approximately one-third of his considerable photographic output employed the panoramic format.

As the twentieth century progressed, landscape photography became more and more about place and the promotion of an appreciation for the beauty of nature and the fragility of the environment. These landscape photographers chronicled the relationship between humans and nature and defended the need to preserve the natural world.

Photography as a Business and the Postcard Era

Entrepreneurship, responsiveness to technological advances, and the development of photography as a business were interdependent. Technological innovations in optics, camera design, and photographic paper changed photography profoundly in the last decade of the nineteenth century. In 1884, George Eastman of Rochester, New York, developed a method to replace the photographic dry-plate with roll film that could be developed easily and rapidly. Eastman introduced the Kodak camera in 1888 followed by the Kodak Brownie in 1901, transforming photography forever.[26] Simpler cameras and improved materials made taking a photograph possible for everyone, anywhere. There are far more images of the Adirondacks made by amateurs, particularly tourists, than by professional photographers. Visitors and locals snapped themselves in the woods or on the waters in order to record happy times in permanent form.

The explosion of amateur photography did not spell the end of professional photography in the Adirondacks. Wooley and his business endeavors exemplify the practitioners of the new technology in

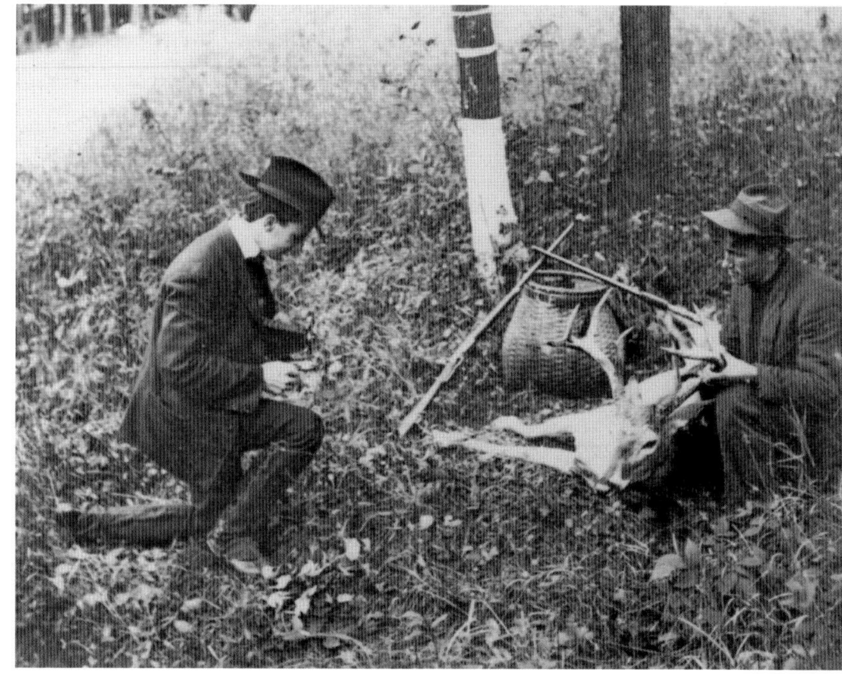

11. *Man Photographing Hunter with Deer.* Courtesy of the Adirondack Experience: The Museum on Blue Mountain Lake, New York, P045040.

the region. Hundreds of professionals took portraits and captured every aspect of life indoors and out in the North Country: hotels and all the means of transportation to get to them; roadside attractions; roads and bridges; civic events and parades; circuses and vaudeville; fire drills and fires, disasters, and accidents; construction and demolition projects; national and local historic sites; civic, ecclesiastical, and domestic architecture; summer camps and their participants; churches and religious ceremonies; schools and graduations; hospitals and doctor's offices; interiors and exteriors of homes; public buildings and private clubs; family rites of passage, including christenings, weddings, and funerals; new technology like airplanes, telegraphs, and telephones; wild and domestic animals; and posed and candid portraits of civil servants, notables, and families.

Photographs and stereo views, which gave a convincing illusion of three-dimensional realism, chronicled places and things to do as well as the rich cultural heritage of the region. They also reflected the extremes of arduous work (logging and mining) and privilege garnered by great wealth (great camps and exclusive clubs). Photographs of lumbering and mining are often more dramatic than views of nature. Among the scenes captured were ghost towns left after industry passed, fire zones and reforested regions, natural disasters, and people—a host of workers who performed back-breaking work in the mines or in the woods. Views of great camps documented extraordinary log and twig architecture that defines the rustic style and how the wealthy "roughed" it in the woods or on the waters. Images of hunting cabins, lean-tos in the woods, and townscapes showcased the variety of other temporary and permanent residences that dotted the settled landscape. Photographs of Saranac Lake's architecture, transformed by cure porches for the treatment of tuberculosis, illustrated the cure industry along with pictures of patients. Photographs also captured international events like the Winter Olympics in Lake Placid in 1932—an event important on its own and also for its transformative change on the village. After the 1932 Games, winter sports attracted large numbers of winter tourists and made Lake Placid into a winter resort.

The first professional photographers often followed the Adirondack tradition of multiple livelihoods. They took pictures and produced for sale a variety of formats: large-sized prints, portraits, cabinet cards, cartes de visite, and panoramas, along with brochures and other commercial publications. By far the most lucrative format after 1900 was the photo postcard.

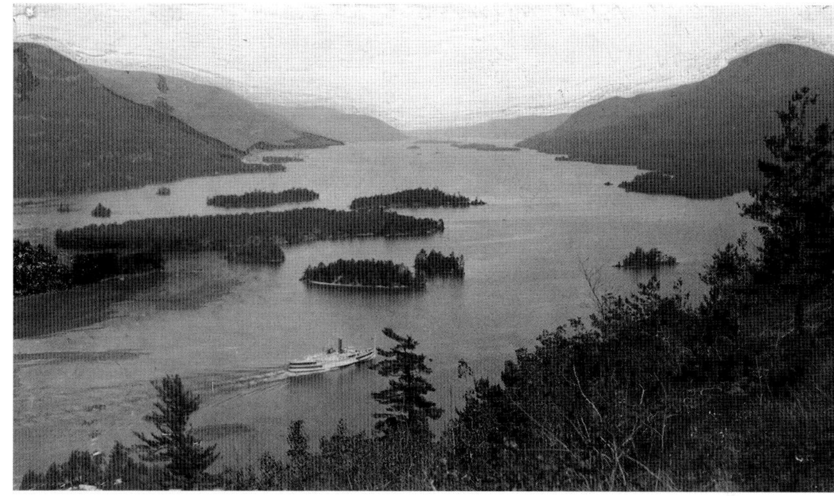

12. *Postcard of the Narrows, Lake George*, J. S. Wooley. Courtesy of the Adirondack Experience: The Museum on Blue Mountain Lake, New York, P036001.

Postcards were originally designed for writing a message and mailing it without an envelope. The earliest known picture postcard was hand-painted in 1840 and mailed in London. The first known souvenir picture postcard was posted in Vienna in 1871 and the first advertising cards appeared in England in 1872 and Germany in 1874. The first American postcard was developed in Springfield, Massachusetts, by the Morgan Envelope Factory in 1873, and the first souvenir postcard advertised the Chicago World's Fair in 1893. By the mid-1890s, picture postcards were all the rage on both sides of the Atlantic. In 1907, Kodak introduced a service called "Real Photo postcards" that enabled people to make a postcard from their own pictures. This touched off a national craze to collect them in albums. No other format produced such an abundance of imagery from everyday life in rural and urban America. By then, photographers were businessmen, providing professional services to document all aspects of family and civic life as well as selling everything needed to take pictures.[27]

The Cirkut panoramic camera became available at the same time as the emerging popular interest in postcards. The size of panoramas, 6.5 inches by 20–46 inches, was widely desired to document large groups of people at graduations, weddings, outings, and conventions, as well as workers or staffs at their places of employment; thus, panoramas became a lucrative business for commercial photographers. Panoramas also recorded Adirondack scenery, hotels, resorts, and clubs. Large-format postcards soon were part of professional photographers' expanding product line.

Dozens of individuals joined Jesse Wooley in making a living from photography in the Adirondacks. Wooley began his own diversified photography business in Ballston Spa after apprenticing in Saratoga Springs. Most of his peers followed a similar career path, including taking portraits and documenting local sites, scenery, and events. Few of his regional contemporaries joined Wooley, who followed his senior peer Seneca Ray Stoddard, in picture-taking tours of the American West, Florida, and Europe, or in his venture as a popular travel lecturer, which reflected the widespread national popular demand for education and entertainment. From 1908 to 1923, Wooley was the official photographer for the Silver Bay Association on Lake George and enjoyed a profitable business creating and selling photo postcards. Wooley's entrepreneurial and diverse business model was mirrored by others in the region with varying degrees of success. What distinguished Wooley from his peers was his success at the business of photography, due in large part to his aesthetic sensibility and ability to capture the beautiful view as well as serve the commercial market. His natural business acumen, responsiveness to advances in technology, and his gifts for promotion assured his success.

Wooley's contemporaries worked throughout the region. In nearby North River to the west of Ballston Spa, Ernest John Ameden (1862–1940) was a self-taught, part-time photographer in addition to managing a general store and being a postmaster in his community. Ameden documented the local scenery in and around North River, people at work in the garnet mines and the woods, the ski trains arriving at North Creek, his friends and neighbors, tourists, and notables, making portraits and photo postcards for sale.[28]

In the western Adirondacks, Henry M. Beach (1863–1943) of Lowville and Remsen traveled the North Country documenting camps, resorts, communities, industries, and groups of people, often with humor. He produced images that he sold as postcards or panoramic photographs in the communities he chronicled. He used glass-plate negatives and printed the images on special postcard paper. His wide-angle views of camps, resorts, hotels, and groups of people were produced using a Cirkut panoramic camera, which enabled him to pan the view and capture the broad view. His scenes of the logging industry are some of the most important records of the business.[29] Beach rivals Wooley in the quality, number, and diversity of his photography.

William Mandeville (1864–1947) stayed close to home as a studio photographer for Lowville for more than sixty years. His focus was entirely local; he documented the people and ways of his town, specializing in portraits and photo postcards.[30] J. Walton Pursell

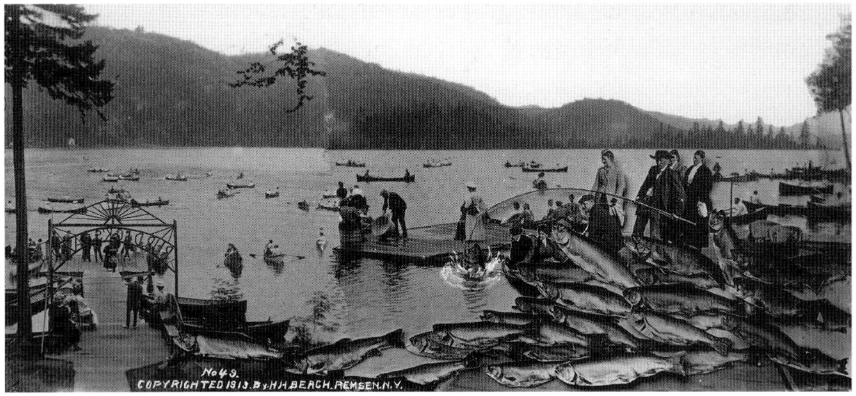

13. *Believe Me. This Is Real Trout Fishing*, Henry Beach. Courtesy of the Adirondack Experience: The Museum on Blue Mountain Lake, New York, P002812.

(1877–1964) of Gloversville also specialized in portraits, nature scenes, and events including weddings, graduations, accidents, and civic functions in his hometown and its neighboring locales. His well-composed pictures of nature were often hand-colored by his wife. His scenes of the Sacandaga Valley document a place now lost beneath the waters of the Sacandaga Reservoir.[31]

In the northern Adirondacks, Katherine Elizabeth McClellan (1859–1934) was an exception in more ways than one. Educated at Smith College, she built a successful photography business in Saranac Lake in the 1890s after her family moved there with her sister, a victim of tuberculosis. Her physician father became the first public health officer for the village. McClellan sold prints of her carefully staged mountain and lake views to locals and in New York City and Philadelphia, where she received critical acclaim. She also produced souvenir books for the tourist trade and mail order and published calendars illustrated with her photographs, an innovation at the time.[32]

William Kollecker (1879–1962) expanded the photography business in Saranac Lake. Born in Brooklyn, he also came to Saranac Lake to recover from tuberculosis. He opened his first photography business in 1905, and by 1920 was well established in a large store in the heart of town. Kollecker was known as "The Kodak Man of Saranac Lake" because he sold Kodak cameras and equipment. Jesse Wooley, fifteen years Kollecker's senior and of similar entrepreneurial bent, became the accredited agent for Eastman Kodak Company in Ballston Spa.[33]

In addition to an extensive souvenir, photo-processing, matting, and framing business, Kollecker made thousands of engaging pictures of the landscape, winter carnivals, tuberculosis patients, and all aspects of village life, business, and recreation in the first decades of the twentieth century, producing an invaluable record of North Country life for sale at his shop on Main Street.[34] Among these images were large-format panoramas of scenery as well as group portraits of all kinds. Wooley's contemporary, Henry M. Beach, also joined Kollecker and Wooley in producing panoramic photographs and postcards for sale.

The first photo shop on Lake Placid's Main Street was a dilapidated building owned by James Brownell. In the early 1900s Henry Kaiser, a travelling salesman of photo supplies, fell in love with the area while selling photo supplies and convinced Mr. Brownell to give him a job. He worked without pay until he doubled the store's business; at that point, he received 50 percent of the profits. This agreement proved successful; within a year, Mr. Kaiser had tripled the profits and bought the business from Brownell. Kaiser became renowned for his pictures and for his business endeavors.[35]

Closer to Ballston Spa, Theresa (d. 1941) and Flora (d. 1953) Sexton, known around Hague as the Sexton sisters, lived a hardscrabble life on a farm on the northern end of Lake George. They began a photography business on Hague's main street around 1915 to supplement their meager income. Always keeping their equipment up to date, they made portraits of wealthy seasonal residents in formal and informal settings on their boats, at picnics, and at parties. The photographs are in albums preserved at the Hague Historical Society.[36]

Among the hundreds of other photographers who continued the tradition of multifaceted professional photographer-entrepreneurs, maintaining studios and documenting the local scene in the first half of the twentieth century, were the following: Fred Hodges (1900–1957) of Blue Mountain Lake, L. H. Fillmore (active 1870s–1880s) of Whitehall and Lake George, George C. Baldwin (active 1860s–1870s) of Keeseville, George W. Baldwin (1848–1930) of Plattsburgh and Saranac Lake, J. F. Holley (active 1870–1920) of Chestertown, and Alonzo L. Mix (1845–1915) of Warrensburg, who specialized in farm scenes and portraits.[37] Biographical information is sparse for many photographers in the region; their surviving work is their testament.

The Adirondack region was (and is) a stage on which many social, cultural, and environmental dramas of national significance have played out: the conservation movement, the democratization of leisure, the development of freshwater pleasure craft in North America, and the survival of subsistence lifestyles into the twenty-first century. Photographs are a rich resource to tell this story, and Jesse Wooley and his contemporaries did it well.

Jesse S. Wooley

American Photographer

PHILIP TERRIE

Jesse Wooley and Ballston Spa

Jesse Sumner Wooley was born to a farm family in the rural town of Wilton, Saratoga County, New York, on May 23, 1867. The 1875 New York state census identifies his parents as Edmund R. and Emily Wooley.[1] His early education was at a one-room schoolhouse, and family income was probably lean; in 1878, when he was only eleven, he landed his first job, working for the summer at a furniture store in far-off Brooklyn, making $1.50 per week. How a farm boy from Saratoga County found himself working away from his family, in Brooklyn, remains a mystery, but the very fact that he did suggests the level of energy and entrepreneurship that characterized his entire life. In 1879, the family moved to the Geysers, a part of Saratoga Springs, about six miles south of Wilton, and briefly in the summer of 1880 he was back in Brooklyn, this time making $2.00 per week.[2] When the Wooleys left their farm in Wilton and moved to Saratoga Springs, they were transitioning from rural America to one of the premier resort towns of the Northeast.[3] By 1890 and probably earlier, his father was an oil dealer.[4]

The Wooleys' move from the Wilton farm to a more settled neighborhood in Saratoga Springs reflected the hard times besetting much of the agricultural economy of the northeastern United States in the decades after the Civil War. Rural villages and the standard of living enjoyed by farm families declined; amenities and opportunities available only in urban centers or larger towns beckoned; previously tilled fields were abandoned; and the nation's agricultural needs were increasingly met by farmers in the Midwest. Pockets of prosperity persisted, of course, and it is impossible to argue with certainty that diminishing opportunity on the farm was the only factor drawing the Wooleys from Wilton to Saratoga Springs.

The Wooley family's move typified a demographic shift that was reshaping American society. The economic life of the Northeast had revolved around agriculture since it was first settled by Europeans, but by the last third of the nineteenth century many families that had farmed for generations saw their children give up on agriculture and either head west or migrate to nearby towns and cities, where they entered the emerging world of industry and commerce. Between 1880, the year of Jesse Wooley's initial contact with the world of professional photography, and 1930, after his retirement, the percentage of New York State's population that was directly involved in agriculture dropped from forty-four to sixteen.[5] Wooley, descended from generations of farmers, proved skillful at adapting to new realities and carved out a prosperous life, combining entrepreneurship and an innate and deftly deployed aesthetic talent. The movement from apparently poor circumstances, as reflected in his working far from his family when he was but eleven, to comfort and ease constitutes a major theme in Wooley's biography.

Shortly after the move to Saratoga Springs, in 1880, Wooley took another job—one that would lead to the career that defined his life—as an errand boy for a pair of Saratoga photographers named Baker and Record; he was thirteen years old. A young man of talent and energy, Wooley quickly moved up the ladder at Baker and Record (which was later known as Baker and Epler). Within a year he had begun an apprenticeship, then was a general shop assistant, and by 1882 he was assistant photograph printer. Two years later, he left Saratoga Springs and moved to Ballston Spa, New York, where he was to live and work—with lengthy interludes of travel and many summers on Lake George—for the rest of his life. He took a job as photograph printer for the Ballston Spa firm of T. J. Arnold and boarded at a lodging nearby.[6]

By 1885, Wooley had been working in the photography business for five years, and he was still a teenager. But only two years after his move to work with Arnold, he borrowed enough capital—$1500, a huge sum for a young man with minimal collateral—to buy out Arnold and take over the business. This was a testament to Wooley's confidence, as well as that of the local bank where he borrowed the money, in both his skills as a photographer and his business acumen.[7] This was a young man on the move. With his rural roots only a few years behind him, at the age of twenty he was an independent businessman, moving smoothly into the professional circles of a bustling town.

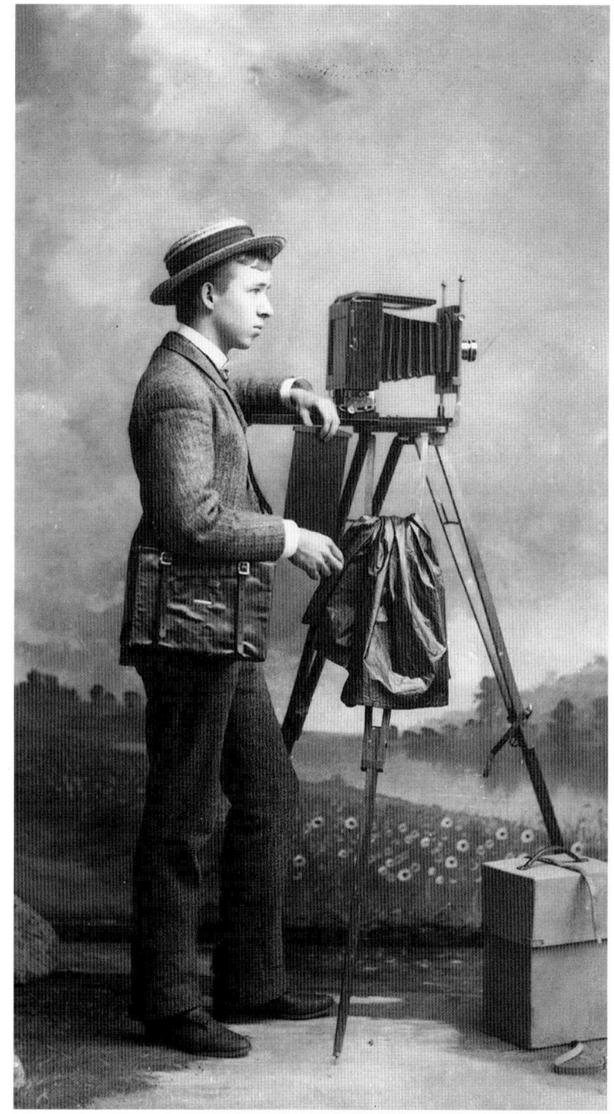

14. *Jesse Sumner Wooley as a Young Photographer.* Courtesy of the Saratoga County Historical Society.

Settled in the eighteenth century and soon known for its medicinal springs, the village of Ballston Spa offered hotels and boarding houses to travelers. The goal of those developing the early tourist economy was, as historian Richard Gassan has written, to "create, in the deep woods of upstate New York, the first American spa culture . . . modeled on European examples," and by the early nineteenth century, it was a prosperous town. In 1809 a southern visitor called Ballston Spa "the most fashionable place in America."[8] A local history notes, "Each succeeding summer brought a constantly increasing number of guests, and wealth began to flow into the coffers of its citizens. The fame of its waters and hotels, and the beauty and healthfulness of the surrounding country attracted visitors from the remote sections of the Union, and even from distant lands."[9] Even after nearby Saratoga Springs established itself as the premier spa in New York, Ballston Spa remained a tourist destination throughout most of the nineteenth century.[10]

In 1817, perhaps as an effort to avoid the pitfalls of being a one-industry town, Ballston Spa secured for itself the prize of the county government for Saratoga County. The combination of continuing tourist trade at the hotels and springs and the commerce inevitably generated around a county seat, all served by railroad lines radiating out in nearly every direction, kept Ballston Spa a thriving community with well-financed schools, elegant churches, and a bustling business district. When the springs began to fail after the Civil War, mills and manufacturing took up the slack. Woolen mills, the manufacture of tools and carriages, tanneries, paper mills, an iron foundry—these and a wide variety of other concerns took advantage of water power and efficient transportation arteries.[11] Ballston Spa was an active center of commerce and activity, a world profoundly different from the dreary and often penurious life of farming districts like Wilton only a few miles away.

This was the town on which Wooley staked his future in 1887 when he borrowed the cash to set himself up as an independent entrepreneur. It was clearly a smart move. Wilton and the uncertainties of northeastern American agriculture were in the past, while Ballston Spa and the emerging culture of specialized professions, of which photography was but one of many, represented the future. Wooley's seemingly effortless transformation of himself from poor farm boy to necktie-wearing professional typified similar makeovers occurring across the country. Most Americans, of course, were unable to make such a leap—financial panics and recession, along with tedious, low-wage jobs and economic hardship, constituted reality for the majority—but Wooley's ascent is a classic American story, achieved during the same era wherein popular novelist Horatio Alger was relentlessly spinning the appealing fable of rags-to-riches success.

As Wooley established himself as a photographer, he became a fixture in the Ballston Spa social and professional world.[12] In 1889, two years after setting himself up as an independent photographer, he married Susie Arnold, daughter of a Ballston Spa dentist (relationship to T. J. Arnold, if any, is unclear), and they set up housekeeping in an apartment in the center of the village; a few months later, they moved to an apartment in the stylish new complex around the San Souci Opera House. He and Susie had two children, Marion, born in 1890, and Carl, born in 1901.

By the early 1890s, Wooley was advertising regularly in the *Ballston Journal* and proudly declaring himself "Ballston Spa's Leading Photographer."[13] A few years later, the paper noted that he was routinely hired by both defense attorneys and the District Attorney to

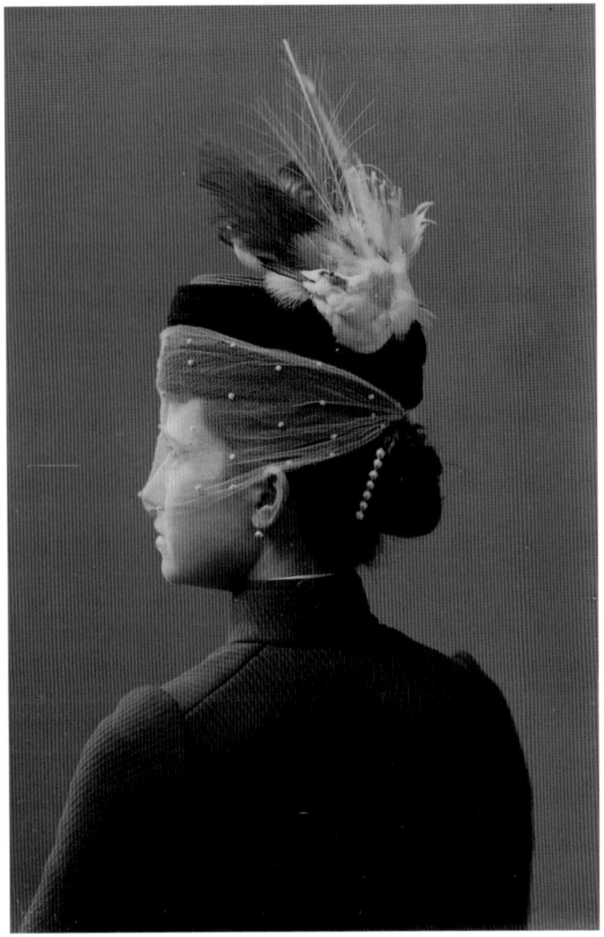

15. *Susan Arnold Wooley.* Courtesy of the Saratoga County Historical Society.

record details of accidents subject to litigation. This work led to his being called to deliver expert testimony at trials.[14]

In 1900, a decade after moving to the San Souci block, the Wooleys were awakened at 2:30 in the morning by the smell of smoke. Living on the third floor, they had to make a hasty dash for the street. Once safe, Wooley ran to his nearby office, secured a light camera, and returned to the fire, which he recorded photographically for the rest of the night. They lost everything they owned, except for a bird and its cage, which they grabbed on the way out of the apartment. They rented a new place for a while before moving into a new combined residence and office at the intersection of Milton Avenue and Washington Street. For the new structure, Wooley designed a skylight to maximize the natural light for studio portraits.

The year Marion was born, Wooley joined a growing and popular national fad and bought his first bicycle. According to the brief biographical sketch by Puckhaber and MacMillin, "It was not uncommon to see Wooley dashing around the village on his bike with all his photo equipment strapped to his person." In 1898, he and a friend mounted their bicycles—and Wooley packed his camera—for a biking expedition from Ballston Spa all the way to Orange, Massachusetts. They pedaled east to Schuylerville, where they crossed the Hudson, then southeast to Hoosick Falls. From there, they headed to the village of Pownal, Vermont, and then south into Massachusetts and the campus of Williams College. They puffed over the Berkshires, down the Deerfield River to Greenfield and finished at Orange, Massachusetts, taking photographs all along the way.[15]

Later, perhaps that same year (photographs similar to those recording the trip to Orange follow immediately in the same album), Wooley and two companions took their bicycles up to Lake Champlain and

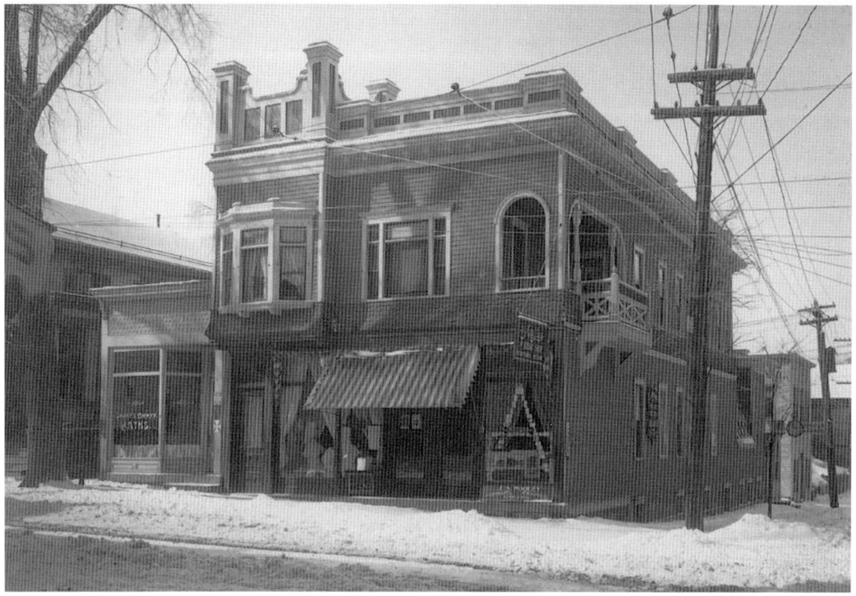

16. *Wooley Photo Studio under Construction.* Courtesy of the Saratoga County Historical Society.

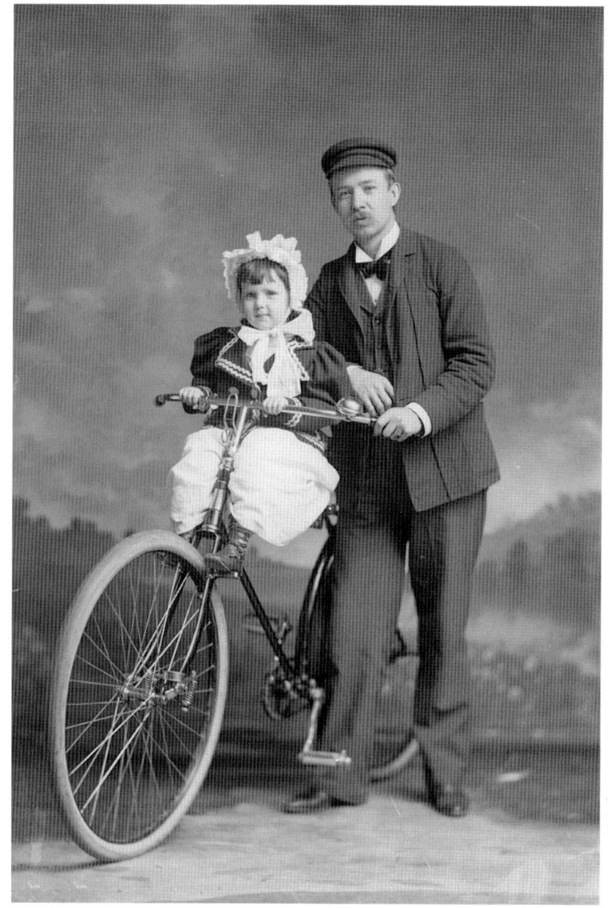

17. *Jesse and Daughter Marion.* Courtesy of the Saratoga County Historical Society.

set out touring from there to the Adirondacks. They spent some time on a Champlain ferry and then made it to Elizabethtown.

From Elizabethtown, they pedaled to Keene Valley and the Ausable Lakes, where Wooley recorded the striking profile of Indian Head and the spectacular scenery around the lower lake.[16] Wooley's enthusiasm for the bicycle (which, because of recent innovations involving weight, chain arrangement, and tires, had become widespread and immensely popular) was similar to his obvious appreciation of advances in camera technology. He was a man who loved the technology of the day.

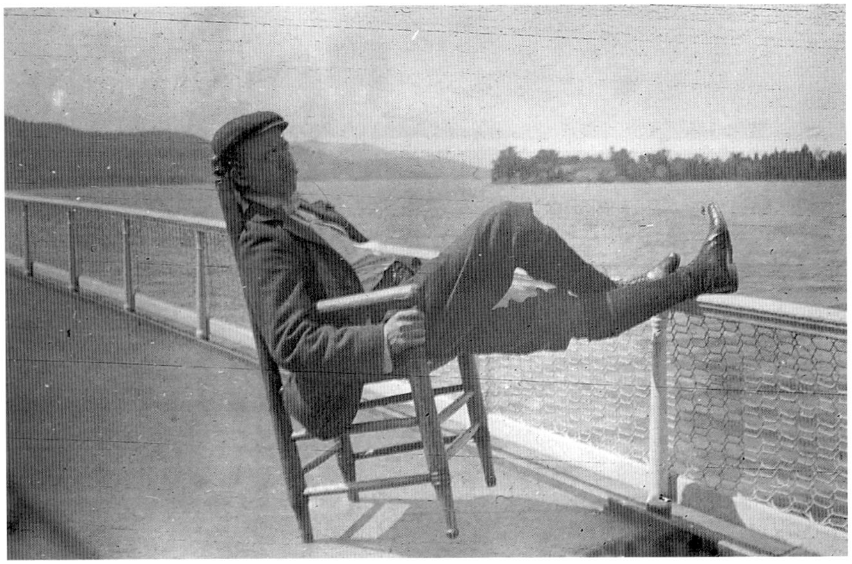

18. *Wooley Enjoying Lake Champlain.* Lance DeMuro Collection.

Throughout his career, Wooley frequently set off from Ballston Spa on expeditions to distant places. These might be by bicycle; they might be by boat, by train, or, later, by automobile. They might be for personal pleasure, collecting images for an album that stayed in the family; they might be designed explicitly to produce images for commercial use, either through sale or as part of an illustrated lecture. In any case, Wooley loved to travel, and spent much of his life on the road (or the rails). A camera was never far from his reach. And he ceaselessly captured the scenes, from picturesque wooden bridges or the mowing machine factory of W. A. Wood in Hoosick Falls, to students at Williams College walking to morning chapel. When a train ran off the rails and crashed near Ballston Spa, Wooley was quickly on the scene. When a new church was built, Wooley took a photograph of its façade. When the local baseball team was on the field, Wooley was there. He was the unofficial recorder of Saratoga County life for several decades.[17]

In Ballston Spa, Wooley was an active member of the Baptist church and served it in a variety of capacities, including as board member and deacon. When illness and old age kept him from weekly services, the church acknowledged his many years of dedication with an honorary deaconship. He was also president of the Ballston Spa Chamber of Commerce, a Rotarian, and a Modern Woodman. During the First World War, he volunteered for the Red Cross and Liberty Loan drives. In 1930, years after his retirement, he contributed photographs for a history of the Battle of Saratoga.[18]

During his career in Ballston Spa, Wooley ran a many-faceted business. At his headquarters on the corner of Washington and Milton, he and his assistants were available for studio work, i.e., formal portraits taken with fixed camera and good natural lighting. From the same location he ran a gift shop, sold postcards, and served as a Kodak retailer; he quickly saw the potential of the Kodak Brownie camera, which was introduced in 1900, and sold these in his shop. The Brownie—simple to use, with film that could be quickly developed and printed by dealers like Wooley—greatly expanded the pool of Americans taking pictures and generated a lucrative business for Wooley and others who developed the film of their Brownie customers.[19] The very existence of the Brownie meant less work for professional photographers, and Wooley, as other village photographers also did, simply replaced one source of income with another. It also meant he could leave his Ballston Spa office in the hands of a shop hand. During his frequent and extended travels away from Ballston Spa, the shop and business were overseen by a succession of employees and assistants. Alongside all these outlets, he also worked

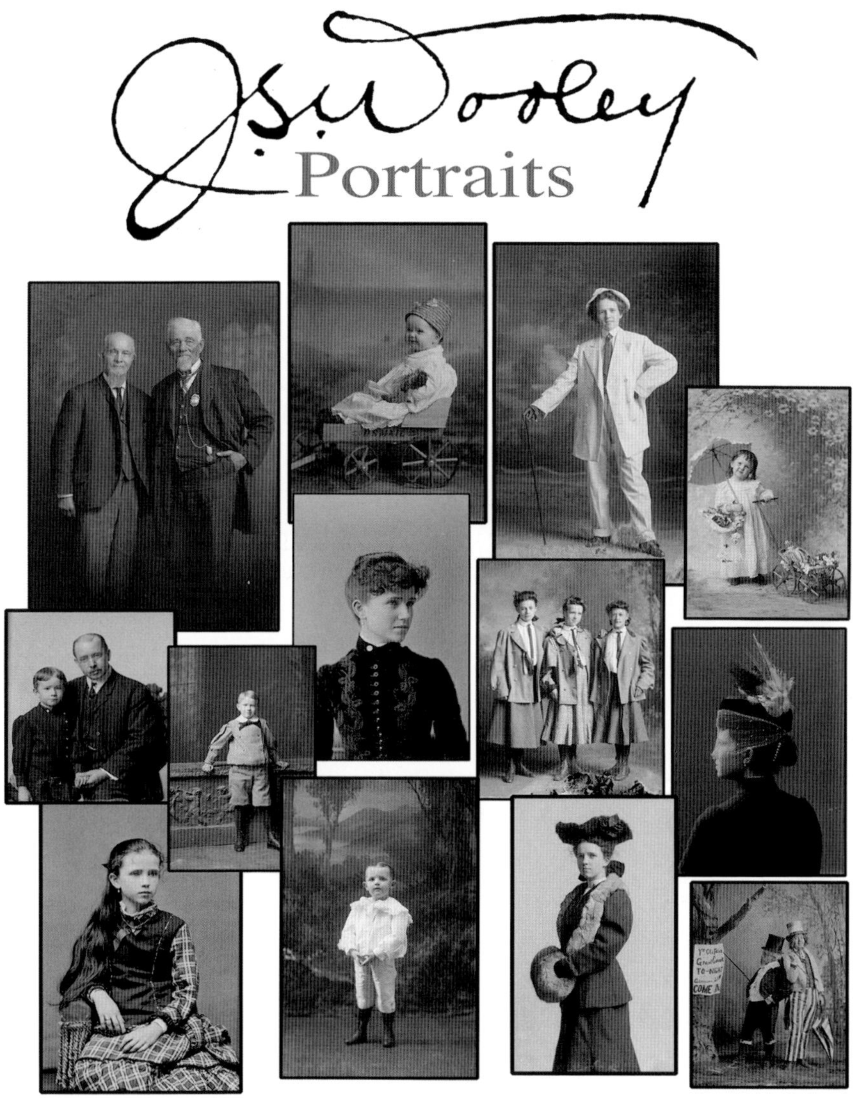

19. *Wooley Portraits.* Courtesy of the Saratoga County Historical Society.

as official photographer for the Delaware and Hudson Railroad (as Seneca Ray Stoddard, also discussed below, had before him).[20]

One sign of his success is the fact that at a relatively young age, he began spinning off parts of his business. In 1915, he sold the Ballston Spa studio business to his assistant Howard Hume, keeping the gift shop. In 1923 he wrapped up his work at Silver Bay (discussed below), and in 1924 he handed the Ballston Spa shop over to his son Carl, beginning a retirement that nonetheless included photography, both near to home and far afield, for the rest of his life. After a career as a professional photographer, he carried his camera with him on vacations, recording the day-to-day travel of his family and friends.

Around town, Wooley was known for clean living—no drinking, swearing, or gambling (notwithstanding a lifelong interest in horse racing and annual visits to the track in Saratoga Springs, where he apparently never placed a bet)—and for his meticulous and tightly organized attention to the affairs of his businesses. He was also among the first in town to try out new inventions. In addition to his early fascination with cameras and bicycles, he and Susie owned the first electric refrigerator in town; he quickly saw the appeal of the radio and phonograph, and added records and players to the inventory of his shop, where they shared the shelves with film and a variety of handheld cameras.

During the 1920s and 1930s, Wooley and his wife spent their winters in Florida, where, predictably, his camera was always at hand. They stayed at a variety of hotels and inns, on both coasts, often with Ballston Spa friends or with their daughter, Marion. In 1940 Wooley suffered a stroke, and in 1942 Susie died. Upon Wooley's death in 1943, the *Ballston Journal* declared that Wooley was one of the town's "most active and progressive citizens." He was, moreover, "[o]f a most attractive and pleasing personality, he had close friends in all walks of life and his energetic disposition kept him always busy yet he never was so busy in private affairs that he could not give much time to public matters."[21]

His local biographers, Puckhaber and MacMillin, admired Wooley: "Jess Wooley was an optimist. He was never depressed and he always looked on the bright side of things. He enjoyed life and he was the kind of person with whom people enjoyed being. He never complained, never got angry and always had a kind word for everyone." He was known for his sense of humor, his charity, and his meticulous care for his appearance: "He never wore work clothes and even when he sat on his porch he wore his panama hat and a white jacket."[22] Of the numerous self-portraits left after his death, none shows him not wearing a tie. From pedestrian origins on a Saratoga County farm, which his lifetime attention to his clothes and to scrupulous neatness suggests he never forgot, Wooley turned successfully to a white-collar career and made himself a pillar of a prosperous community.

Over the course of his busy and active career, Wooley took pictures of people, vistas, buildings, train wrecks, and steamboats. He carried a camera through town on his bicycle and captured images of storefronts, churches, and houses. He recorded the insides of houses, hotels, and inns. A lakeside view from the side of a country road, a group of boys playing in the street, bridges across the Hudson, historic battlefields, street views in New York City—he photographed virtually everything he saw. Just as hundreds of village photographers were doing across the country, Wooley recorded the life of small-town America.

Among the thousands upon thousands of images Wooley left in his studio and house and others now owned privately or by museums and libraries are many that had no apparent commercial value. He took pictures because he liked to, because he was clearly fascinated by photography's combination of technology, skill, and personal perception of the physical world. We have very little in Wooley's own voice concerning the culture in which he lived and worked, other than notes neatly inscribed on some—but far from all—of his negatives and prints, and nothing at all uncovering his inner, psychological life. But the quantity and variety of his photographic corpus reveal a man inspired by the infinite details of his physical environment and determined to leave a sharp record of that reality as he understood it.

Jesse Wooley and Seneca Ray Stoddard

Early in his career, Wooley saw the opportunities for combining camera work with travel. Inspiration for this insight may have come from another New York photographer with roots in Wilton: Seneca Ray Stoddard, who was born in Wilton in 1843—also of a farming family, though one with ties to a prominent name in colonial New England—twenty-four years before Wooley. Whether Wooley's family and Stoddard's were acquainted is impossible to say for sure, but given their proximity in a small rural village, it seems almost certain that they were. What we do know is that Wooley and Stoddard occasionally collaborated, at least as early as 1893.[23] The relationship between Wooley and Stoddard, who was roughly a generation older than Wooley, is both important and difficult to assess; neither left any extant records of their time together. We know that they collaborated early in Wooley's career, and we know that Wooley made several career moves that appeared to follow in Stoddard's footsteps. Was Wooley consciously adopting Stoddard's model, or do the similarities in their careers simply reflect the options available to a talented and hard-working village photographer in the late nineteenth and early twentieth centuries?

In 1864 Stoddard was working as a house and sign painter in Glens Falls, New York, a ride of a couple of hours from Wilton. After the Civil War, he learned the complex details of wet-plate photography, and in a stroke crucial to his subsequent career and enduring fame, he was the first photographer to recognize the commercial possibilities for images of Adirondack scenery. As early as 1867, Stoddard was advertising his stereoptic views of Lake George and the Adirondacks.[24] Stereoptic images were small pairs of photographs of the same scene: viewed through a special device, the stereopticon, the scene appeared to display in three dimensions. The stereopticon was a popular device, found in American parlors throughout the country, and regional photographers like Stoddard and Wooley quickly saw the market for mass-produced stereo images of local landscapes.[25]

During the 1870s and early 1880s, Stoddard traveled extensively in the Adirondacks and northern New York, lugging heavy equipment and bottles of chemicals. He produced images of the Adirondack region that were aesthetically stunning and remain today among the most successful efforts of scores of nineteenth-century artists to capture the grandeur of New York's northern wilderness. In addition to producing postcards, guidebooks, souvenir albums, and travel writing, Stoddard also was a major force in calling for conservation in the Adirondacks. In 1892, he delivered a lecture to the New York Assembly, accompanied by a magic lantern slideshow, that helped alert legislators to the need for protecting New York's forests; it was a critical factor contributing to the establishment of the Adirondack Park that same year.[26]

Like many others, Stoddard recognized the multiple potentials for photography, in addition to the obvious application in a studio for formal portraits, and he explored a wide range of outlets for his talents. He produced attractive panoramas, many of scenes in the Adirondacks, which he sold from his Glens Falls headquarters. And he delivered illustrated lectures inspired by his travels, which ranged as far as the Middle East and Russia. He produced travel brochures and recorded the architectural details and everyday life of his town. He also became a distributor for Kodak film and cameras.[27] All of these activities would be picked up by Wooley.

Stoddard's most acclaimed photographs depict his Adirondack travels in the 1870s and 1880s. This is the corpus that led art historian John Wilmerding to include Stoddard's images in a landmark exhibition on American Luminism at the National Gallery of Art in 1980.[28] Beginning around 1890, Stoddard devoted himself increasingly to illustrated lectures, based on trips to the American West in 1894, the Mediterranean in 1895, and Europe in 1897 and 1900. These drew large paying crowds and made Stoddard a much better living than had his more aesthetically successful work.[29] Wooley's career followed a similar trajectory.

Wooley's earliest known expedition to gather materials for a lecture was to New York City, in April 1889; the occasion was the centennial celebration of George Washington's first inauguration as president, at Federal Hall, April 30, 1789.[30] In the summer of 1893, Wooley joined Stoddard on an expedition to the central Adirondacks. Both used the images of that trip for illustrated lectures. Their collaboration led quickly to further travel, this time to Chicago for the 1893 World's Columbian Exposition, and another lecture series, "The Great White City."[31] After an 1895 trip down the Hudson, their final work together appears to have involved a similar expedition, also followed by a slide show, to Vermont in 1897.[32]

Wooley's time with Stoddard—whether he was an apprentice, studying in the salon of an older, established expert, or an equal collaborator, invited by Stoddard because of his energy and talent—was important to Wooley's subsequent career. Wooley went on to establish a prosperous life, replicating many of the media so carefully and successfully cultivated by Stoddard. In particular, Wooley was a deft photographer of lakes and mountain vistas, as Stoddard was. A critical part of Wooley's professional life and certainly a key source of income, moreover, was his use of his own images in illustrated lectures. In 1894, shortly after his first known collaboration with Stoddard, Wooley bought a Bessler Stereopticon Projector (now on display at the Brookside Museum in Ballston Spa) to use in his lectures.[33] Finally, Wooley adopted Stoddard's scheme of working closely with lucrative businesses, providing brochures and other advertising. Neither Stoddard nor Wooley was unusual in any of these pursuits; regional photographers across the country were always looking for avenues to expand their business.

Like Stoddard and like hundreds of other American photographers, Wooley devoted much energy and time to cultivating a trade in postcards. In the days before personal cameras like the Brownie were introduced, postcards were one of the main ways that traveling Americans could capture a sense of locale in the distant—or not-so-distant—places they visited. For professionals like Wooley, the production of postcards was a valued source of income. Beginning with the 1893 Chicago World's Fair, when the United States Postal Service relaxed its rules governing rates, this new form of communication quickly became a mass medium, a popular obsession that lasted roughly until World War I. Depicting everything from street scenes to mountain vistas, postcards were enthusiastically mailed and collected. In 1906, almost a billion postcards were mailed in the United States, and one company was manufacturing three million postcards per day.[34]

As Robert Bogdan has meticulously described in *Exposing the Wilderness: Early-Twentieth-Century Adirondack Postcard Photographers*, Wooley was one of several postcard producers active in this region a century ago. In northern New York, as throughout the country, postcards were collected as souvenirs, and many middle-class American parlors were stocked with postcard albums that were treasured and perused for decades. Wooley's postcards—hundreds of which can be found to this day in museums, antique shops, and private collections—helped to establish an image of the Adirondacks, especially around Silver Bay and the rest of Lake George, as a scenic vacation destination.[35]

The Magic Lantern Slideshow

An important thread linking Wooley's career to Stoddard's is the magic lantern slideshow, lectures on distant, often exotic lands with illustrations. In the decades after the Civil War and up to the time when cinema became widely available, roughly around the era of World War I, the magic lantern slideshow was a well-known and popular form of entertainment. One historian has asserted that "the magic lantern [was] as much a part of Victorian life as the horse and buggy."[36] With roots in the late seventeenth century, the basic technology of the magic lantern was simple: a bright light shining through a specially colored piece of glass onto a white surface. The image on the glass automatically becomes enlarged and projected. Before photography came along, such images were hand drawn and painted. The original light source—mainly candles—was primitive, unreliable, and insufficiently bright.

In 1802, American chemist Robert Hare experimented with igniting a mixture of oxygen, hydrogen, and lime and discovered a shining, incandescent light. Other tinkerers refined this, while still others experimented with electricity; by mid-century, it was possible to project brilliantly bright light through a hand-painted glass slide. At the same time, the Langenheim brothers of Philadelphia saw the potential for using these light sources with the new technology of the daguerreotype and began offering public exhibitions, using transparencies of photographs and engravings. Their innovations were a great hit at the London World's Exposition of 1851. With the advances accomplished by the Langenheim brothers, the magic lantern slide was soon a commercially viable medium for both entertainment and education.[37]

The potential of the marriage of photography with the magic lantern show was obvious, and entrepreneurs were soon coloring glass negatives of everything from European cathedrals to archaeological sites in the Middle East. When the lighting technology further improved to the point where it was portable and reliable, a new medium of popular entertainment had arrived. In the 1870s, an American photographer and lecturer, S. J. Sedgewick, made a name for himself by turning images of the American West—over 2,000 by 1875, many of them by photographers other than himself—into slides and using them in popular presentations. One of Sedgewick's main draws was "Across the Continent," which anticipated a similar lecture that Wooley would develop a few decades later.[38] (Like Sedgewick, Wooley also advertised a number of slide shows using purchased images.[39])

Sedgewick eventually had a repertoire of seven lectures, each "complete in itself," lasting about two hours, and available for $100.[40] During the same period, photographer Matthew Brady lectured on the Civil War, using slides made from his famous images created on or near the battlefields of Virginia.[41] By the time Jesse Wooley started advertising his illustrated lectures, this medium was widespread across the United States, and thousands upon thousands of Americans attended lectures in churches and meeting halls. Before it was replaced by the movies, the magic-slide lecture, combining education and aesthetic pleasure, was one of the most popular forms of indoor entertainment in the country.[42]

The combination of ostensible education about distant lands and people (easily digestible and requiring no effort on the part of the consumer) and the entertainment value of what was for the time a high-tech innovation drove ticket sales. Imagery of the exotic and splendid American West, for example, could be projected in huge dimensions with dazzling light, accompanied by riveting commentary. The public saw these displays as deeply edifying and imagined themselves traveling through a landscape it was unlikely they would ever get a chance to see personally. One satisfied customer even wrote that the illustrated lecture was more enlightening than reality itself: "Far more can be learned of the country from these lectures than by taking the ordinary trip over the road."[43]

The eclectic nature of Wooley's magic lantern lectures is shown in an ad printed in the *Ballston Journal* in 1893. An evening of music and entertainment was to be offered at the Ballston Spa Baptist Church on May 2, 1893. After a musical prelude on the church organ by "Miss Fenton," followed by a "Recitation" (of poetry, perhaps) by "Miss Hart," Wooley offered an illustrated lecture of travels and more, with views from Saratoga County, the Hudson Valley, New York City, Washington, DC, Florida, Bermuda, Mexico, and Niagara Falls. The slides from Florida, Bermuda, and Mexico are attributed to photographers other than Wooley. After these views of scenery, the show continued with "thirty-five fine portraits of eminent men, presidents, statesmen, authors, etc.," followed by twenty-five "miscellaneous views, plain and colored, comic, mechanical, statuary, animals, etc." and "twelve highly colored slides, superbly illustrating that grand hymn, Rock of Ages." Admission to this multimedia event was "25 cents, with Reserved Seat, Without a ticket 35c, and take chances for a seat."[44]

By 1899, when the *Ballston Journal* published a centennial edition to commemorate the paper's founding in 1798 and included a series of short articles on prominent local businesses, Wooley's lectures were noted as a major part of town life:

> He is somewhat of a traveller and stereopticon lecturer, and never goes without his camera, and is therefore the possessor of a large and valuable collection of views taken on his trips from the Atlantic to the Pacific, and from the St. Lawrence to the Gulf of Mexico. From his thousands of negatives thus secured he has prepared several very fine illustrated lectures, which comprise, "Picturesque Adirondacks," "Florida Illustrated," "The Hudson River, from its source to the Sea," "The Empire State," "From Ocean to Ocean" and "California and Yellowstone National Park," and the summer of 1900 will find him "kodaking" in foreign lands.[45]

The Adirondacks

By the 1890s, the Adirondack region of northern New York was the focus of intense interest throughout the state, and both Stoddard and Wooley developed popular slideshows featuring Adirondack scenery.

Encouraged by William H. H. Murray's *Adventures in the Wilderness*, a 1869 best seller, downstate anglers and hunters sought their sport in the state's last wilderness, and the Adirondacks became a tourist mecca. In addition to its bounteous offerings in field sports, the Adirondacks drew throngs of travelers searching for—and finding—spectacular scenery. Artists and photographers, including Stoddard and Wooley, were quick to appreciate the aesthetic appeal of the Adirondack landscape. Opulent hotels and less expensive lodging houses offered both wealthy and middle-class families an escape from the heat, pollution, and frenzy of the crowded and rapidly industrializing cities. By the time Wooley was an apprentice photographer, the Adirondacks had become one of the country's most beloved and popular vacation destinations.[46]

At the same time, loggers were cutting millions of cords of Adirondack pulpwood. Wasteful and irresponsible logging threatened the viability of the Adirondacks both as a vacation retreat and as a reliable reservoir of water needed for vital transportation arteries like the Hudson River and the Erie Canal. In the 1880s and 1890s, the state of New York began to protect what remained of its Adirondack assets. In 1885, the state established the Forest Preserve comprising all state-owned lands in the Adirondacks and Catskills. In 1892, the legislature created the Adirondack Park, which included both state and private lands, and in 1895, a new state constitution asserted that the Forest Preserve would be "forever kept as wild forest lands."

These were matters of statewide interest, debated in the press, in the legislature, and in the constitutional convention in the summer of 1894.[47] When Stoddard and then Wooley developed illustrated lectures on the Adirondacks, they were tapping into a subject certain to generate ticket sales. Many New Yorkers, including some who would likely never get to the central Adirondacks, were well aware of both the scenic majesty of their state's northern counties and the steps the state legislature was taking to protect this treasure for future generations. They were interested in the Adirondacks and eager to see Wooley's images and hear his account of traveling through the North Country.

Wooley's slideshow, which he titled "A Summer Tour through the Adirondack Mountains and Lakes," incorporated at least a few

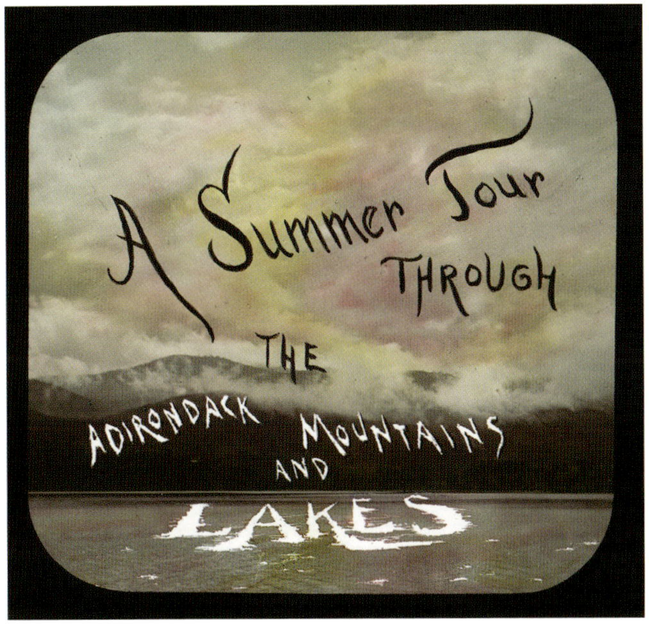

20. *Title Slide for "A Summer Tour through The Adirondacks and Lakes."* Courtesy of the Saratoga County Historical Society.

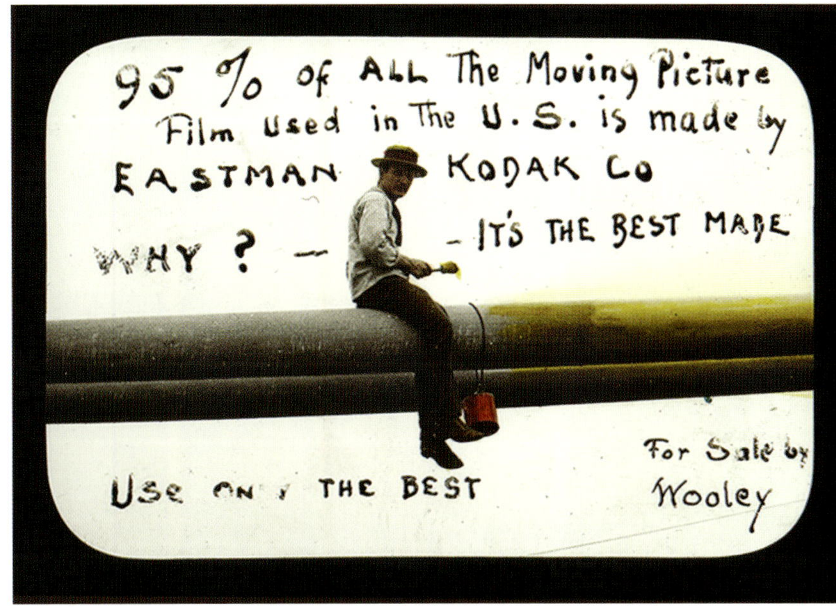

21. *Lantern Slide Advertisement.* Courtesy of the Saratoga County Historical Society.

images generated by Stoddard's camera.[48] With some of the Adirondack slides in the Wooley collection at the Saratoga County Historical Society's Brookside Museum in Ballston Spa, it is nearly impossible to tell which are Wooley's and which are Stoddard's. In any case, the lecture tapped efficiently into the statewide enthusiasm for the topic. With both black-and-white and hand-colored slides, he gave his viewers a tour of Adirondack scenery and local life packaged in an entertaining, easily digestible, vicarious tourist's experience, involving no uncomfortable wagon rides, no stormy afternoons, and no black flies.

After a slide advertising Kodak film "For sale by Wooley" (Wooley's slideshows often included such promotions, either for his own goods and services or for those of local merchants), the lecture displays a variety of images, including the characteristic piece of Adirondack craftsmanship, the guideboat.

We also see images of guides, dead deer, and a variety of lakeshores. Throughout his career, Wooley was drawn to elegant hotels, and he showed slides of many of the grand hotels of the Adirondacks; this was an age when great hotels like the Ampersand on Lower Saranac Lake and the Prospect House on Blue Mountain Lake were among the nation's premier tourist destinations. He also showed

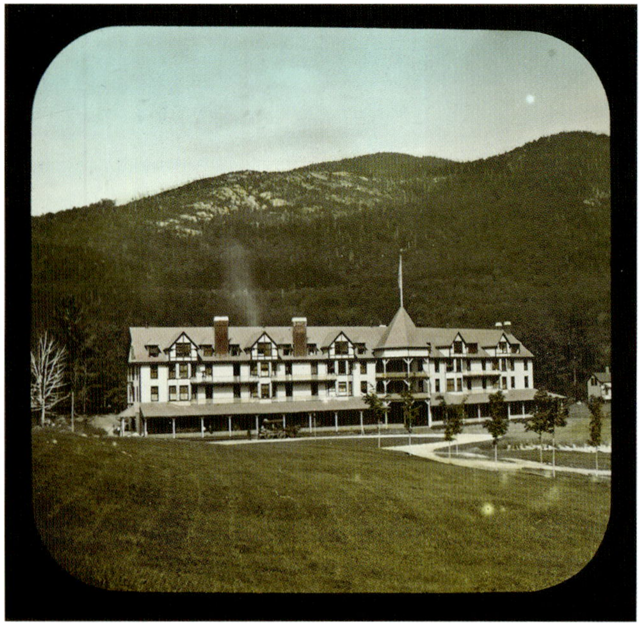

22. *Ausable Club.* Courtesy of the Saratoga County Historical Society.

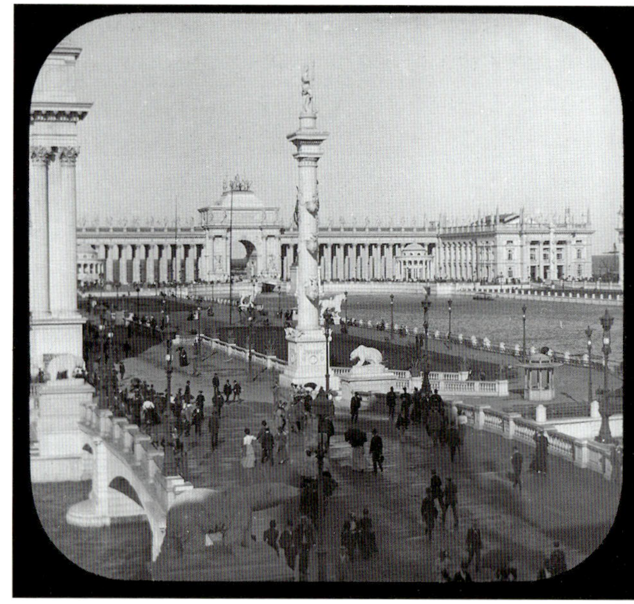

23. *Lantern Slide from Chicago World's Fair.* Courtesy of the Saratoga County Historical Society.

people camping at Adirondack lean-tos, the scenic wonders of Ausable Chasm, lakesides, and docks. People traveled by boat along the region's waterways or by stagecoach or wagon on rough roads, and Wooley showed both the elegant launches, like Raquette Lake's *Killoquah*, and various coaches.

Chicago

In 1893, Wooley accompanied Stoddard to Chicago for the World's Columbian Exposition. This was a significant event in American cultural history, and it is not surprising that Wooley would have taken the time to travel from Ballston Spa to Chicago and to use the photographic work gathered there in a slide-and-lecture presentation. The Exposition had been in the news for years, as Chicago, reconstructed and feverish with commerce and activity after the devastating fire of 1871, invited the world to the shores of Lake Michigan to see pavilions erected by many of the world's nations, as well as the first Ferris wheel.[49]

Wooley's chief interest in Chicago was the spectacular architecture of the fair. The result of his time in Chicago is largely a record of the elaborate pavilions and other gargantuan structures, many designed by the leading architects of the day. Albums and other evidence at Brookside show that Wooley undertook similar expeditions to Buffalo for the Pan-American Exposition of 1901 and to Montreal in 1912.[50]

Not only was the World's Columbian Exposition a showcase for industry, commerce, and international cultures, it was also an important moment in the history of photography. The Eastman Kodak Company hosted its own exhibit, showcasing its latest cameras, one of which, designed especially for the Exposition, was the "Kodak Kolumbus." Armed with the latest in camera technology, amateur photographers, along with professionals like Wooley and Stoddard, made Chicago's world's fair one of the first American spectacles recorded on film by and for the mass culture.[51]

South Carolina and Florida

The 1890s were busy years for Wooley. He seems to have been constantly traveling. In 1895, he steamed down the Hudson, capturing images along the way.[52] And on January 27, 1896, Wooley sailed out of Brooklyn with three Ballston Spa companions. After a stopover at Charleston, South Carolina, their destination was Florida, where Wooley spent several weeks collecting images for an illustrated lecture, which he titled "From Ice and Snow to Flowers and Fruit."[53]

The colored slides in Wooley's Florida lecture are thought to be among the earliest photographic images of Florida in color ever shown in a popular medium, while the lecture he built around them was the first-ever "complete stereopticon slide lecture series about the state of Florida."[54] The Florida lecture is especially important to us because the notes that Wooley used as he delivered it have survived; this is not the case for any of Wooley's numerous other lectures. These notes are written on small postcard-sized, black-and-white photographs, which he turned over, one after another, with a running commentary on the slides. In addition to simple reminders on locale and events, the commentary provides a rare window to his perception of each scene, including his sense of humor, a lamentable degree of racism, and his sense of what was important. For the most part, while the images are striking and always interesting, Wooley's verbal account of any slide's significance is pedestrian and predictable. He had the eye of an artist but the unexamined racial politics of a man who may have spent too much time at traveling minstrel shows.

Wooley opened his lecture with a map of Florida and followed with a short series depicting the ship and its departure from New

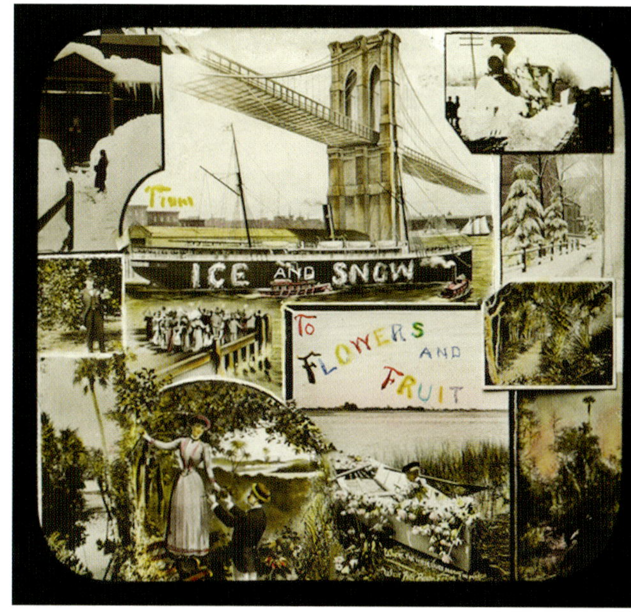

24. *Title Slide "From Ice & Snow, to Flowers and Fruit."* Courtesy of the Saratoga County Historical Society.

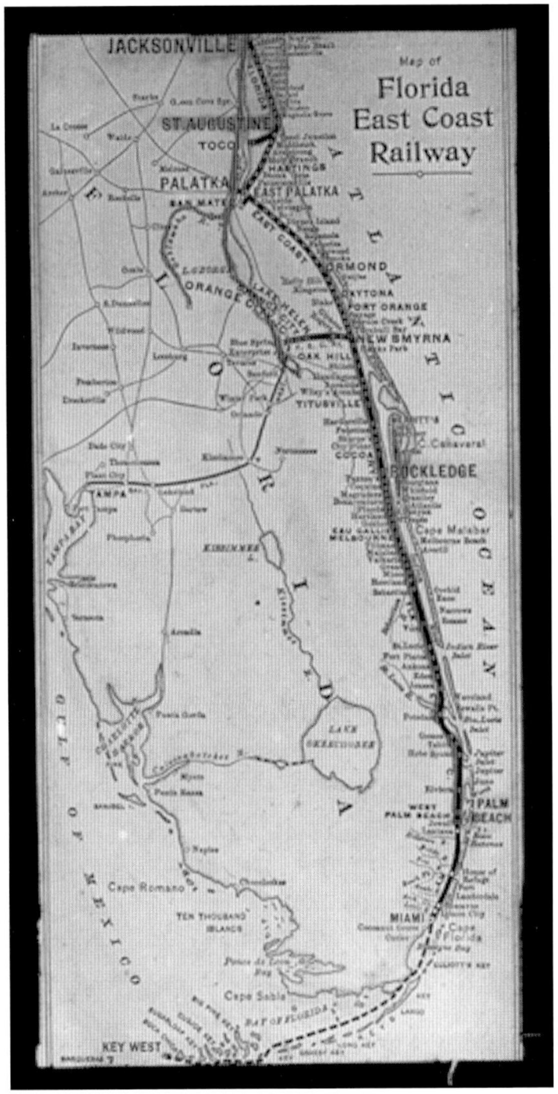

25. *Lantern Slide, Mapping Trip to Florida.* Courtesy of the Saratoga County Historical Society.

York harbor. The tone of his commentary can be seen in his account of a misty image of a sailing sloop and the Statue of Liberty, "who with uplifted hand points our way out to sea and bids us *bon voyage*."[55] This cheery, awkward bonhomie runs throughout the lecture.

Wooley's commentary on Charleston includes tour-book snippets of information about old churches and public and commercial buildings. Here as throughout his career, Wooley was fascinated by architectural detail—domestic, religious, commercial, government—and captured many images of houses and other buildings. For the most part, the architecture that interested him was formal and ornate, not vernacular. Along the Battery, for example, he recorded "the fine residence quarter overlooking the harbor—a fine street lined with typical old Southern houses, high walls with imposing gateways." When wandering along the poorer "King Street—the Colored Section," he retreated to overt racism, including, for example, a photo of a young African American, and commenting: "Nature seems to have furnished the average darky with a mouth especially built for eating watermelon."[56]

From Charleston, the *Algonquin* sailed for Florida and the wharves of Jacksonville. As any New Yorker would be on a winter visit to Florida, Wooley was immediately delighted by the warm climate, the palmettos, and the Spanish moss. From Jacksonville, it was a thirty-five mile train ride to St. Augustine, where Wooley was duly impressed by the Spanish ambiance (reflected in place names), the climate, the antiquities, and the "palatial hotels." It was, he declared, "the favorite winter resort of the Western Hemisphere." Drawn to St. Augustine's charm, Wooley would return there many times in the 1920s and 1930s with Susie.

He was especially taken with the Hotel Ponce de Leon. This hotel was indeed a wonder. Recently built by Florida developer and railroad tycoon Henry Flagler, it was an ornate, huge example of Spanish Renaissance architecture, with interior details designed by Louis Tiffany.[57] Wooley called it the "most magnificent building in the world" and continued, "the magnificent towers rise 150 ft and can be seen from any part of the city. And when seen, as I saw them, by night, glistening with a flood of colored electric light it was never to be forgotten." He devoted ten slides to the Ponce de Leon, with detailed commentary on decorative devices, amenities, gardens, and the extensive interior courtyards.

The lecture closed with a summary of the trip and the observation that while "We enjoy Florida," with its scenery and climate, the charms of the South were transient when compared to New York's: "We long to see a hill or mountain, a crystal brook or lake with pure sweet water. . . . We are of the opinion that the Empire State is a little ahead of anything we have yet seen." Such a conclusion was an almost guaranteed part of such a lecture. It reassured his audience that while Florida was exotic and appealing in so many ways to the tourist, the familiar and comforting features of home offered stability and progress. Like a Chautauqua lecture, a magic lantern slideshow should educate, to a degree, but not challenge received, tacitly understood conventions about the superiority of one's hometown.[58]

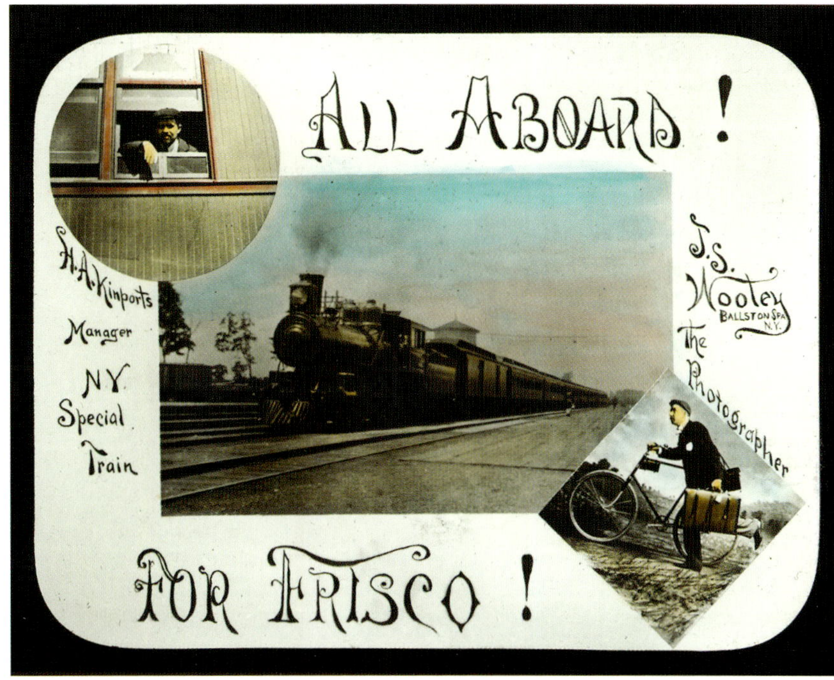

26. *Title Slide, "All Aboard for Frisco."* Courtesy of the Saratoga County Historical Society.

The American West

A trip to Europe followed in July of 1897, and later that same year Wooley took a tour group on a trip to California by way of Yellowstone National Park. This western trip was announced in a brief notice in the *Ballston Journal* on July 3 of that year: "J. S. Wooley left today for a tour of the continent. He will visit Chicago, Ill., Denver, Col., Salt Lake City, San Francisco, and returning visit Portland, Oregon, Seattle, Wash., Yellow Stone [*sic*] Park, and St. Paul, Minn."[59]

Wooley turned group trips into complex business opportunities. He acted as travel agent, tour guide, and photographer, recruiting people from Saratoga County and beyond to join him on elaborate expeditions. He organized or joined large tour groups, entertained his companions along the way, sold them souvenir photographs, and then put together a magic lantern lecture show on his return. He also assembled souvenir albums, which he sold to fellow travelers after they were home.

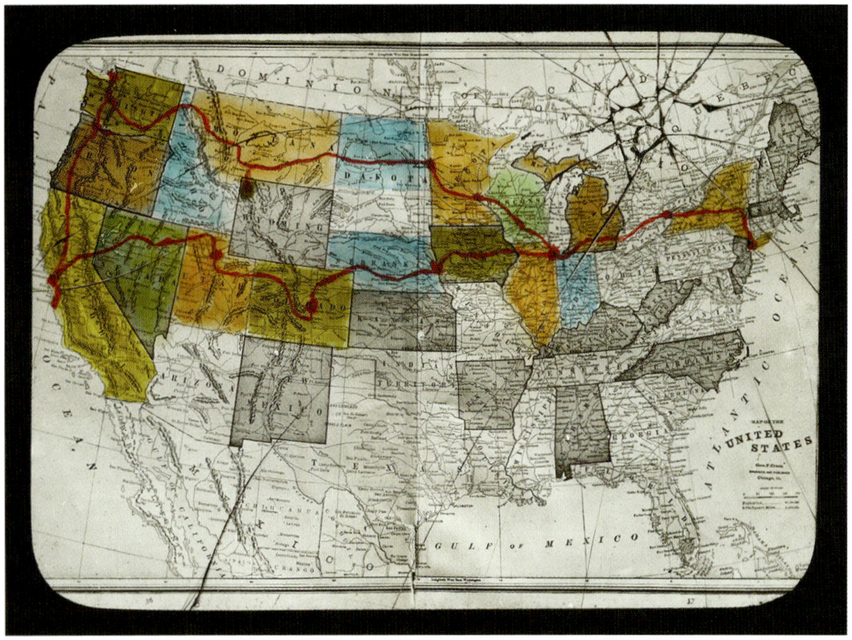

27. *Lantern Slide Map for Western Trip.* Courtesy of the Saratoga County Historical Society.

In the Brookside archives, for example, is a typed letter from Wooley addressed to "Dear Friends of California Party" with an advertisement to the group for prints and albums for sale; these accompanied a sample album. Wooley notes that he took 700 images, of which 450 were worth printing; the difference is attributed to equipment failures, bad film, and other unforeseen problems. "Price will be six cents each [for prints] or Five dollars per hundred unmounted." In the same file is a list of the people on the trip, who were to forward the album along to the next name after deciding what to order. The images in the sample album cover the whole itinerary.[60]

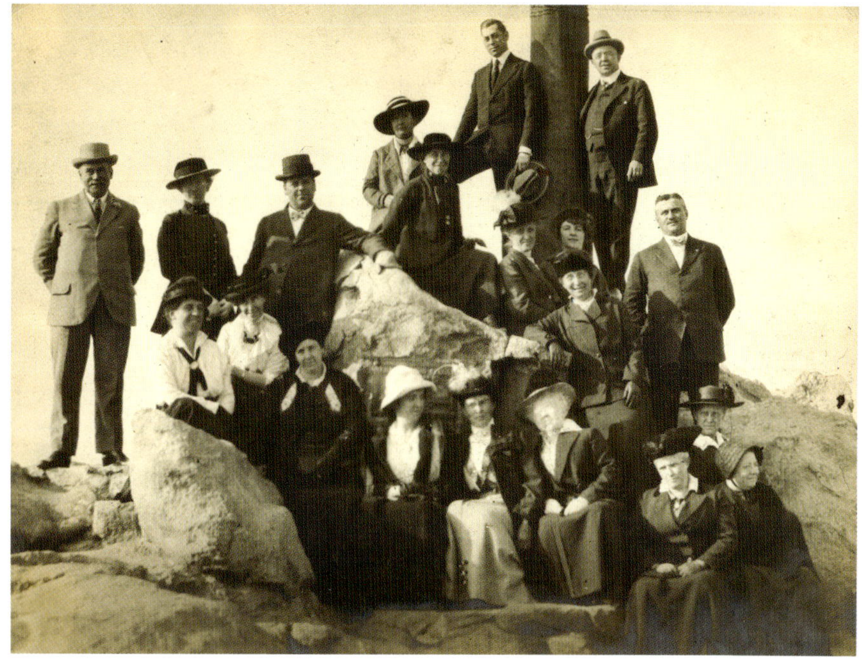

28. *Western Travel Group.* Courtesy of the Saratoga County Historical Society.

Every element of the whole affair was both a business opportunity and an aesthetic challenge. His slideshow, moreover, includes both photographs taken by him and commercially available glass slides of popular tourist attractions.

Europe

In July of 1900, he led a party from Ballston Spa to Europe, sailing from Baltimore on July 5 on the steamer *Rhein.* This was a grand tour of over two months. After arriving at Southampton, they spent about ten days in England, with stops in London, Windsor, Warwick, and

Stratford. Then it was off to the continent and a seemingly frenetic march from city to city, castle to castle: the Low Countries, Germany (with a stop to see the Passion Play at Oberammergau), Austria, Italy, Switzerland, France (with two weeks set aside for Paris and the World Exposition staged there that year). According to a notice in the *Ballston Journal* concerning this trip, Wooley recruited his Ballston Spa group to join a larger tour: "It is purely a pleasure trip for the whole party with the exception of Mr. Wooley, who combines business with pleasure, and carries four cameras and films sufficient to make fifteen hundred negatives. . . . It is safe to assume that Ballston will hear more about the doings of this small party in Europe later on."[61] There is no mention of Susie or their daughter Marion, who would have been ten. Wooley's travels, which were extensive, were, until his retirement, undertaken without family. On returning to Ballston Spa, Wooley employed a familiar pattern, assembling a magic lantern slideshow with images that he had shot himself, combined with purchased glass slides of the castles, cathedrals, and scenery they had seen along the way.

Lake George

Growing up and working in Saratoga County, Wooley probably visited Lake George early in his career—at the latest by 1893, the summer of his first known collaboration with Seneca Ray Stoddard. That year, they worked in Saranac Lake, Lake Placid, Tupper Lake, Long Lake, and Keene Valley during August, and it seems unlikely that they would have passed up the opportunity to admire the scenic wonders of nearby Lake George along the way. (It seems equally unlikely that Wooley, a photographer since his teens, would not have been to world-famous and nearby Lake George even before then.) Stoddard had been photographing Lake George at least since 1871, well aware of both the opportunities for aesthetically challenging work and the national reputation of Lake George as one of the country's most treasured natural wonders.[62]

During the first century or so of European settlement in what is now New York, Lake George was known mainly as part of a trade route—and hence as a much contested and critical strategic artery—linking the Hudson and St. Lawrence Rivers. But by the era of the American Revolution, a few tourists had begun making the then somewhat arduous journey to see its historic sites and scenery. One of the first was none other than Thomas Jefferson, who, in 1791, while on a vacation tour, wrote to his daughter, "Lake George is, without comparison, the most beautiful water I ever saw; formed by a contour of mountains into a basin thirty five miles long, and from two or four miles broad, finely interspersed with islands, its waters limpid as crystal, and the mountain sides covered with rich groves of thuja [cedar], silver fir, aspen, and paper birch down to the water edge; here and there precipices of rock to checker the scene and save it from monotony."[63]

Ever since Jefferson's day, Lake George has been a popular destination for tourists and a vacation retreat for thousands of American families. Its scenery has been the subject of countless paintings, photographs, novels, and travel narratives. Hudson River artists, Luminists, photographers, and novelists have all been drawn to its combination of history and majesty, while hotels, camps, cottages, and mansions have lined stretches of its once pristine shores.[64] At the same time, lengthy shorelines and vast ridges and forests have been saved from any sort of development by their inclusion in the Forest Preserve. Lake George offers culture and wilderness, and both Seneca Ray Stoddard and Jesse Wooley secured their artistic reputations with photographs of its glories.

On Lake George, hotels welcomed the wealthy, and rustic boarding houses put up the less affluent.[65] A roughly ten-mile stretch of shore on the west side, above Lake George Village at the south end, became known as Millionaires' Row, with a long series of opulent palaces mostly built during the years of Wooley's association with the lake. At their private beaches and at exclusive clubs, the wealthy and their children participated in sailing regattas, canoe races, and other sports; these became common subjects for Wooley's camera.

Silver Bay

Wooley's chief connection with the Lake George area was via the Silver Bay Association, on the west shore about twenty-five miles north of the busy village. Wooley's relationship with Silver Bay was a long one, beginning in 1908 and running through 1923. He was the official photographer for Association events, and he ran a photo and gift shop. He also apparently had plenty of time and opportunity to travel around the lake, always—if we judge from the huge collection of images he left behind—on the lookout for subjects. Distant vistas, roadsides, steamboats—these and just about everything one could find on or near an Adirondack lake in the summer became the subjects of what is perhaps his finest work.[66]

The Silver Bay Association grew out of the YMCA movement. The connection between the Y and Silver Bay was a young man named Luther Wishard, born dirt poor in Indiana in 1854. Smart and relentless, Wishard managed to get an education at Princeton while also associating closely with the American Y. After several years of missionary work outside the United States, Wishard saw that both he and the Y needed a facility for training future missionaries and other young men devoted to evangelical Protestantism. After some introspection and some ill health, he persuaded Silas Paine, a wealthy

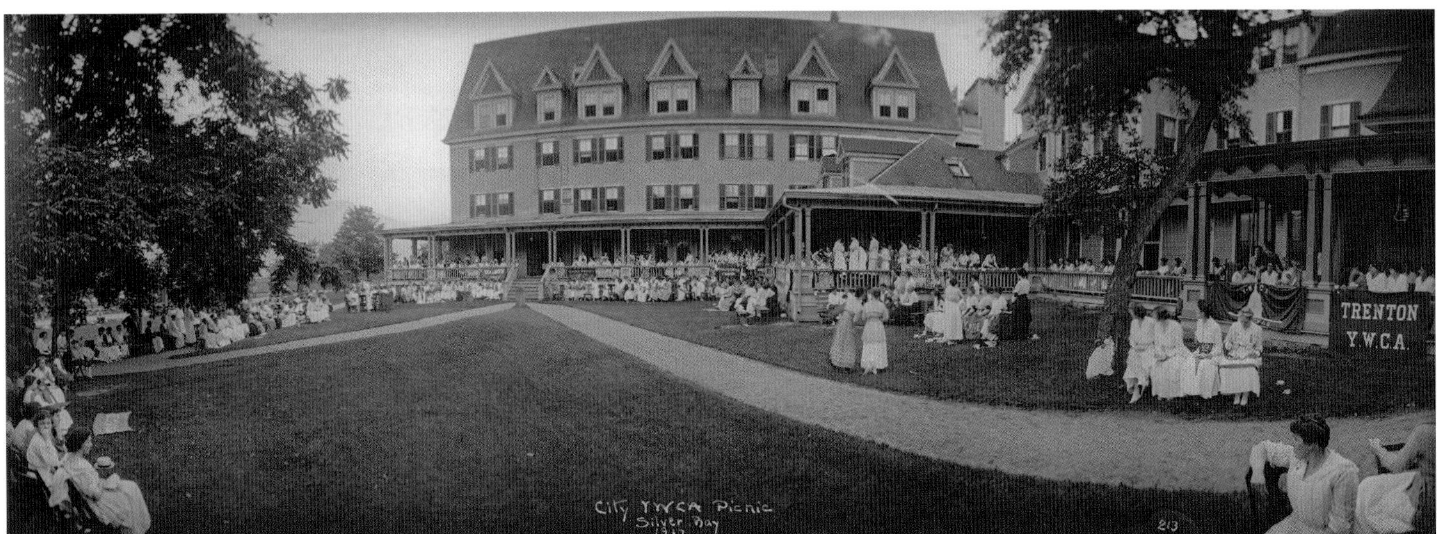

29. *City YMCA Picnic Silver Bay 1917.* Courtesy of the Matt Finley Collection.

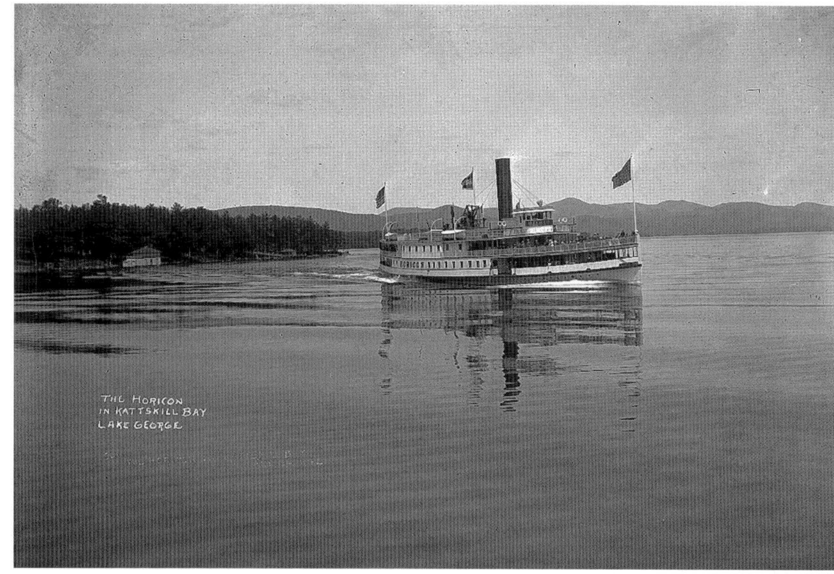

30. *The Horicon in Kattskill Bay Lake George.* Courtesy of the Matt Finley Collection.

businessman and an officer of John D. Rockefeller's Standard Oil Company, to donate a hotel and land he owned on Lake George to establish a conference and training center. This was the origin of the Silver Bay Association, which held its first meeting on Lake George in 1902.[67]

Silver Bay was a good fit for Wooley. The Association was patriotic, optimistic, earnest, and Protestant, an institution characterized by seriousness of purpose but leavened with jovial good humor. He spent sixteen summers as resident photographer there. He captured activities, people, and visiting luminaries, creating a remarkable record of an institution that to this day continues to play a significant role in the cultural life of the southeastern Adirondacks. The juxtaposition of the seriousness and relatively Spartan atmosphere at Silver Bay, near the north end of Lake George, with Millionaire's Row and the bustle of Lake George Village to the south, all set against the magnificent backdrop of the surrounding mountains, moreover, made for a richness of subject matter that immediately caught Wooley's shrewd eye. It was an ideal opportunity to advance his business interests, while at the same time it challenged and inspired his artistic sensibility.

Wooley seemed especially drawn to steamboats, which had been plying the waters of Lake George since 1817, when the *James Caldwell*, an eighty-footer with engine and boilers salvaged from a Lake Champlain wreck, began plying the lake.[68] A lifelong enthusiast for technological innovation, Wooley took to Lake George steamboats with the same spirit he approached new cameras, bicycles, radios, and other inventions of the day. When small floatplanes began landing on Lake George's waters, they instantly and predictably seized his attention.

Around Lake George, Wooley and his cameras captured a diverse array of subjects. In addition to steamboats, both plowing the lake and moored at docks, he recorded all sorts of recreational activities, especially swimming and boating. He boarded many of the steamboats in order to capture images of the shoreline and the great hotels from mid-lake, and he found lookout points from the ridges and other high spots from which he could shoot down toward Silver Bay, Sabbath Day Point, and other popular spots. As always, he was drawn to the houses of the affluent, leaving hundreds of images of the opulent summer homes along the Lake George shoreline. Hotels, both palatial, like the Fort William Henry or the Sagamore, and more modest, like Braley's Inn at Bolton Landing or Rising House at Hague, caught his eye and lens. The lavish interiors of the more expensive hotels—the Sagamore, for example—provided studies in shadow and light.

One locale that especially conveyed an important tradition of the region was the Lake George Club, a bastion of wealth and class privilege on the west shore about twenty miles south of Silver Bay and four miles north of the village. Wooley photographed the club's buildings, its members, and their activities on many occasions. Established on its current site in 1908 (the same year that Wooley first came to Silver Bay) as a venue for regattas, tennis, golf, and other sports associated with lakeside clubs, the Lake George Club soon had a clubhouse designed by the well-known architectural firm of Ludlow and Peabody of New York. In the 1930s, the Club was famous for sponsoring speedboat races, but its main focus since then has been sailing.[69]

At Silver Bay, Wooley routinely recorded daily and special activities and the Association's rich combination of architecture and open space. He photographed sailing and other modes of boating, swimming, ball games, camping, fire drills—all the ordinary events of a summer camp. Special events included elaborate weddings and circuses held on the Silver Bay campus and visits of dignitaries, like that of New York Governor Charles Evans Hughes (a native of nearby Glens Falls) in 1909. When Hughes walked from the dock, where his private yacht, the *Pocahontas*, was moored, to the main building, the sidewalk was lined with scores of white-shirted, bow-tied young men, standing rigidly at attention and singing "Onward Christian Soldiers."[70] The Silver Bay Association often invoked such a quasi-military atmosphere, and the formal raising of the flag was a daily ritual. All such photographs made for popular souvenirs and generated income in Wooley's Silver Bay shop, as Silver Bay attendees packed up after a week or two of training and began heading for home.

The Lake George Panoramas

While Wooley was assembling images of people and places that he could sell as postcards or prints and fulfilling his duties as resident photographer for the Silver Bay Association, he was always on the lookout for intriguing combinations of light, proportion, and shade. These became the black-and-white panoramas that constitute his lasting artistic achievement. The panoramas nearly always involved water, with sunsets, storms, distant ridgelines, cloud patterns, and boats—steam or other—set off against the famous Lake George water. The collection also included more intimate photographs of roadsides, clusters of trees, and architecturally interesting buildings.

Judging from the quantity of images, it seems safe to say that Wooley must have spent day after day driving around the lake or waiting patiently at docks and assessing the light. Working with tripod as well as handheld cameras, he recorded both scenery and human activity, carefully and creatively playing with light, shadow, cloud patterns, the wakes of steamboats, architectural ornament, and all the myriad details of a locale combining nature and culture. But the artistically captured image was seldom, if ever, the whole point: surviving prints often show tape marks where he (or someone working in his studio) cropped them for the manufacture of postcards. Wooley's Lake George canon constitutes a paradigm of his career: a sharp aesthetic vision always married to the need to generate income.

In *America by the Yard: Cirkut Camera Images from the Early Twentieth Century*, Robert MacKay, a historian of photography, discusses the popularity and technology of panoramic photography in Wooley's day. Among other things, he points out that although the panorama had appeared as early as the 1840s, soon after wet-plate

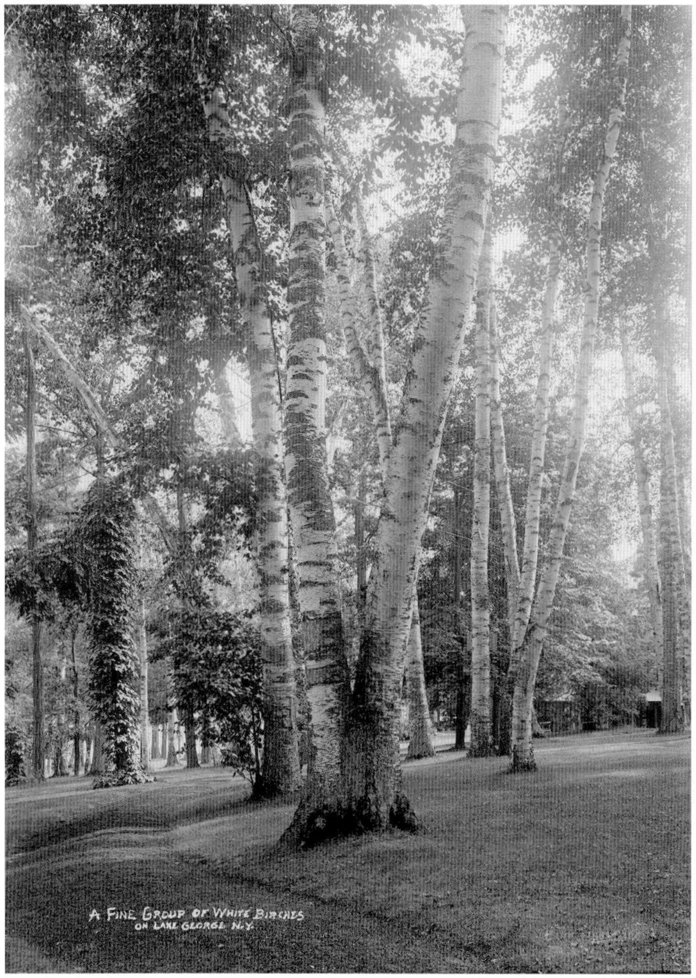

31. *A Fine Group of White Birches on Lake George, N.Y.* Courtesy of the Matt Finley Collection.

photography was invented, it was especially popular at precisely the time of Wooley's tenure on and near Lake George. In part, this was due to George Eastman and his introduction in 1889 of "flexible celluloid film," easier to work with than either wet or dry plates and particularly suited to panoramic cameras. Another technological development that led in a roundabout way to the popularity of panoramas was the rapid and widespread availability of cheap handheld cameras; because so many amateurs were using these, professional photographers like Wooley were on the lookout for work that could be produced only with more expensive, more technically demanding equipment.[71]

For a generation, moreover, Americans had been enjoying the magnificent photography of the American West. The great western surveys of the 1860s through the 1880s often had professional photographers as members of the crew, and their work was fundamental in establishing a narrative of the meaning and significance of the West in the popular culture. As historian Martha Sandweiss observes, "in the West, nineteenth-century photography found its most distinctive subject."[72] Photographers like Timothy O'Sullivan, Eadweard Muybridge, and William Henry Jackson captured the grandeur of the West, which most Americans would never have a chance to see for themselves, in magnificent panoramic images; these were displayed in galleries and other venues in Eastern cities and became the medium by which many Americans acquired their first impressions of scenic wonders like the Grand Tetons, Yellowstone, and the Grand Canyon. It seems likely that Adirondack photographers, beginning with Stoddard and including Wooley, were intensely aware of the precedent established in the West and set out, consciously or otherwise, to create a sense of the Adirondacks as equally scenic, equally deserving the lens of a panoramic camera.

Among Wooley's panoramas are fairly conventional group shots of people visiting Silver Bay—for example, a photo of some sixty or seventy young men, *YMCA Summer School Men on Summit of Black Mt. Aug. 13 1910 Altitude 2665* (p. 94). Black Mountain is a peak on the east side of Lake George, about five miles south of Silver Bay. Known for its bare summit and spectacular views of the entire lake, it was doubtless a popular destination for Silver Bay hikers. This particular panorama shows tape marks, where someone cropped it for reproduction, probably for sale as a souvenir to all the men in the photo.

Silver Bay also served as a retreat for groups other than those with a YMCA affiliation. In 1912, for example, Wooley recorded the presence of forty women from Mount Holyoke College, all in long white dresses, and four neatly dressed men, perhaps professors, visiting Lake George for a summer gathering. And in 1920, he photographed a baseball game at Silver Bay between Middlebury College and the United States Military Academy. A fine variation of the group shot is a 1917 photograph titled *YMCA Men at Silver Bay on Review by Gov. Whitman Aug. 14 1917* (p. 93): in a characteristically semimilitary arrangement, a line of young men, all in white shirts and trousers, white caps, and dark ties stretched toward the lake and the ridgeline on the far shore. Wooley seems to have especially appreciated the opportunities for abstraction and composition presented by group photos wherein the individuals were dressed similarly and monochromatically.

As Wooley circulated among the many clubs, camps, and other institutions on Lake George, he was always on the lookout for opportunities to create souvenir photographs that he could sell to patrons and staff—e.g., the staff and counselors at Camp Iroquois, 1918 (p. 118); Camp Ronah, 1919 (p. 119); the golf course at Glenburnie Club (p. 115); the Lake George Club (pp. 68–71); the Fort William Henry Hotel (pp. 58–59); the Sagamore Hotel (pp. 62–63); and a swimming competition at Hague (pp. 102–3).

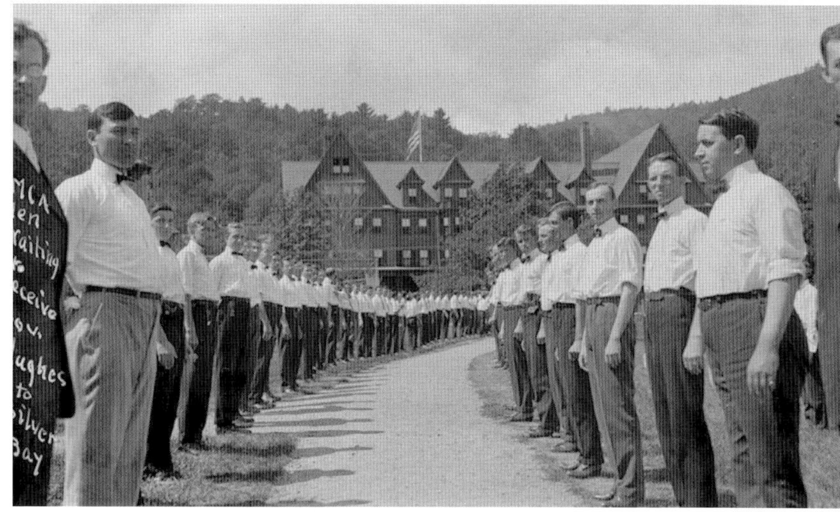

32. *YMCA Men Waiting to Receive Gov. Hughes to Silver Bay.* Courtesy of the Matt Finley Collection.

But the best are shots across or over the lake surface, often taking advantage of a distant ridgeline. *Lake George from Ft Wm Henry Hotel French Mountain* (pp. 52–53), for example, is a characteristic Wooley composition, with a steamboat just left of center and distant shore- and ridgelines on either side. It is a photo perfectly suited either for a museum exhibition or for reproduction as a mass-produced postcard. *Fort William Henry on Lake George From The Air* (p. 61), taken from an airplane, combines Wooley's frequent use of lake surface and architectural display with his fascination with the latest technology, in this case the small floatplanes that were becoming popular on Lake George.

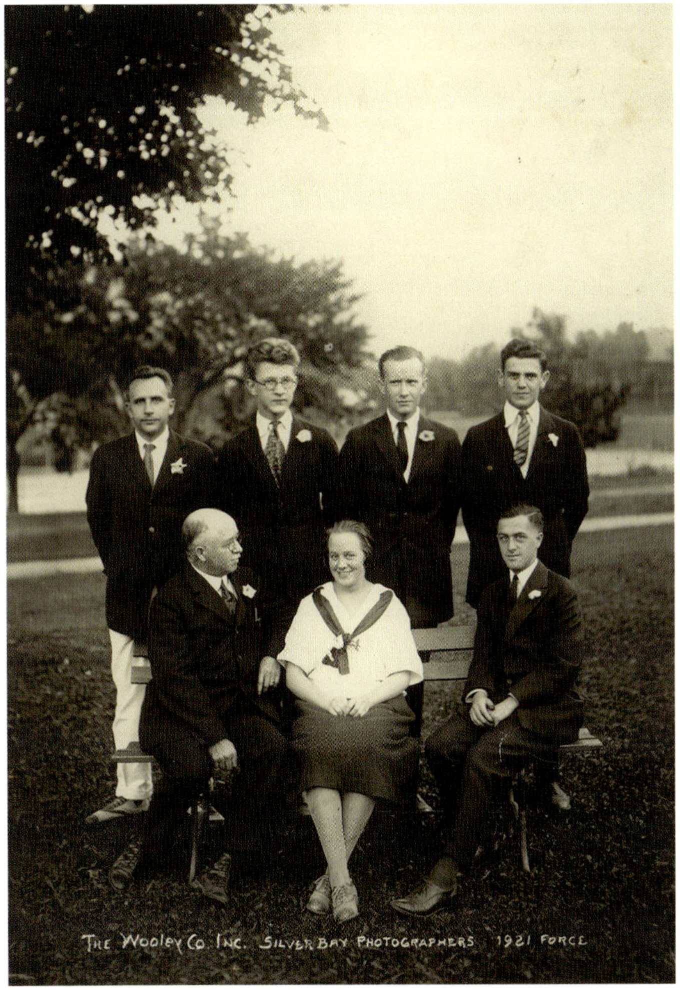

33. *The Wooley Co. Inc. Silver Bay Photographers 1921.* Courtesy of the Saratoga County Historical Society.

Further afield, Wooley worked at Lake Champlain, beginning with Ticonderoga, the historic link between Lakes George and Champlain, where he photographed ruins, monuments, and buildings for postcards. In 1909, during the tercentenary celebration of the first European incursion on Lake Champlain, he was on the scene in Crown Point and then Plattsburgh to record the ceremonial visit of President William Howard Taft. This involved parades down the main street in Plattsburgh, official appearances of foreign dignitaries, and a pageant wherein actors playing Indians and Frenchmen portrayed the deadly 1609 encounter between Samuel de Champlain and his Algonquin allies and Iroquois near what is now Crown Point. President Taft and Governor Hughes traveled from Plattsburgh to this event on the steamboat *Valcour*. Indifferent to historical accuracy, the enactment showed "Indians" camped in "tepees" on the shore of Lake Champlain.

Over a period of several decades, Wooley deliberately made his way around Lake George, visiting villages and scenic points, always on the alert for the combinations of light and shadow that evoked his most compelling images, producing a body of work that secures him a permanent place in the history of New York photography. He was, moreover, an invaluable chronicler of the culture and life of this corner of the Adirondack region. He was not especially interested in the deep woods, but he studiously recorded the summer life of a popular American resort. Equally important, he captured the light, the architecture, and the magnificent scenery that has appealed to every successive generation of Americans. What follows in this book is a carefully considered selection of his characteristic and best work, emphasizing Wooley's images of the villages, waters, and scenic vistas around Lake George.

J. S. Wooley

Technique and Aesthetics

JAMIE YOUNG

LIKE PAINTERS, photographers have always had a range of tools from which to choose. Each generation's photographic aesthetics have been shaped by the camera technology available to them, and each kind of camera gave a particular look to the work. The camera is just a tool, one controlled by the artist, a means to an end. On the other hand, the tool may shape the finished product, which was certainly the case with Wooley's use of the Al-Vista panoramic camera.

Jesse Sumner Wooley, like other photographers of his day, used different cameras and formats for different types of work. He shot a range of subjects, including studio portraits, images for lantern slideshows, scenic postcards, and panoramic images. He shot with a stereo camera and made stereo views, a popular commercial practice at the time. His image collection indicates he regularly shot with a small, easy-to-carry travel camera, a stereo camera, a 5 x 7 camera, and a 3½ x 5½ in. postcard format camera. He also owned a 10 in. Cirkut camera, as a Cirkut group shot of his has been found. Wooley owned an art and photography supply store connected with his portrait studio in Ballston Spa and became a Kodak dealer early on, so he could have experimented with lots of different cameras, depending on the projects he had at the time.

The advent of, first, the dry plate and then flexible roll film made the turn of the twentieth century a revolutionary time for photographers, giving them the freedom to create new kinds of images.

The introduction of flexible roll film allowed for the development of the first commercially produced swing lens camera, the Multiscope

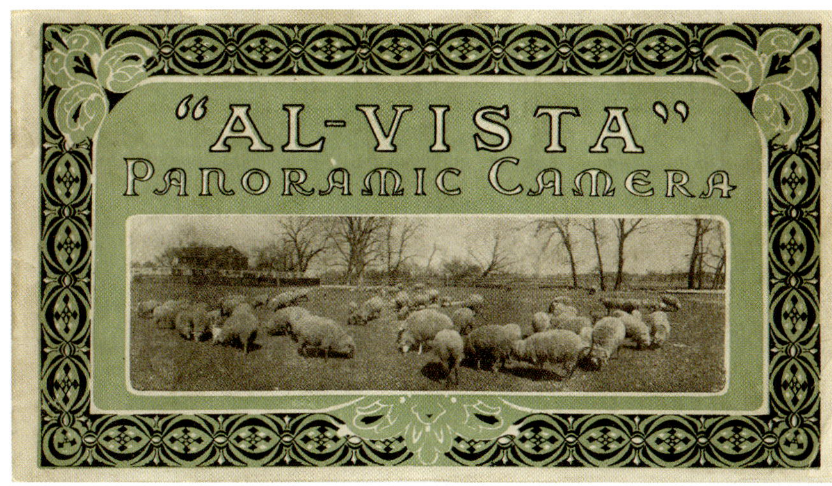

34. *Al-Vista Camera Catalog Cover,* 1903. Courtesy of Jamie Young Photography.

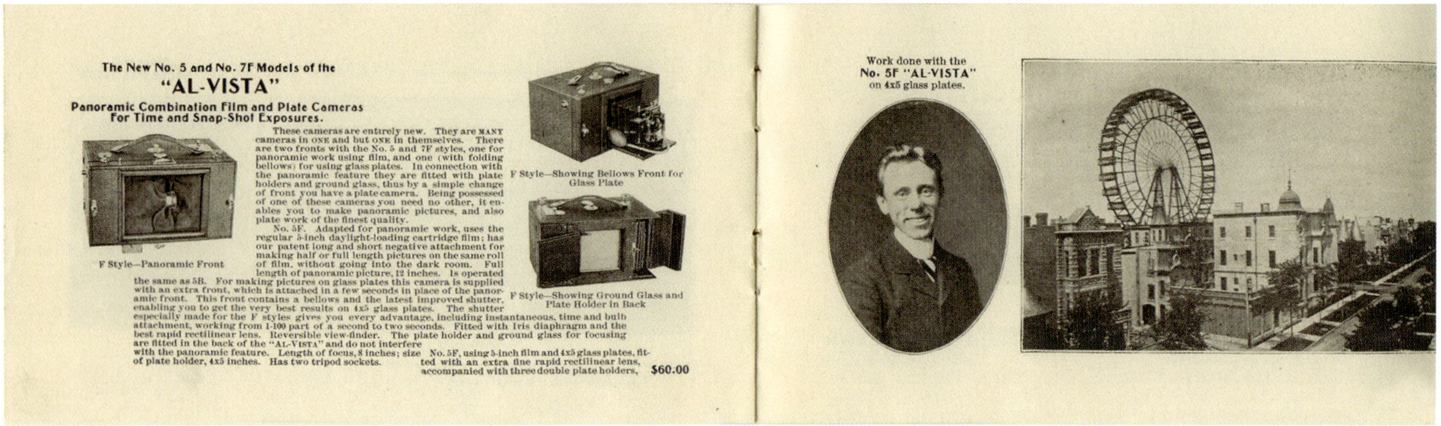

The New No. 5 and No. 7F Models of the

"AL-VISTA"

Panoramic Combination Film and Plate Cameras
For Time and Snap-Shot Exposures.

These cameras are entirely new. They are MANY cameras in ONE and but ONE in themselves. There are two fronts with the No. 5 and 7F styles, one for panoramic work using film, and one (with folding bellows) for using glass plates. In connection with the panoramic feature they are fitted with plate holders and ground glass, thus by a simple change of front you have a plate camera. Being possessed of one of these cameras you need no other, it enables you to make panoramic pictures, and also plate work of the finest quality.

No. 5F. Adapted for panoramic work, uses the regular 5-inch daylight-loading cartridge film; has our patent long and short negative attachment for making half or full length pictures on the same roll of film, without going into the dark room. Full length of panoramic picture, 12 inches. Is operated the same as 5B. For making pictures on glass plates this camera is supplied with an extra front, which is attached in a few seconds in place of the panoramic front. This front contains a bellows and the latest improved shutter, enabling you to get the very best results on 4x5 glass plates. The shutter especially made for the F styles gives you every advantage, including instantaneous, time and bulb attachment, working from 1-100 part of a second to two seconds. Fitted with Iris diaphragm and the best rapid rectilinear lens. Reversible view-finder. The plate holder and ground glass for focusing are fitted in the back of the "AL-VISTA" and do not interfere with the panoramic feature. Length of focus, 8 inches; size of plate holder, 4x5 inches. Has two tripod sockets.

No. 5F, using 5-inch film and 4x5 glass plates, fitted with an extra fine rapid rectilinear lens, accompanied with three double plate holders, $60.00

F Style—Panoramic Front

F Style—Showing Bellows Front for Glass Plate

F Style—Showing Ground Glass and Plate Holder in Back

Work done with the No. 5F "AL-VISTA" on 4x5 glass plates.

35. *Al-Vista Camera Catalog*, 1903. Courtesy of Jamie Young Photography.

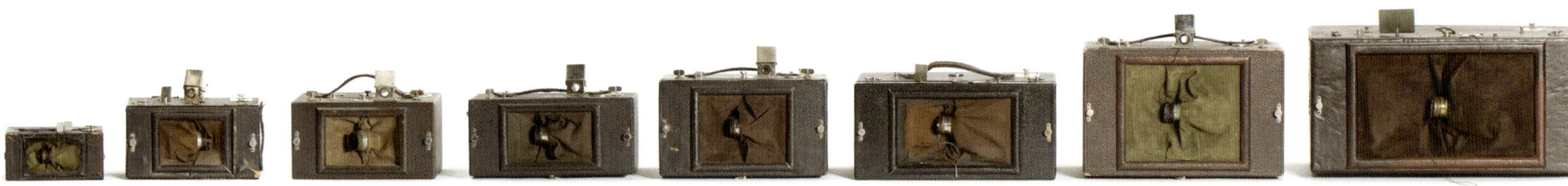

36. *Al-Vista Cameras*. Courtesy of Jamie Young Photography.

Al-Vista camera; it could capture 140-degree views, which is close to the visual range people see. By contrast, a normal camera lens takes in only 40 or 50 degrees, and except for a few rare specialty lenses, even a wide-angle lens can capture only 90 to 100 degrees. The flexible film was bent in a curved half circle, and the lens would pivot or "swing" at its center at a certain distance from the film plane, painting the image onto the film through a vertical slot attached to the back of the lens.

Wooley knew the swing lens camera could show the landscape and culture of the Lake George region in a whole new way, and he often shot with his 5 x 12 in. Al-Vista swing lens panoramic camera.

This camera was unique, manufactured in Burlington, Wisconsin, sometime between 1898 and about 1910. A look today at the inner workings would suggest they were assembled by a watchmaker or clock maker rather than a camera manufacturer. A set of layered gears connects the moving lens to the fan, which controls the shutter

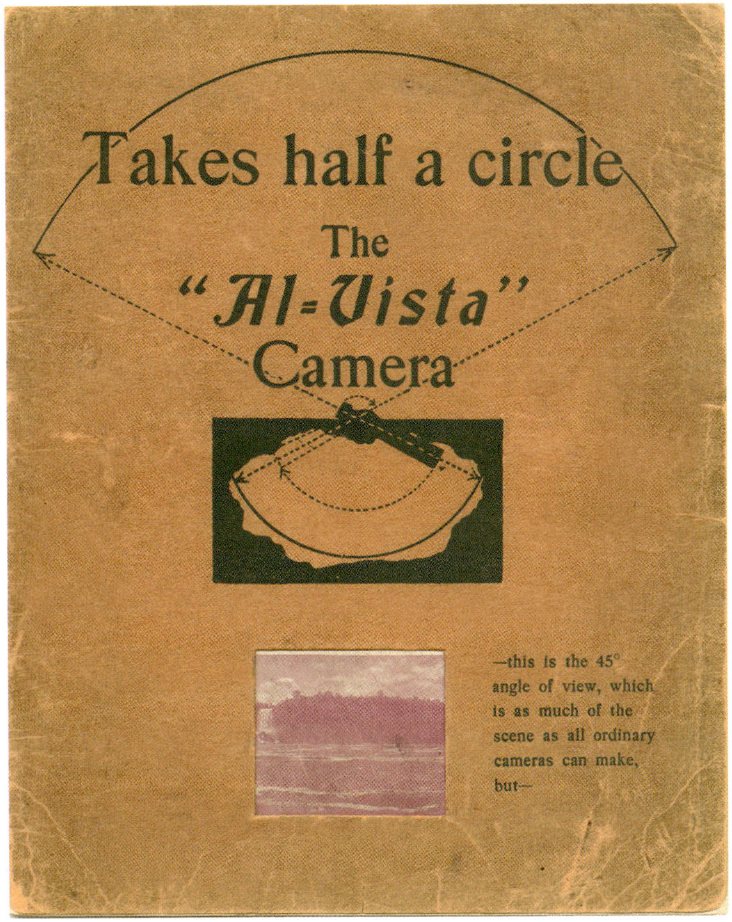

37. *Al-Vista Half-Circle Diagram.* Courtesy of Jamie Young Photography.

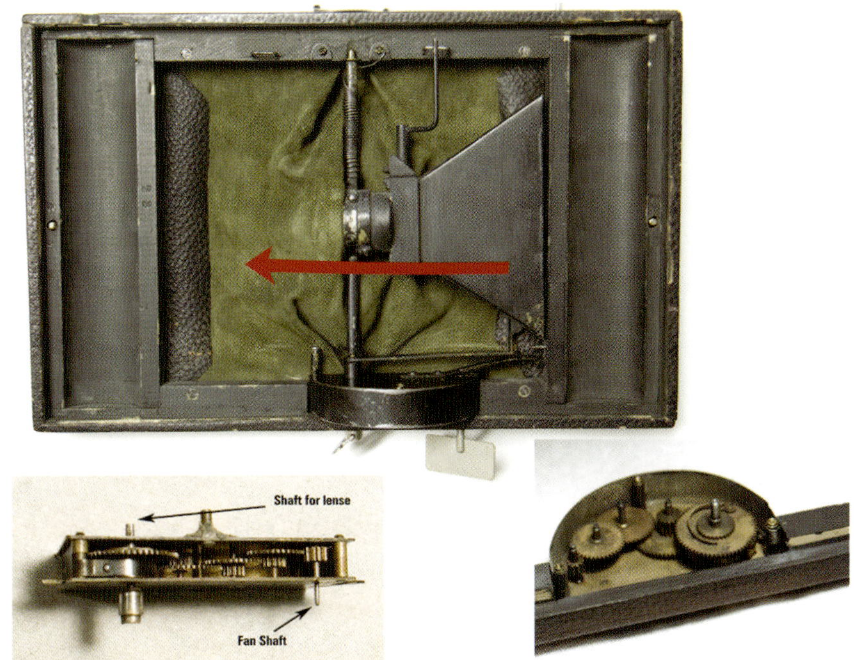

38. *Al-Vista Exposure Mechanism.* Courtesy of Jamie Young Photography.

speed. The vertical slit that makes the exposure rides on a shaft wrapped with a spring so primitive by today's standards that it is hard to believe any kind of consistency in exposures is possible. The lens points to one side, covered in brown suede that acts as a flexible bellows, and is framed by a rectangular box covered in Moroccan grain leather.

This odd-looking camera was designed by German immigrant Peter N. Angsten, who was born in Koblenz in 1855. While still in Germany, Angsten conceived the idea of a camera with a turret-like, spring-driven lens that would turn in an arc of almost 180 degrees.

But he had one big problem: there was no flexible film to work with at that time. Angsten came to America in 1882 and settled in Chicago, where he worked as a painter and decorator. By that time, Eastman Kodak had introduced the emulsion-covered film that solved his dilemma. Angsten patented the camera on September 8, 1896, and began manufacturing it on a small scale in Chicago.

One afternoon while he was taking pictures in Chicago, an industrialist from Burlington, Wisconsin, spotted Angsten using the camera and became so fascinated with it that he rushed back to Burlington and persuaded four friends to buy the patent and put the Al-Vista camera into production in Burlington. Their effort blossomed into the Multiscope & Film Company, the first company to mass-produce an easy-to-use panoramic camera that used readily available roll film.[1]

Photographers like Wooley chose these specialty panoramic cameras when they wanted to show a more complete aesthetic view of the world. A panoramic photo tells a story composed of a number of separate scenes or vignettes, which together become something more than just the combination of the individual parts. A group panoramic portrait holds portraits of individual people but also offers an overall portrait of a community and a sense of place. A panoramic landscape can create a complete, layered narrative of a place, while also highlighting specific moments or spots within that view. Panoramas of events give an authentic sense of place and community, along with an energy that is hard to capture with a traditional camera.

Wooley was able to use the Al-Vista to depict the life and energy of the Lake George community in a dazzlingly complete way. Lake George was more than just a beautiful place, and Wooley chose a camera that could best portray the special feeling of the community and locale. He found a commercial market for these images in summer visitors, selling group shots, events, and panoramic postcards of the area.

Wooley and other photographers using the Al-Vista would set up the camera on a tripod and level it with the built-in level so the horizon would be flat and straight. This was especially important when doing lake views as the lake horizon would be tilted and curved if the camera wasn't level. A rotating viewfinder would let the user see the overall composition. Some cameras also had marks pressed into the leather to show the angle of view. Most cameras had waterhouse stops (metal disks with holes of a specific size) that could be placed inside the lens to control exposure and depth of field.

Some of the very last Al-Vistas, produced around 1908, were fitted with a more modern diaphragm. The film was a flexible base nitrocellulose film with paper backing on a roll. A photographer would remove the camera front, allowing access to the film slots and the inside of the camera, and place the film into the camera. He or she would then feed the leader paper through grooves on the curved film plane and wind it onto an empty film spool. (Because the film plane was so long, some Al-Vista cameras required an additional film leader attached when loading film.) Then the photographer would replace the camera front and advance the film roll until the film was fully in the curved film plane. He or she would determine the exposure and choose a fan blade to produce the correct shutter speed. The fans were rectangular pieces of metal centered on a press fit shaft, which would fit onto a spindle in the camera mechanism; the larger the fan, the slower the shutter speed.

The fan was fitted, the spring mechanism cocked, and the lens cap removed. The photographer would press the shutter button on top of the camera, releasing the pivoting lens and letting it swing from left to right at the proper speed. When the lens got to the end of its swing, an internal shutter gate would close, keeping light from entering the camera and exposing film while the lens moved back into position to take another shot. (Replacing the lens cap during transport and after the exposure helped make sure no light leaked in.) The photographer would then advance the film for the next shot, using the film counter on top of the camera. There was a lot of friction when advancing film in these cameras, and one had to unwind the film spool while winding the takeup spool; the film would come out of the tracks if this was done incorrectly. There was also a marking pin in the camera that would let the photographer mark the place between exposures, in case there were different processing requirements. When the roll was done, the photographer would wind it fully onto the takeup spool to be removed from the camera.

The swing lens pan camera did have some limitations compared with a regular camera. It needed to be set on a tripod, and wasn't good for handheld candid shots. The effective shutter speed was limited by the clockwork spring mechanism, the lenses were slow, and the camera could not shoot very fast or very slow exposures. With the slow film emulsions of the day, interior shots were difficult to achieve. The lens on a swing lens camera was built into the camera design and couldn't be switched for a different lens. One would have to buy a whole new camera with a different lens designed around it.

Negative processing and printing was the same as for any other roll-film camera. Kodak offered developing kits for roll film, but people often developed by hand by rolling the film back and forth through a tray. A contact print was created by laying a negative directly onto print paper and exposing it to light. Print enlargements were generally rare, and photographers would use a camera that made a negative the same size as the desired print. Wooley's camera used stock Kodak #4 cartridge roll film or #104 film, and the film would take four exposures on a stock fifty-two-inch roll. He also made a lot of photographic postcards with special "postcard" photo paper in regular and panoramic sizes.

Visual artists have been interested in the panorama for centuries. The term panorama (formed from the Greek πᾶν "all" + ὅραμα "sight") was coined around 1790 by Robert Barker to describe his large cylindrical painting installations. These installations were popular attractions, and likely influenced photographers to look for ways to create similar kinds of images. Almost from the start of the medium, in fact, photographers began creating mechanical cameras that could extend the limited view of the camera lens. In 1843, Joseph Puchberger of Retz, Austria, created a 150-degree swing lens daguerreotype camera. A year later, Frederic Martens made a very similar camera, which he used to shoot scenes in Paris. Other photographers followed, making their own one-of-a-kind devices to create seamless images beyond a normal camera's ability. The sensitizing materials were coated on glass or metal and the cameras required a curved film plane. People developed many ingenious methods to deal with this problem, but shooting with these cameras remained a complex and difficult process.

Another common way to make a panoramic image was segmented photography, which let people shoot many consecutive images with a regular camera and place them side by side to create a panoramic image group. Eadweard Muybridge, Carlton Watkins, H. H. Bennett, and W. H. Jackson often used this technique.

Throughout the nineteenth century, resourceful photographers continued to pursue labor-intensive specialty solutions to create seamless panoramas, but it wasn't until around 1890, when George Eastman developed flexible film, that anyone could buy and use a panoramic camera easily.

Gallery of Selected Photography by J. S. Wooley

Richard Timberlake, *Curator*

The images contained in this gallery are from the private collection of Matt Finley of Bolton on Lake George.

Introduction

Jesse Wooley's Selected Views

CAROLINE M. WELSH

THE PHOTOGRAPHER'S ART lies in the ability to capture a moment of reality, whether staged or witnessed, and turn it into an image that is interesting and beautiful. Photographers select rather than conceive their subjects; the quality of the photograph results from their ability to anticipate and recognize the best moments and make them permanent. The decisions a photographer makes about composition or the arrangement of visual elements and the content or meaning distinguish a simple document from a personal creative expression. Cameras capture an image; photographers take a picture.

Jesse Wooley had an artist's eye for identifying the picturesque qualities in his panoramic landscape compositions. His natural talent for composing the view along with his ardent love for taking pictures and fascination with the technology of photography assured his success. His views of Lake George and its environment suspended moments of natural beauty for his viewers and compose an impressive body of work.

Jesse Wooley captured Adirondack scenery by selecting the view for visual impact and employing perspective and composition (establishing fore-, middle-, and backgrounds while selecting the visual elements to be included); the expressive qualities of light, shadow, atmosphere, texture; and balancing linear and volumetric elements in order to achieve an aesthetic effect.

The "Irresistible Charm" of Lake George the Beautiful (pp. 72–73) is a good example of Wooley's eye and aesthetic decisions. The dark woods and the breakwater wall along with the strong angle of the dock on the right foreground dynamically drive the eye across the lake to the mountains and sky in the background; expressive light and shadow achieved by contrasted lights and darks dramatize the sun peeking through the clouds above the distant mountains, the light sculpting the birch trees, the empty chair and bench sheltered under the trees, the empty boats, and the dock reflected in the still water; the mass of the woods and stone is balanced by the calm expanse of water and the visual interest created by the details of the boats and dock; the near view woods and wall and the distant mountains contain the view. The effect is one of peace and tranquility at the same time as it, as the title suggests, captures the "irresistible" beauty of a moment in time on this storied lake.

Dimensions, not subject matter, make a photograph a panorama, as Professor Bogdan points out in *Adirondack Vernacular: The Photographs of H. M. Beach* (Syracuse, NY: Syracuse University Press, 2003, 35). For most commercial photographers, large groups of people on outings, celebrating, or at work were their best sellers, not the scenery. Henry M. Beach (1863–1943), Jesse Wooley (1867–1943), and William Kollecker (1879–1962) were Adirondack photographers who all used panoramas to chronicle everyday life, industry, recreation, events, architecture, people, and the landscape. Seneca Ray Stoddard's (1843–1917) photography is not in panoramic format; his panoramic experience comprises 200 panoramic views from the tops of Adirondack mountains while working for Verplanck Colvin as a photographer for the New York State Topographical Survey in 1878. Jesse Wooley began to use wide-format photography for a wide variety of purposes in addition to landscapes in 1908 and continued into the 1920s.

Living in a time of great social and technological change, Wooley's keen eye for detail in all aspects of his physical environment served the documentation of myriad subjects. Status and dress are seen in portraits of notables and families. Wooley's changing world is chronicled through images of the architecture of everyday life, wealthy summer residences or historic buildings, images of the past and nostalgic views of disappearing landmarks, the juxtaposition of the old and the new, and horse-drawn vehicles and automobiles, steamboats and flying boats, speedboats, and airplanes. All aspects of civic and social life in the towns around the lake were captured by the photographer's eye—camps and their events and activities, especially the Silver Bay YMCA, hotels and clubs, interiors and exteriors, grounds and structures, and people at work and play.

On one hand, the panoramic format offered Wooley the opportunity to capture more comprehensive and detailed views of subjects, whether in group portraits or events or landscapes. The wider field of view and the eye-level viewpoint gave the photographer the chance to capture more information. On the other hand, it could freeze an unexpected vantage point or moment in time and create an opportunity to teach his viewers to notice visual elements and details in a scene. The photographer created meaning by what he chose to include and exclude from the picture.

The gallery is organized geographically by the towns around Lake George where Jesse Wooley captured views of the spectacular scenery, people at work and play, events and reunions, hotels, cottages, and mansions, everyday life, and structures with a reporter's and artist's eye.

Lake George Village

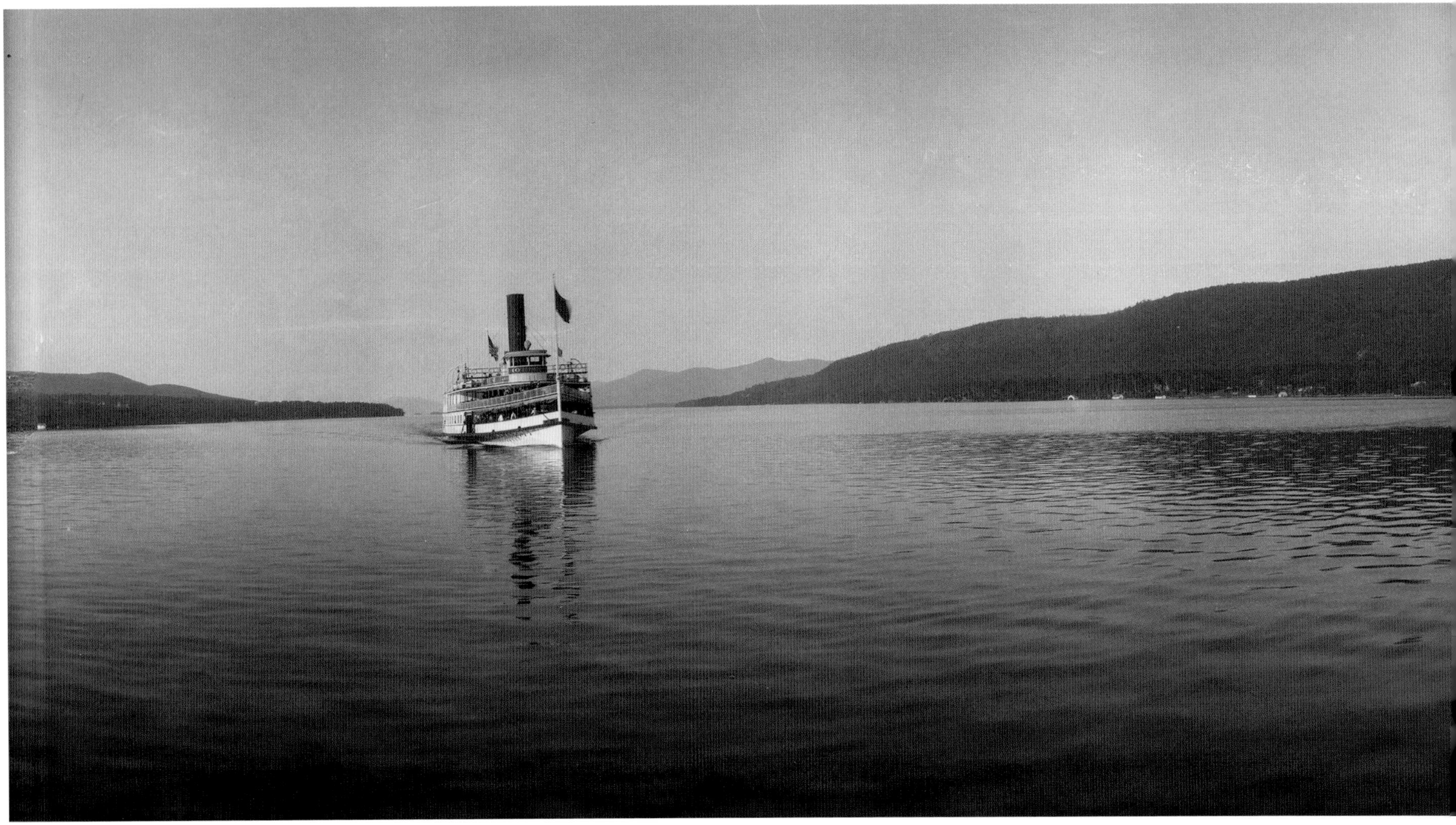

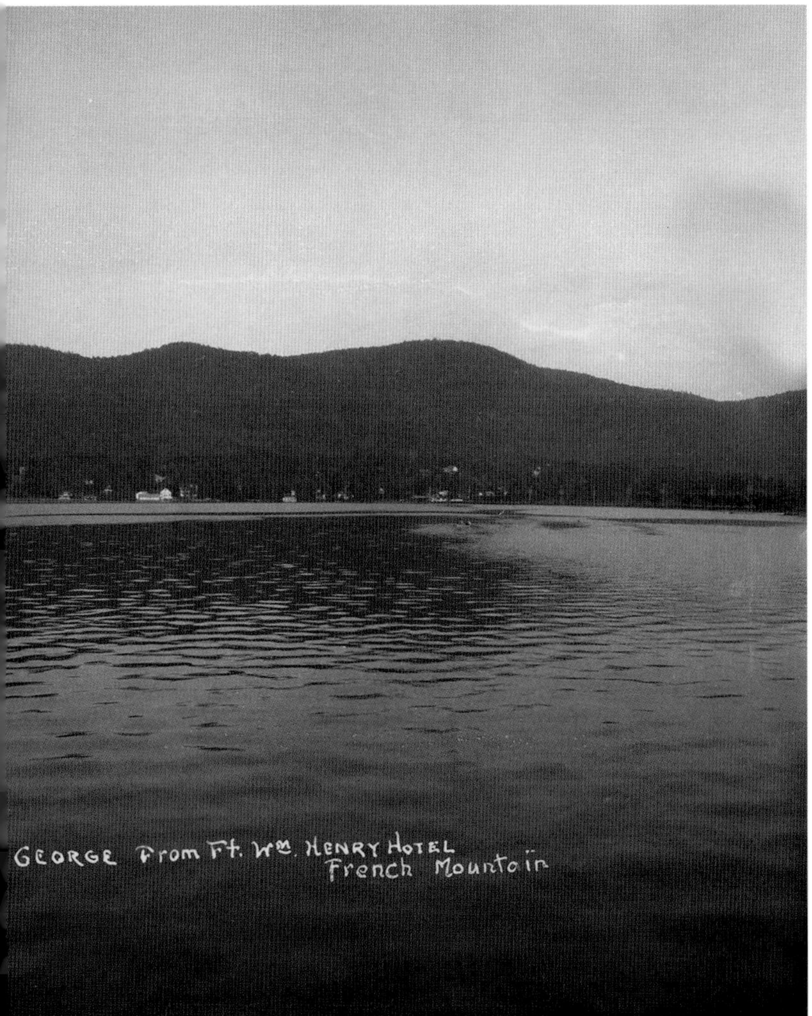

G1.1. *Lake George from Ft Wm Henry Hotel French Mountain*

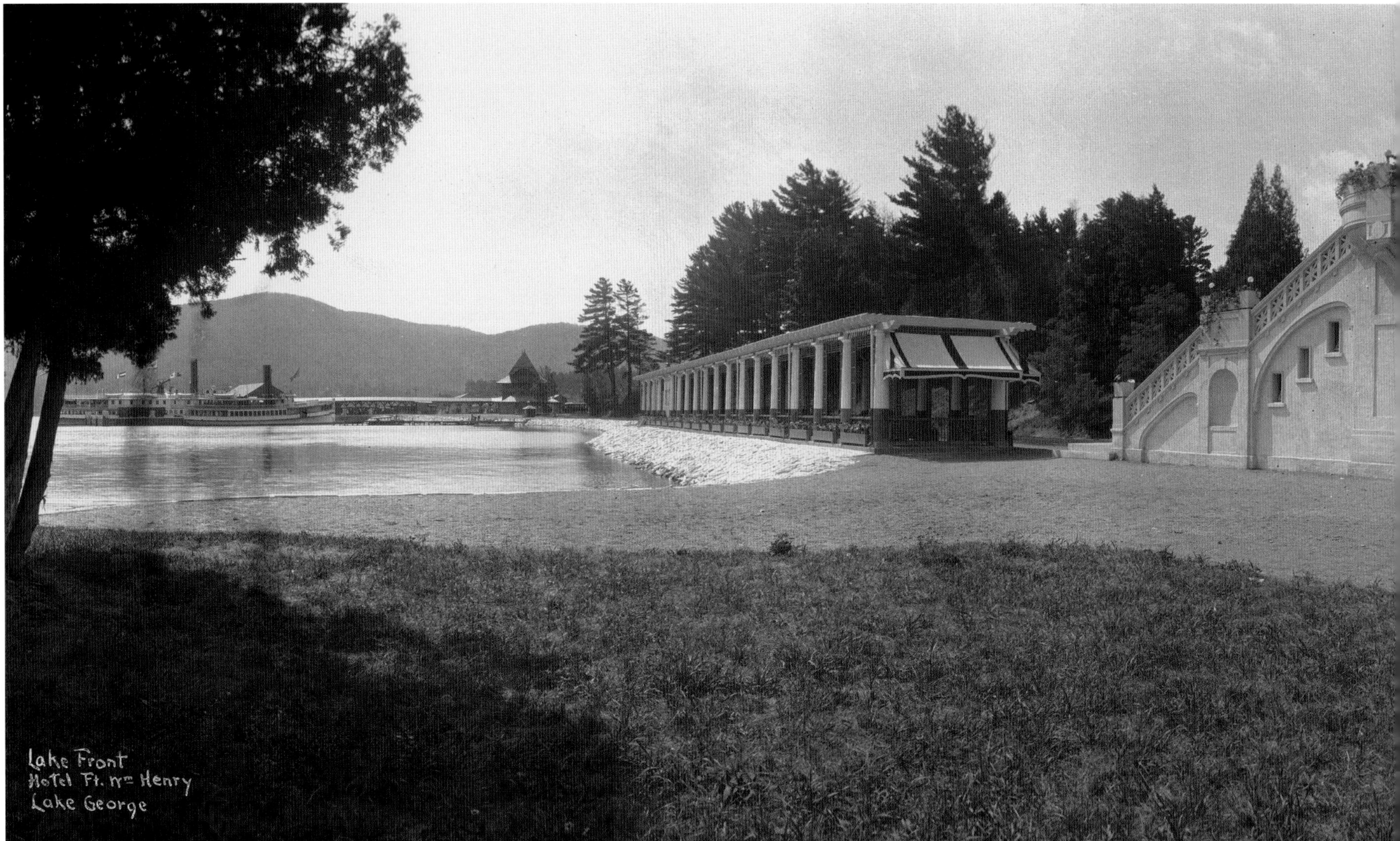
Lake Front
Hotel Ft. Wm Henry
Lake George

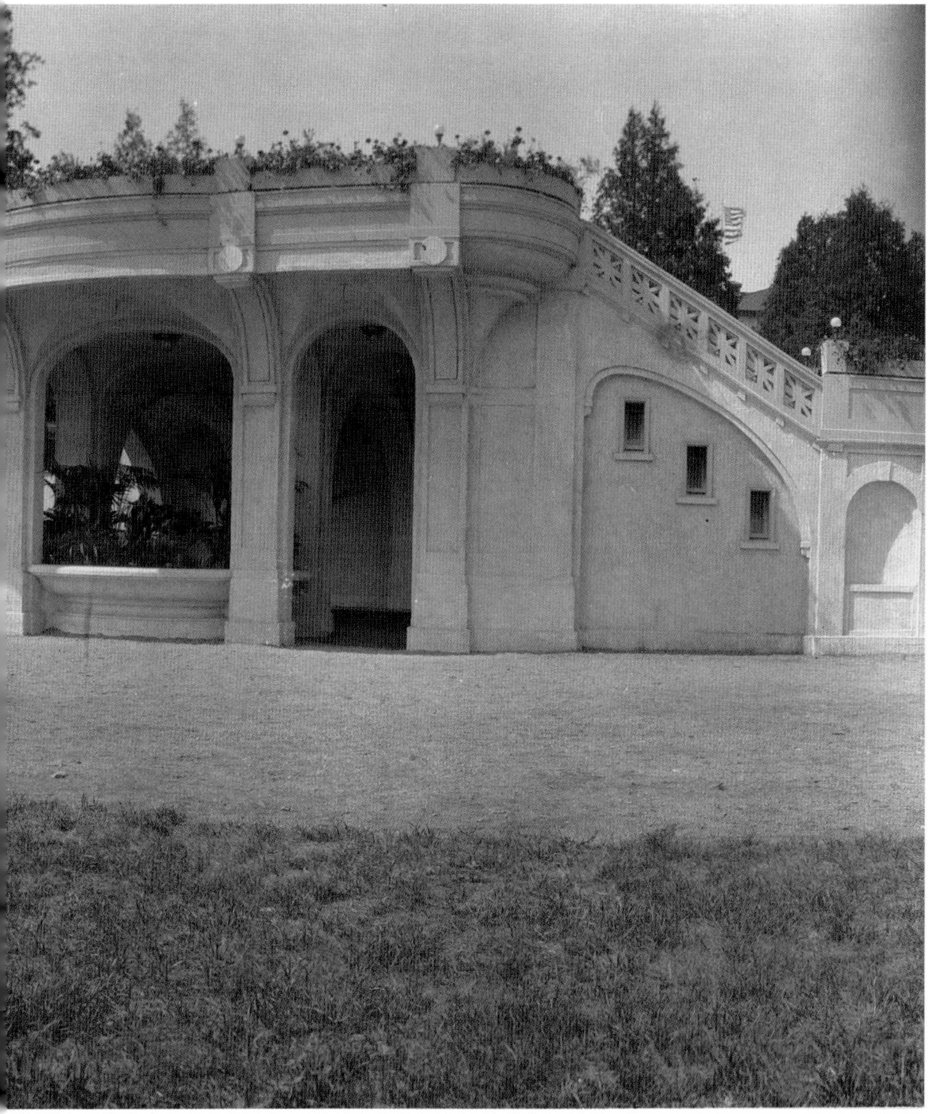

G1.2. *Lake Front Hotel Ft Wm Henry Lake George*

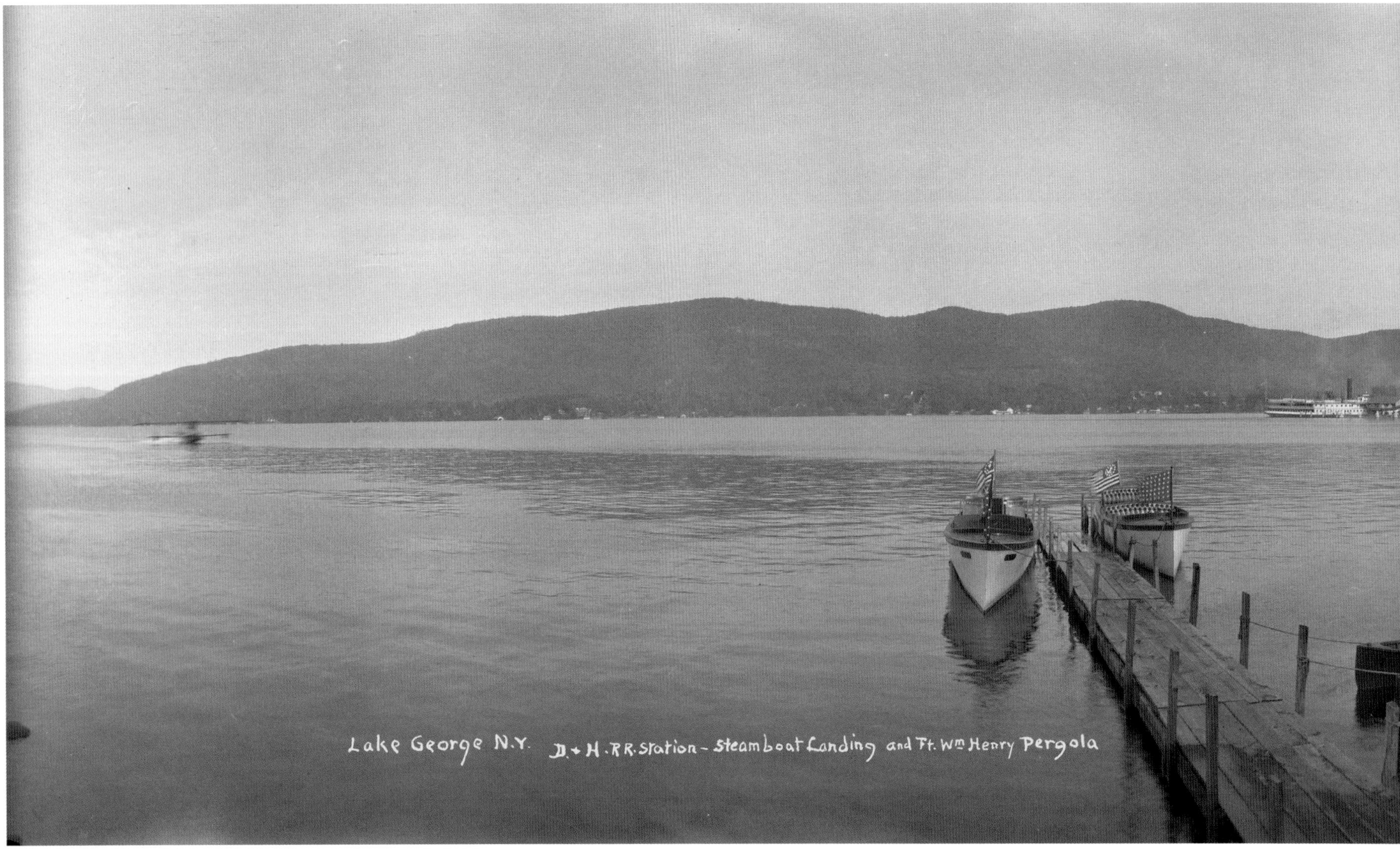
Lake George N.Y. D.+H. R.R. Station - Steamboat Landing and Ft. Wm Henry Pergola

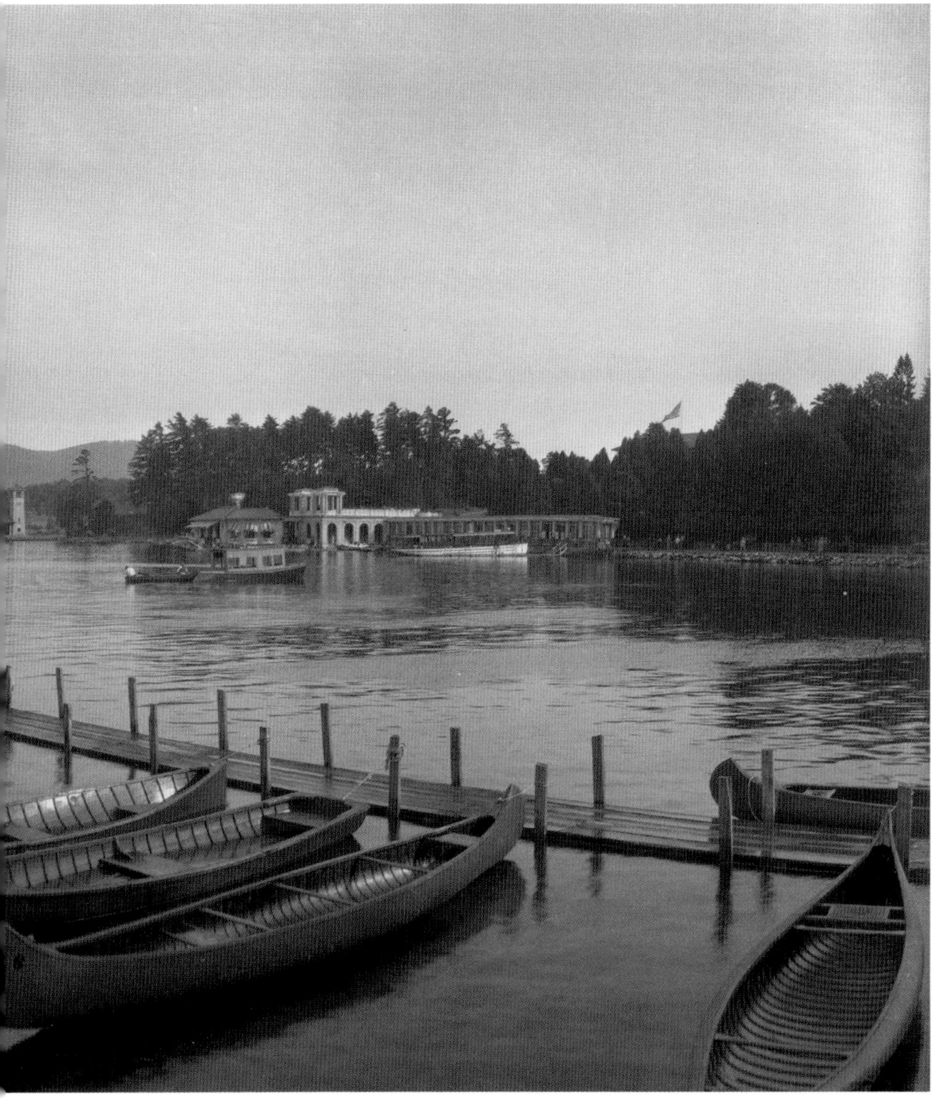

G1.3. *Lake George NY, D&H R.R., Station-Steamboat Landing and Ft Wm Henry Pergola*

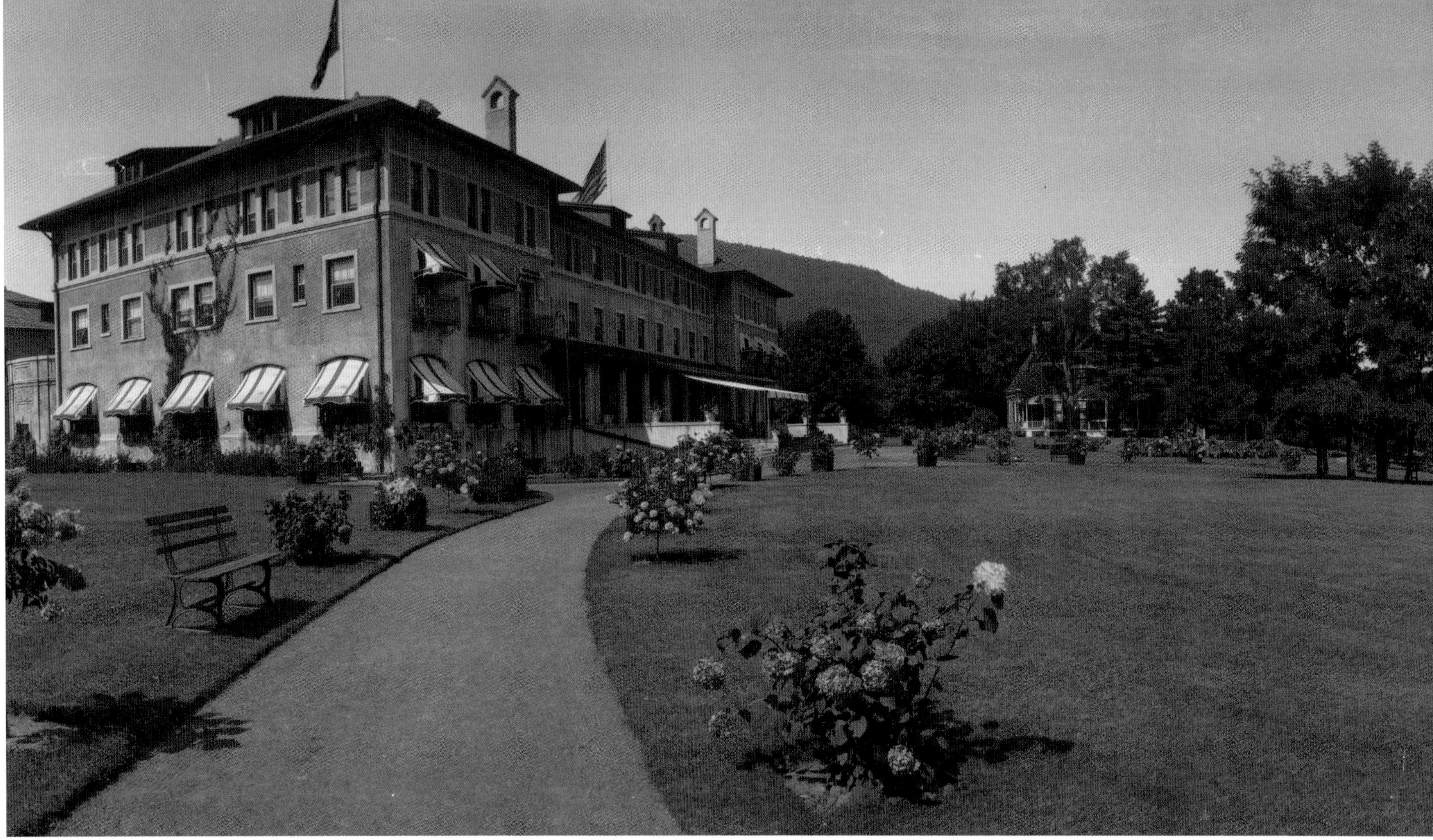

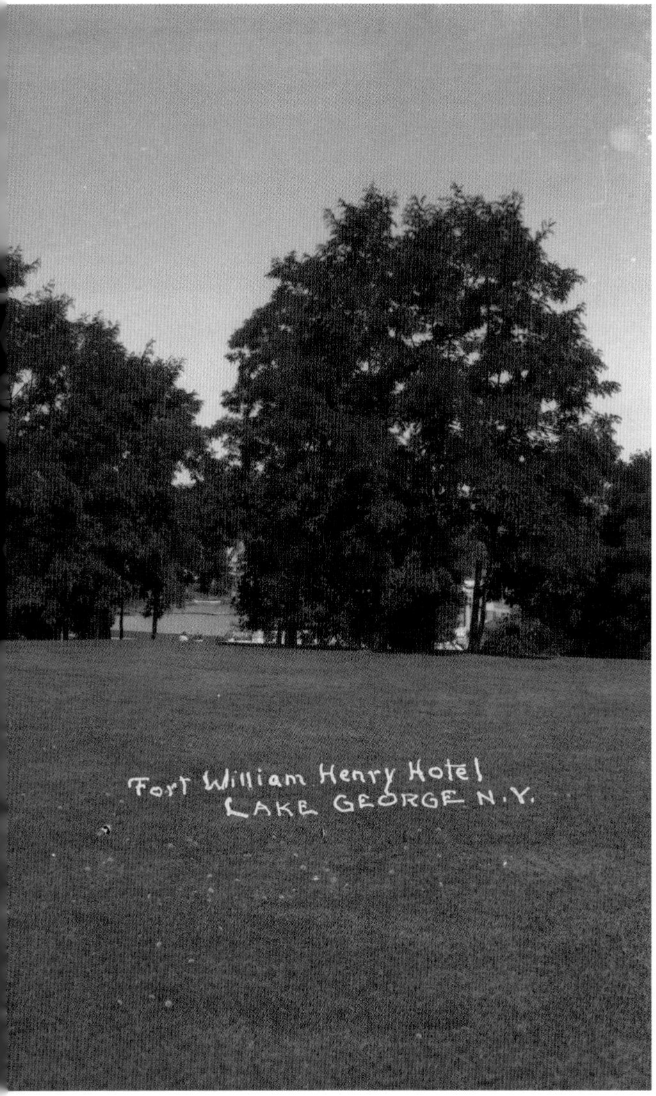

G1.4. *Fort William Henry Hotel Lake George N.Y.*

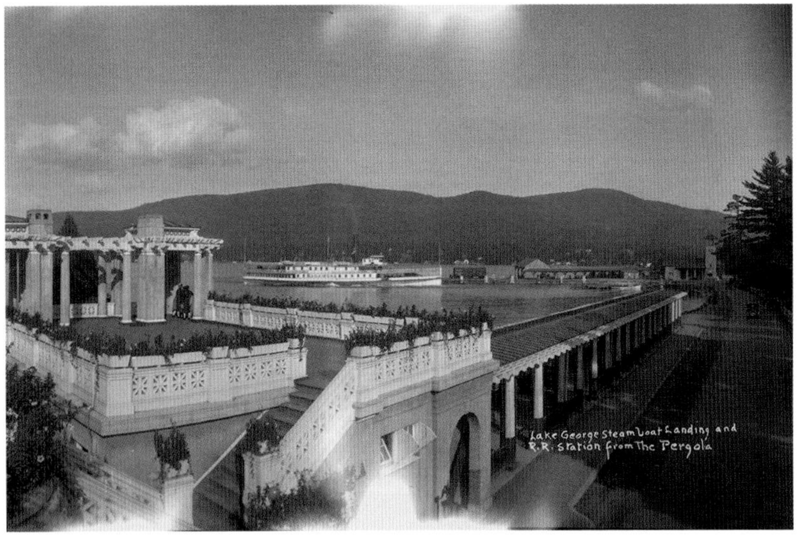

G1.5. *Lake George Steamboat Landing and R.R. Station from the Pergola*

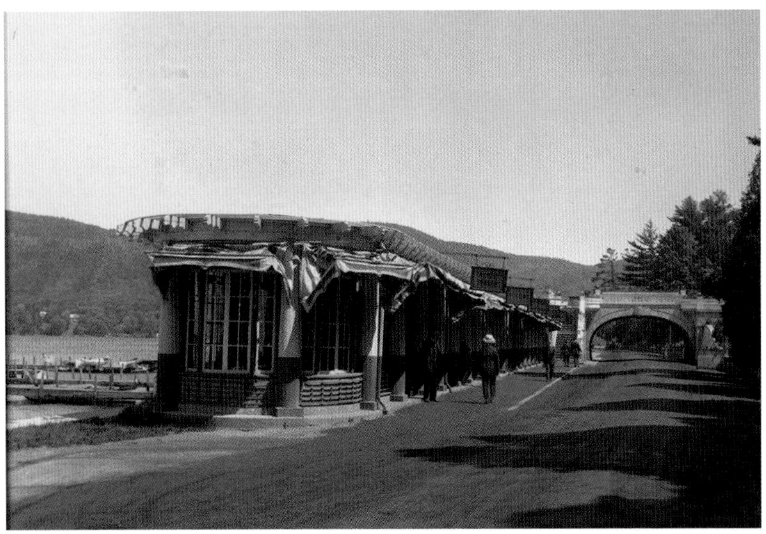

G1.6. *Lake George Pergola*

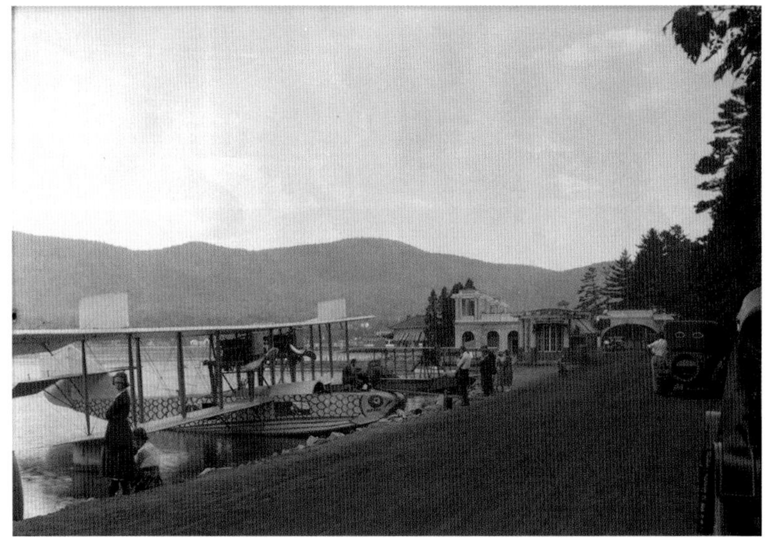

G1.7. *Flying Boat Rides*

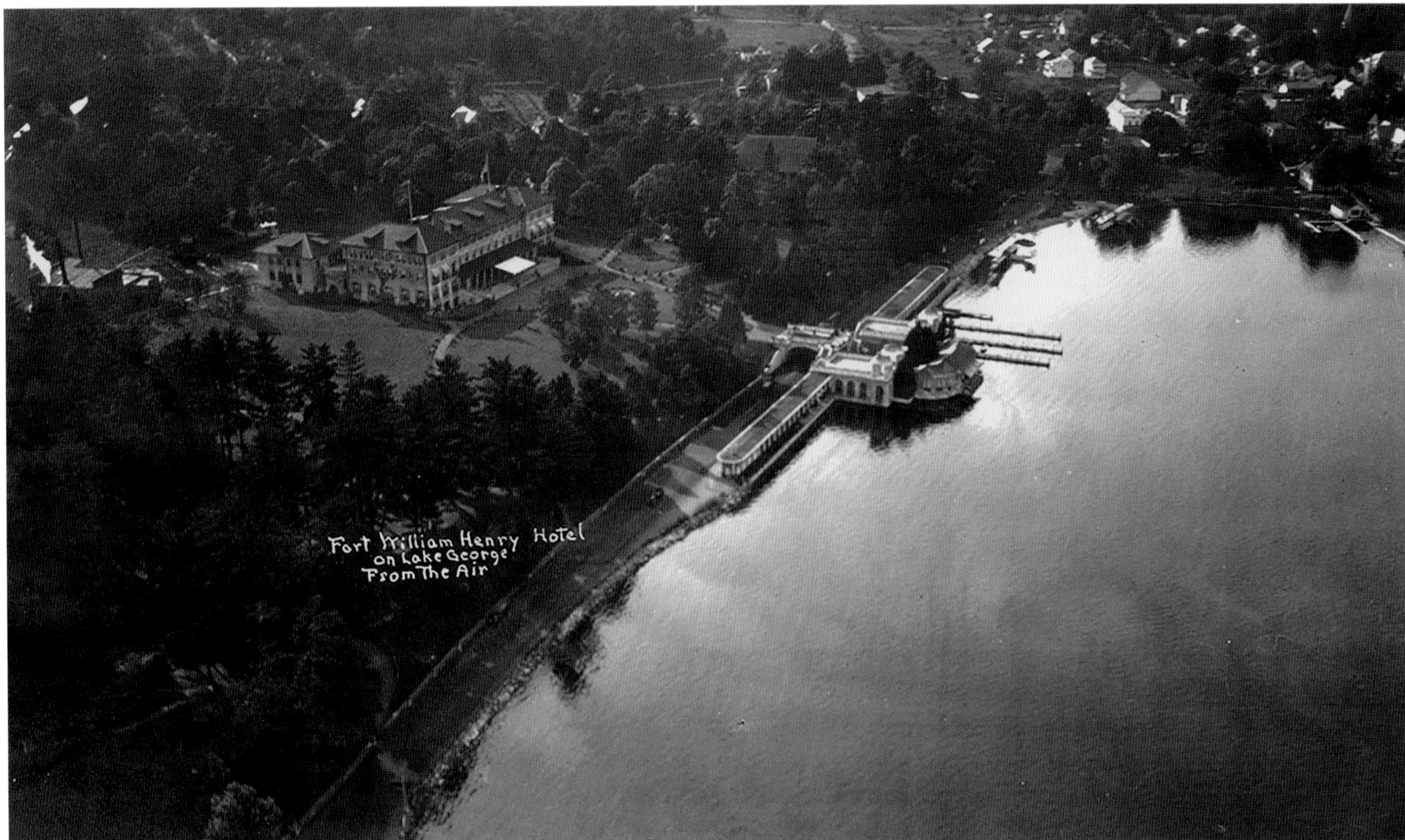

G1.8. *Fort William Henry on Lake George From The Air*

Bolton

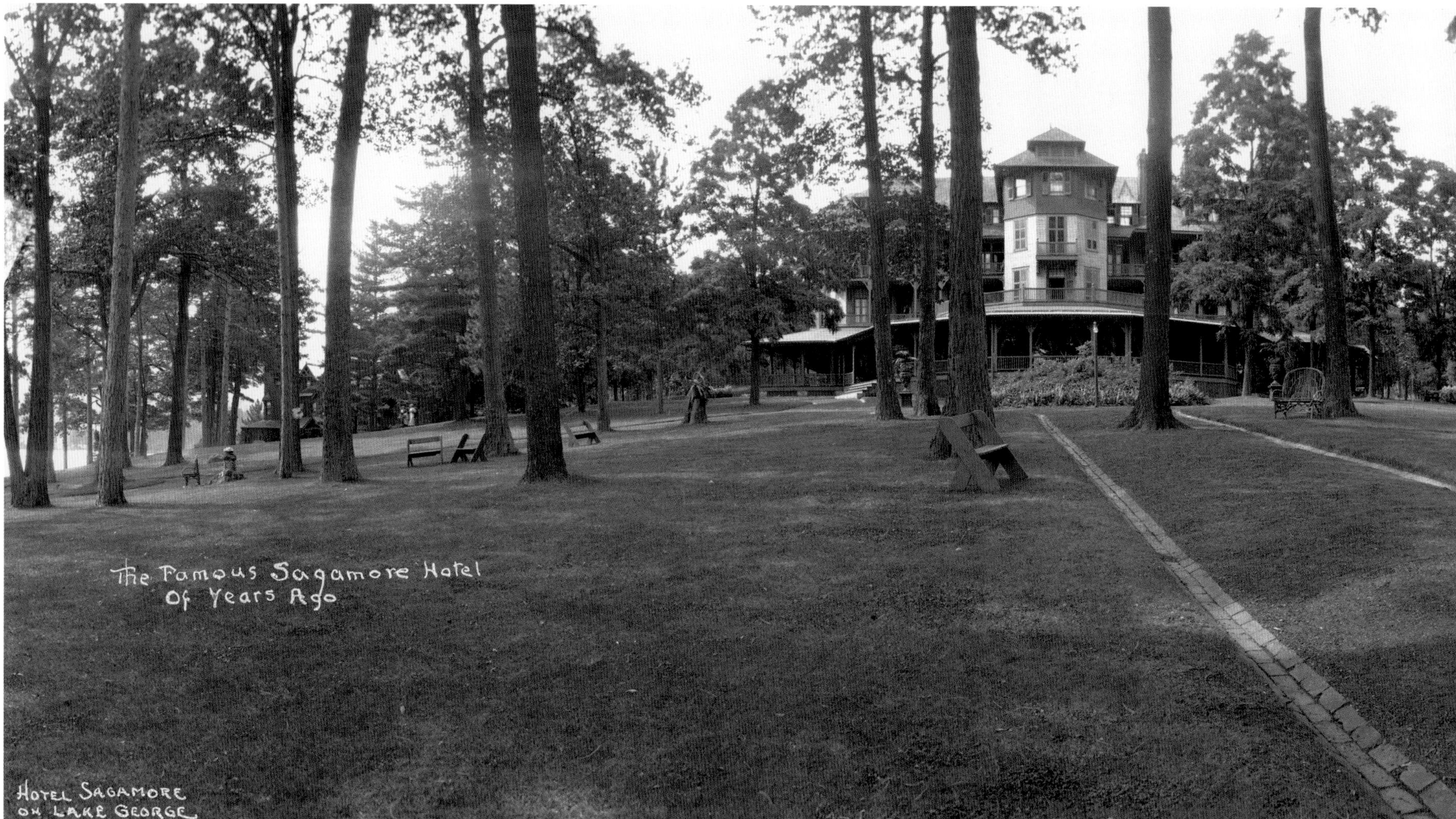
The Famous Sagamore Hotel
Of Years Ago
HOTEL SAGAMORE
ON LAKE GEORGE

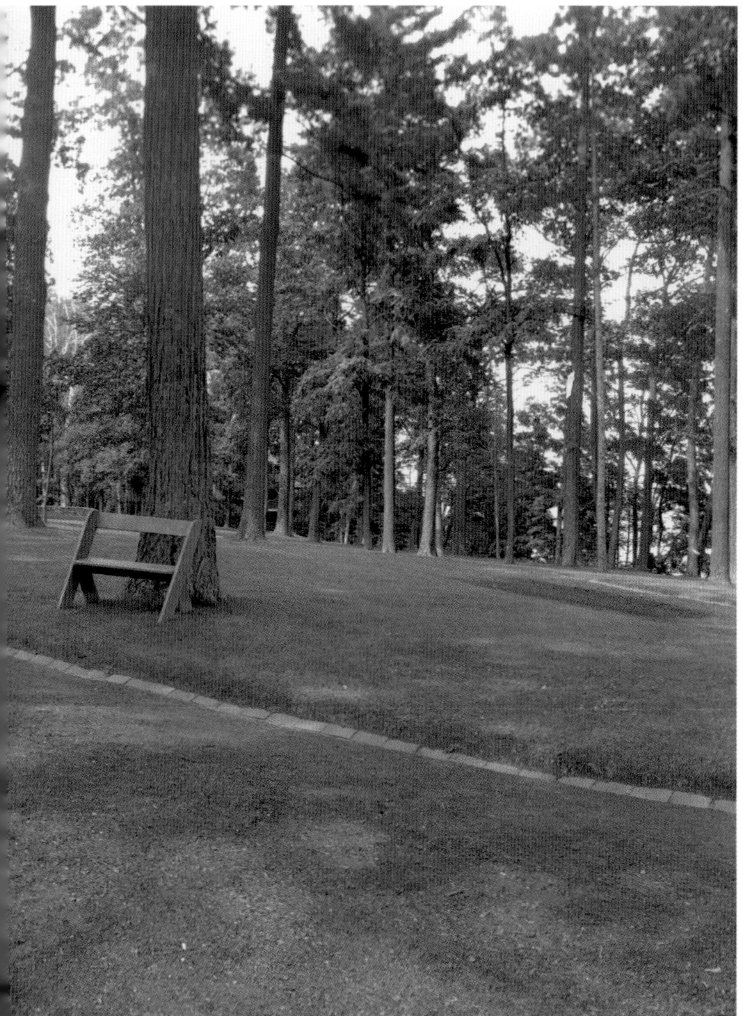

G2.1. *The Famous Sagamore Hotel of Years Ago*

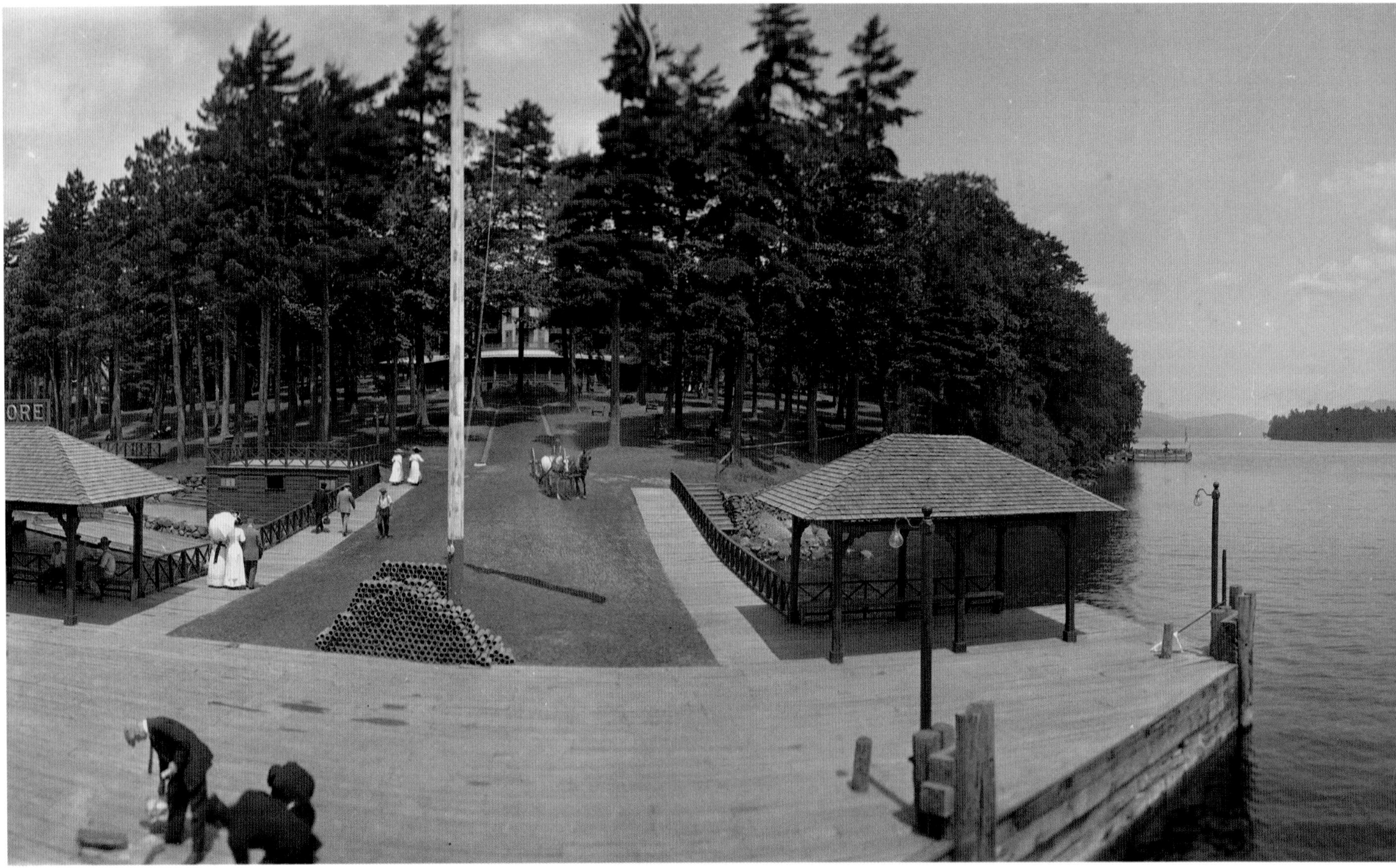
ORE

G2.2. *Lake George North from the Sagamore Hotel Dock*

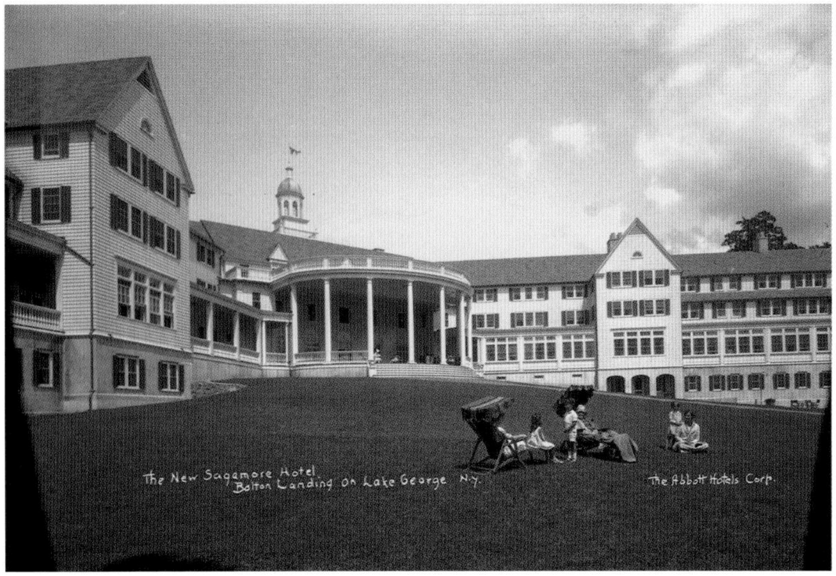

G2.3. *The New Sagamore Hotel, Bolton Landing on Lake George, N.Y.*

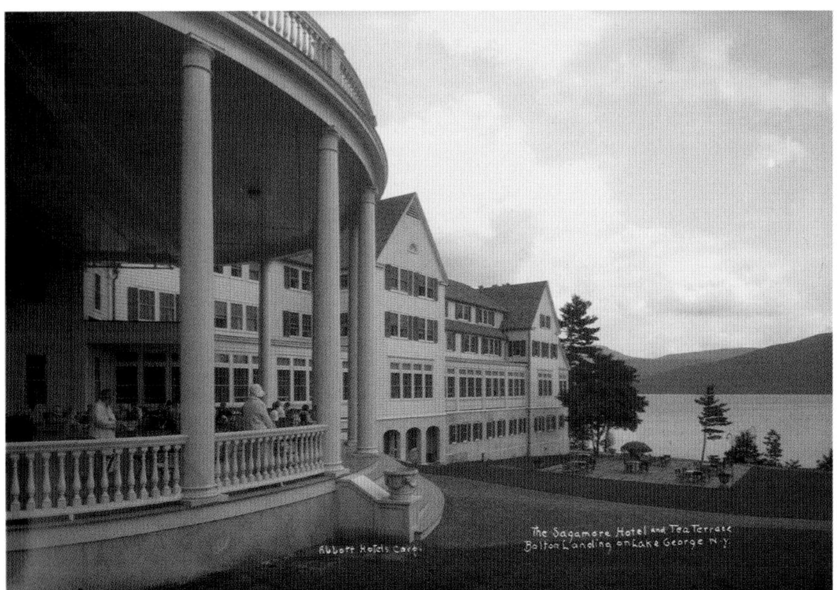

G2.4. *The Sagamore Hotel and Tea Terrace, Bolton Landing on Lake George N.Y.*

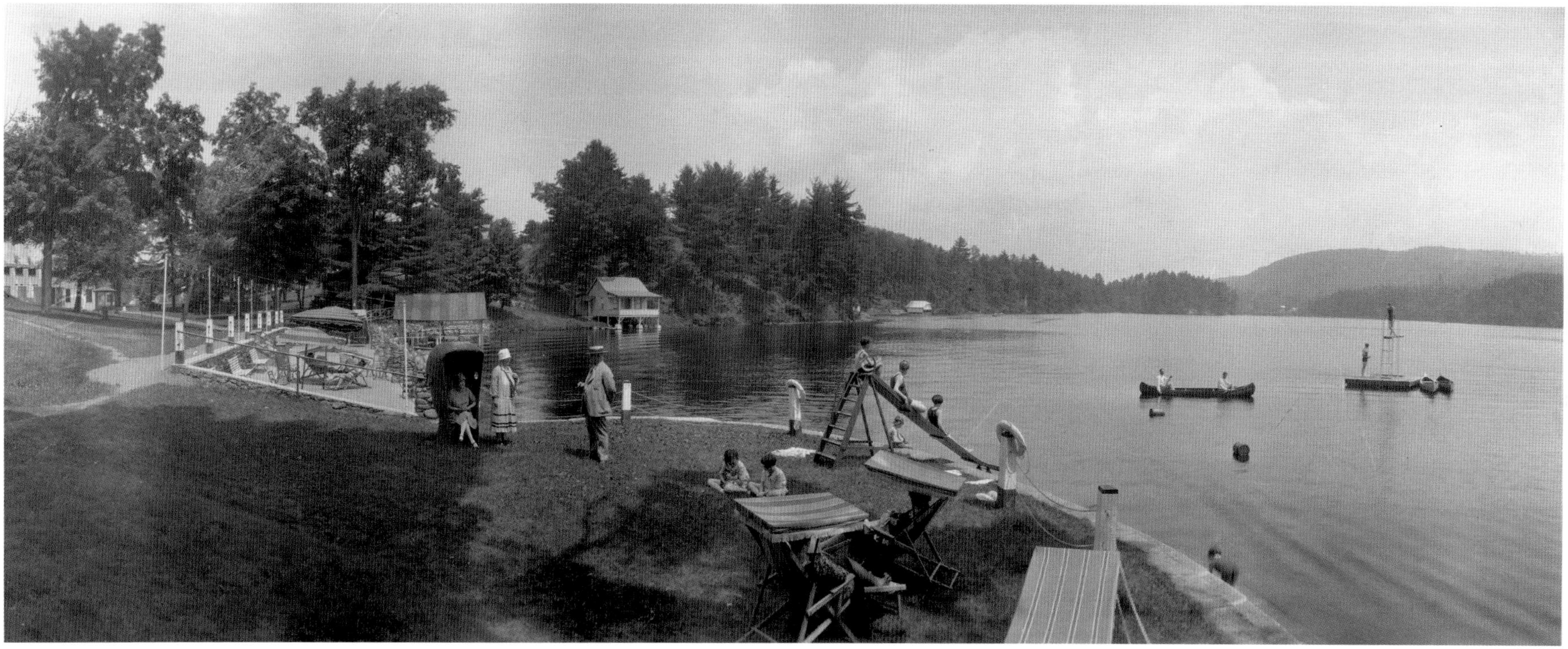

G2.5. *A View North from the New Sagamore Hotel Grounds*

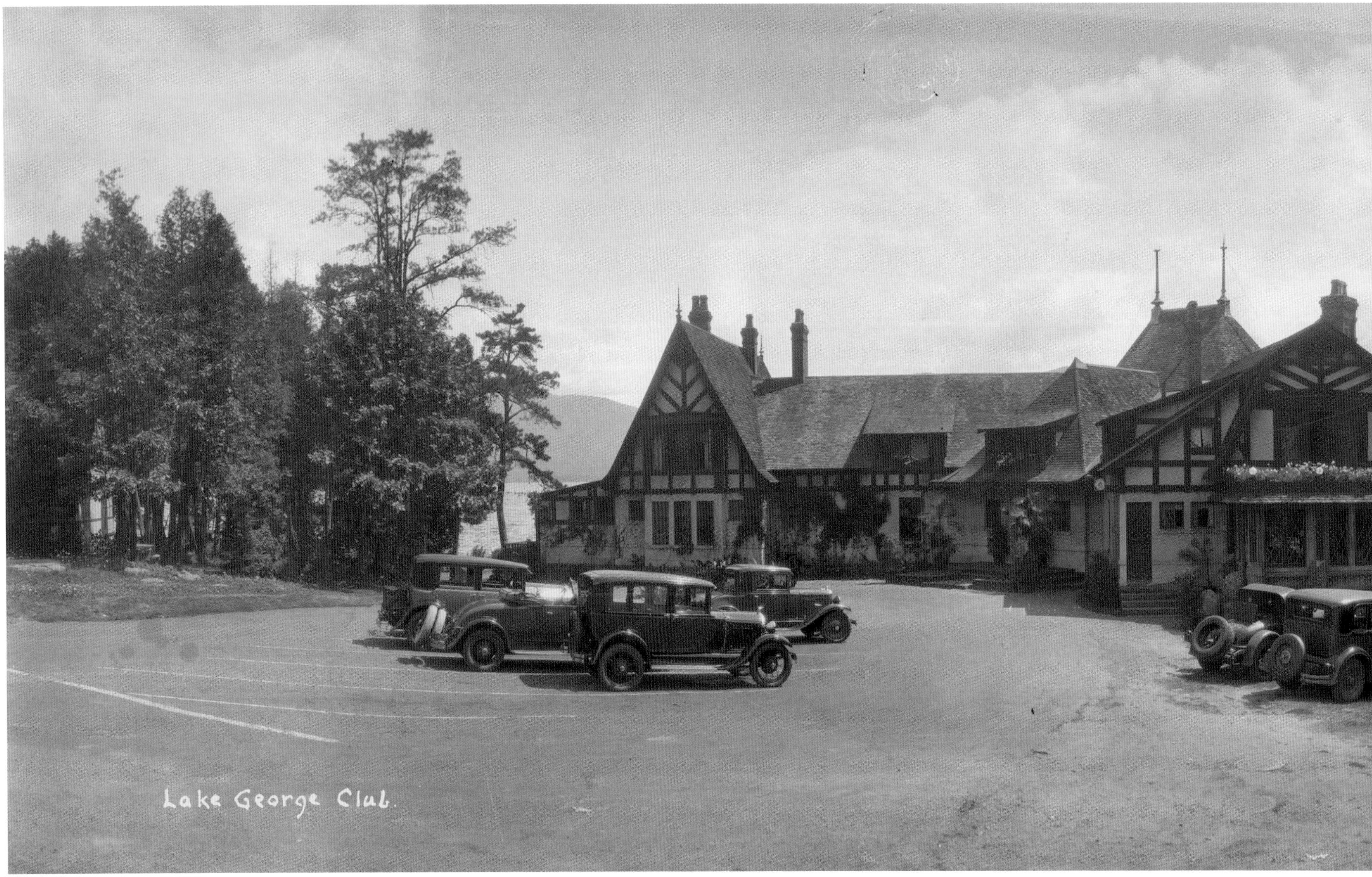
Lake George Club.

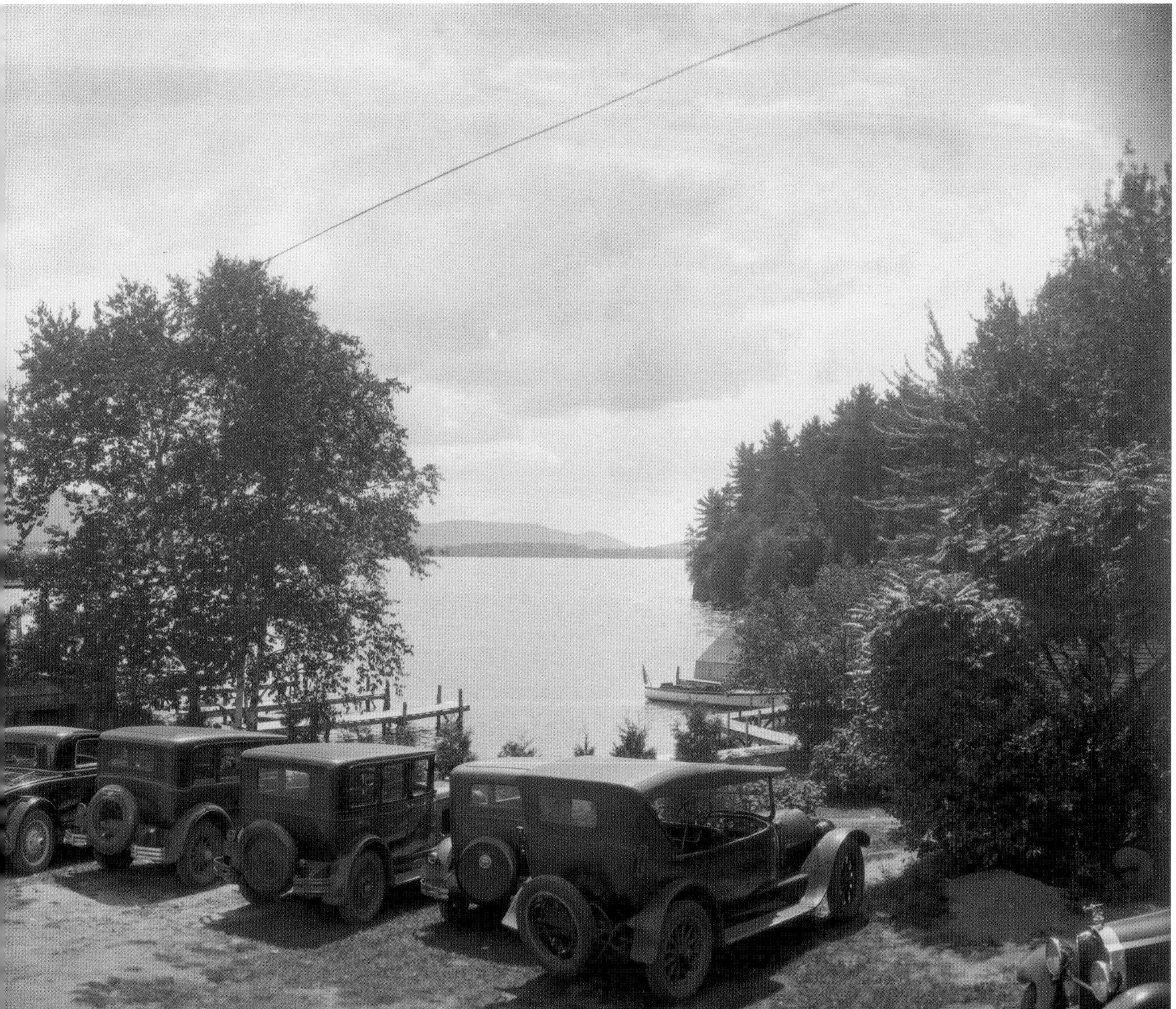

G2.6. *Lake George Club*

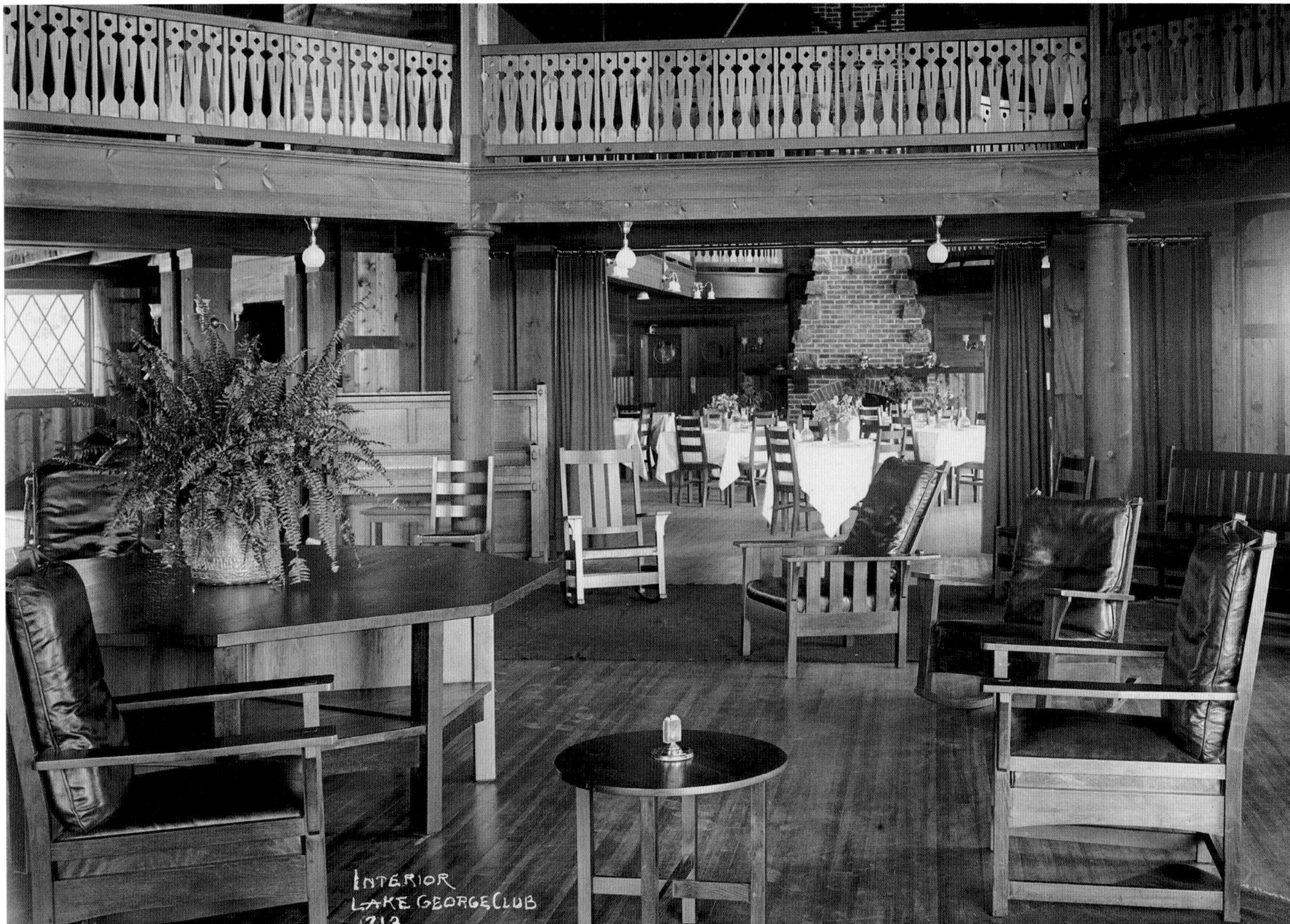

G2.7. *Interior Lake George Club*

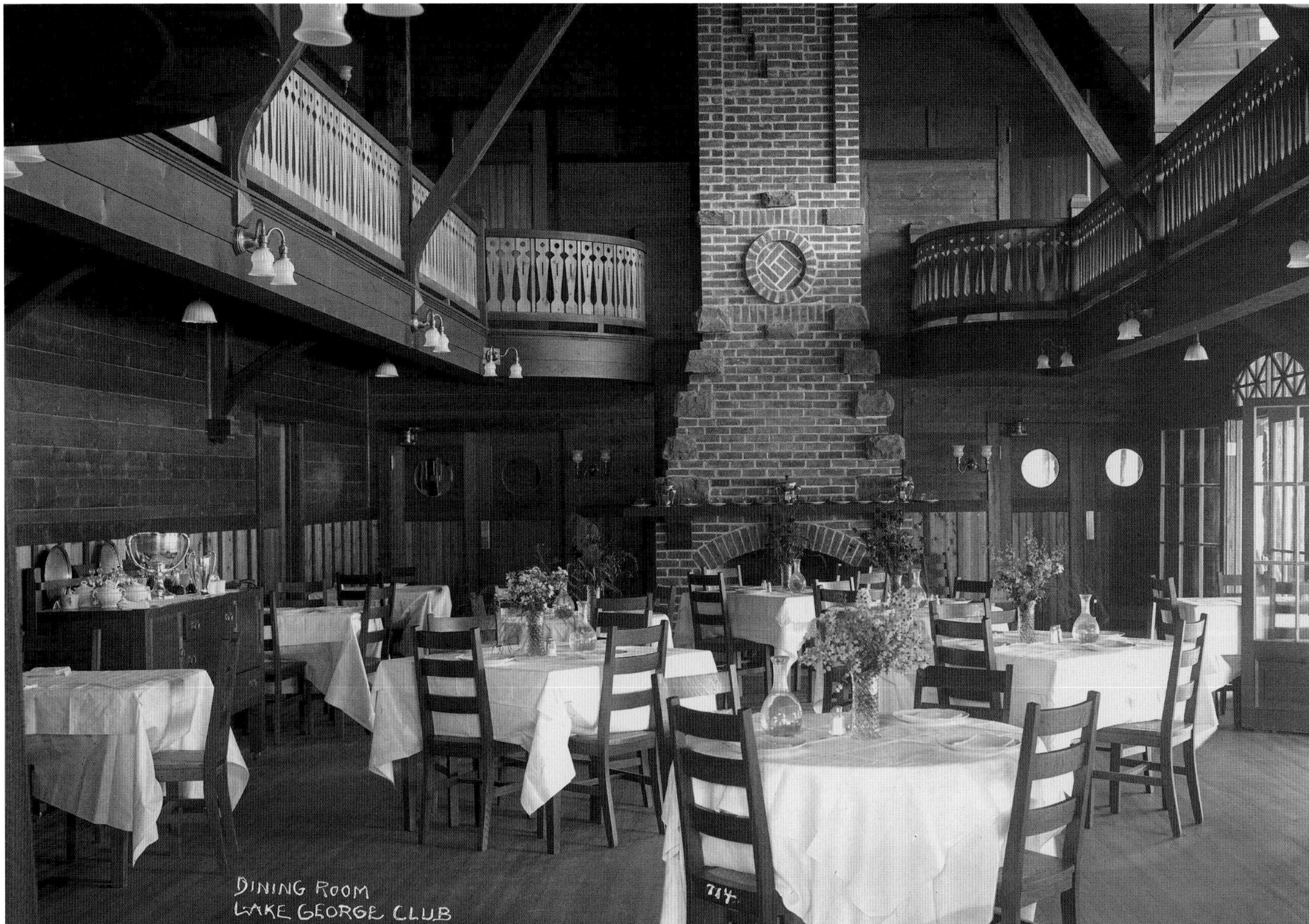

G2.8. *Dining Room Lake George Club*

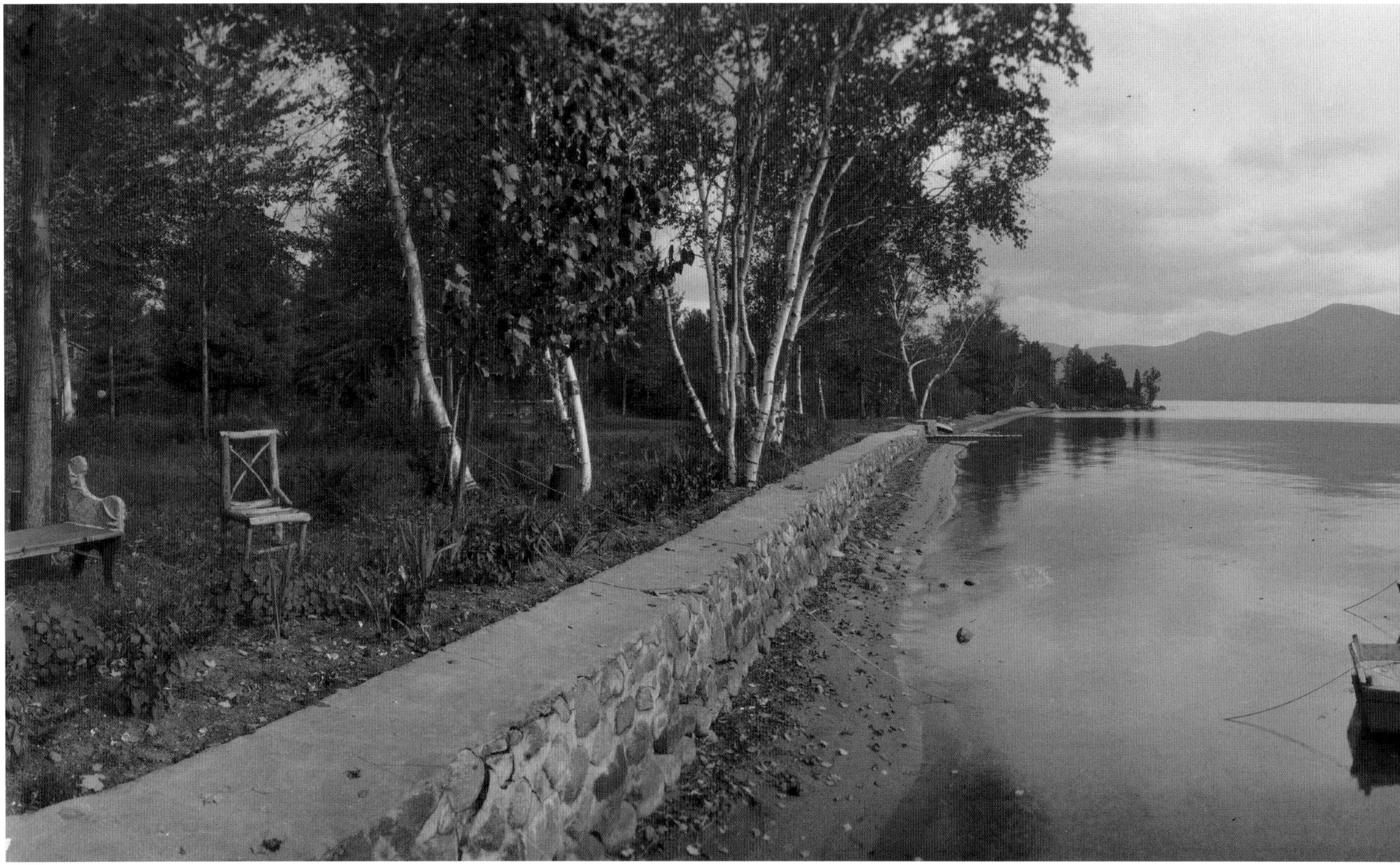

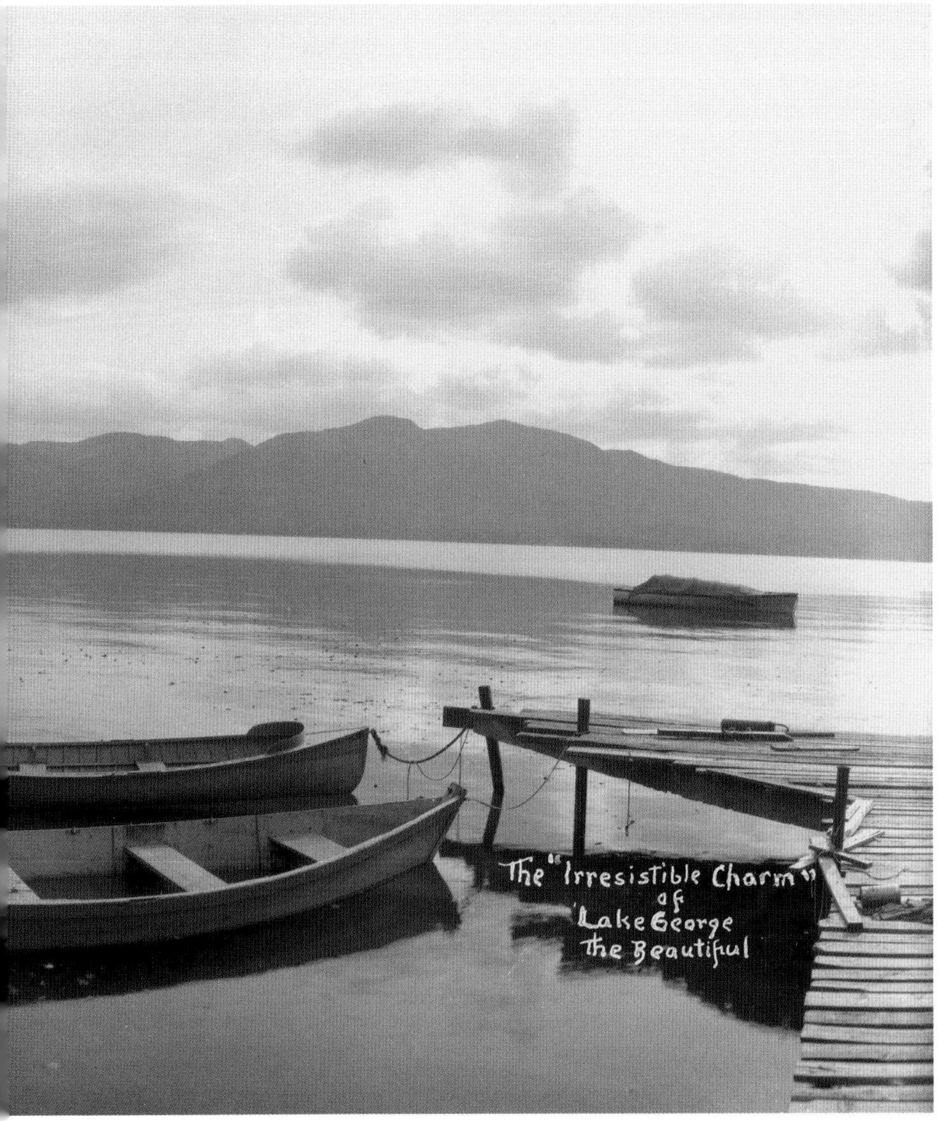

G2.9. *"Irresistible Charm" of Lake George the Beautiful*

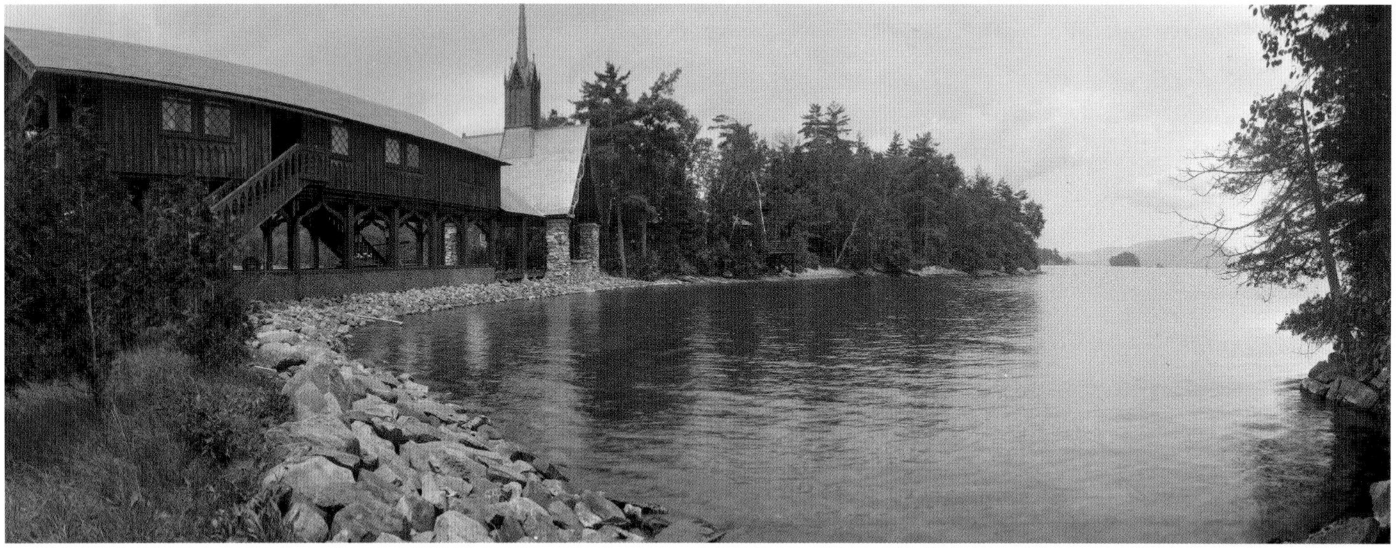

G2.10. *Three Brothers Island*

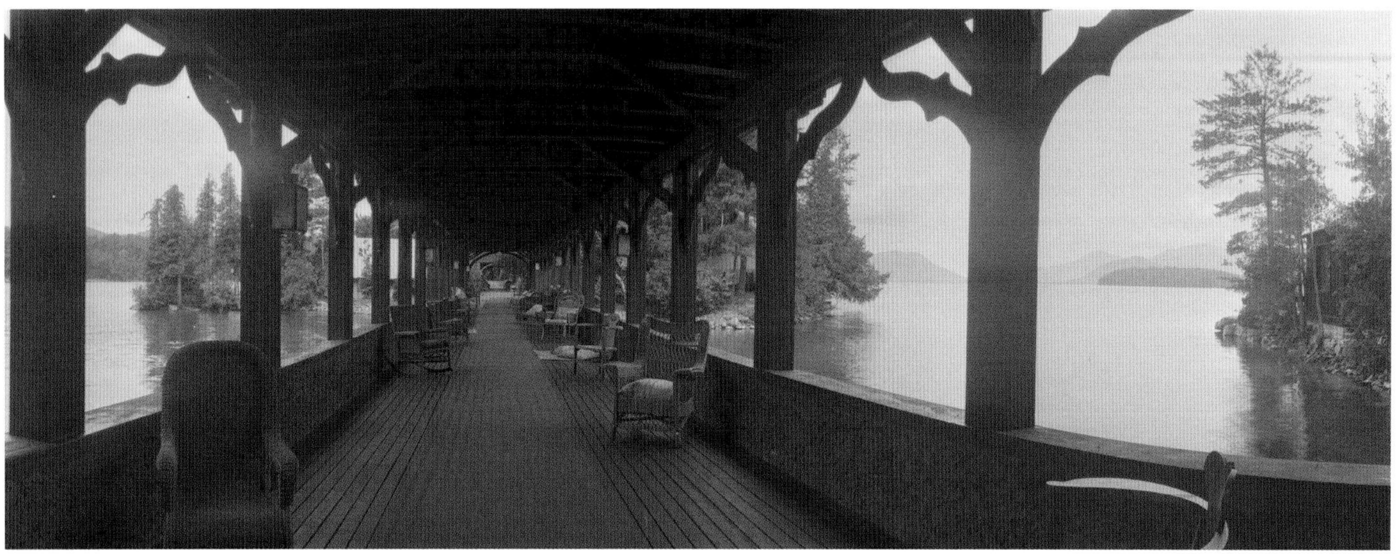

G2.11. *Three Brothers Island*

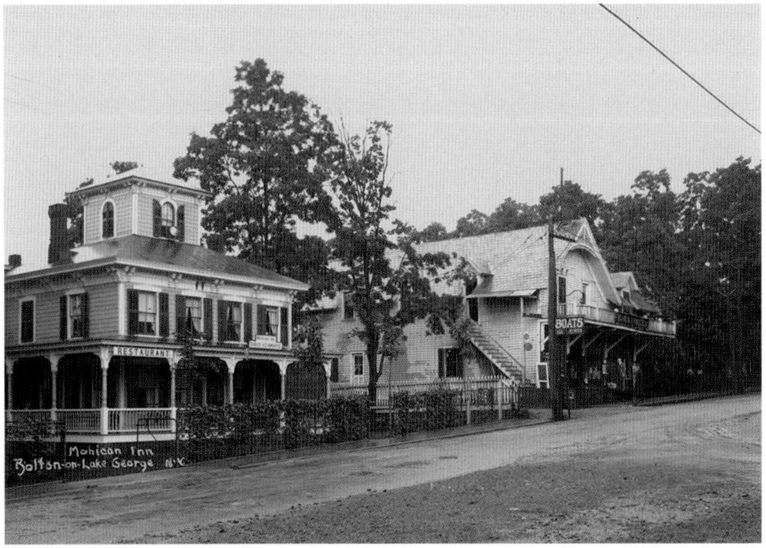

G2.12. *Mohican Inn Bolton on Lake George N.Y.*

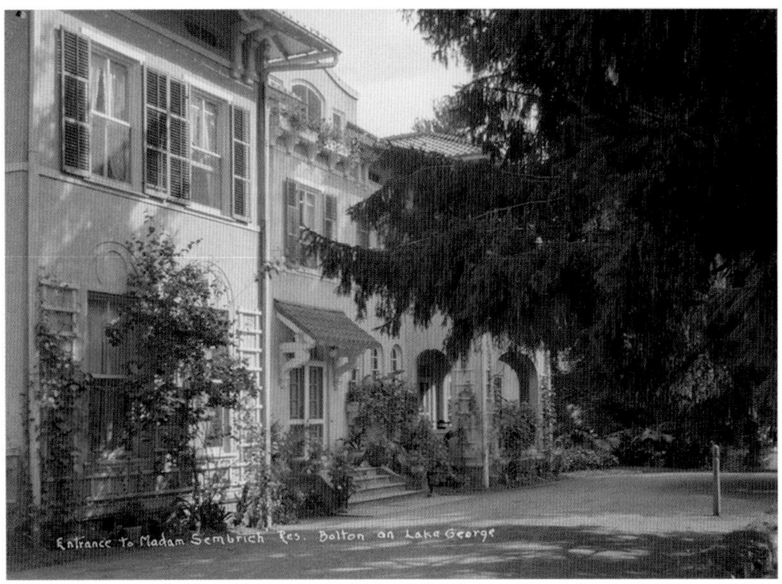

G2.13. *Entrance to Madam Sembrich Res. Bolton on Lake George*

Sabbath Day Point

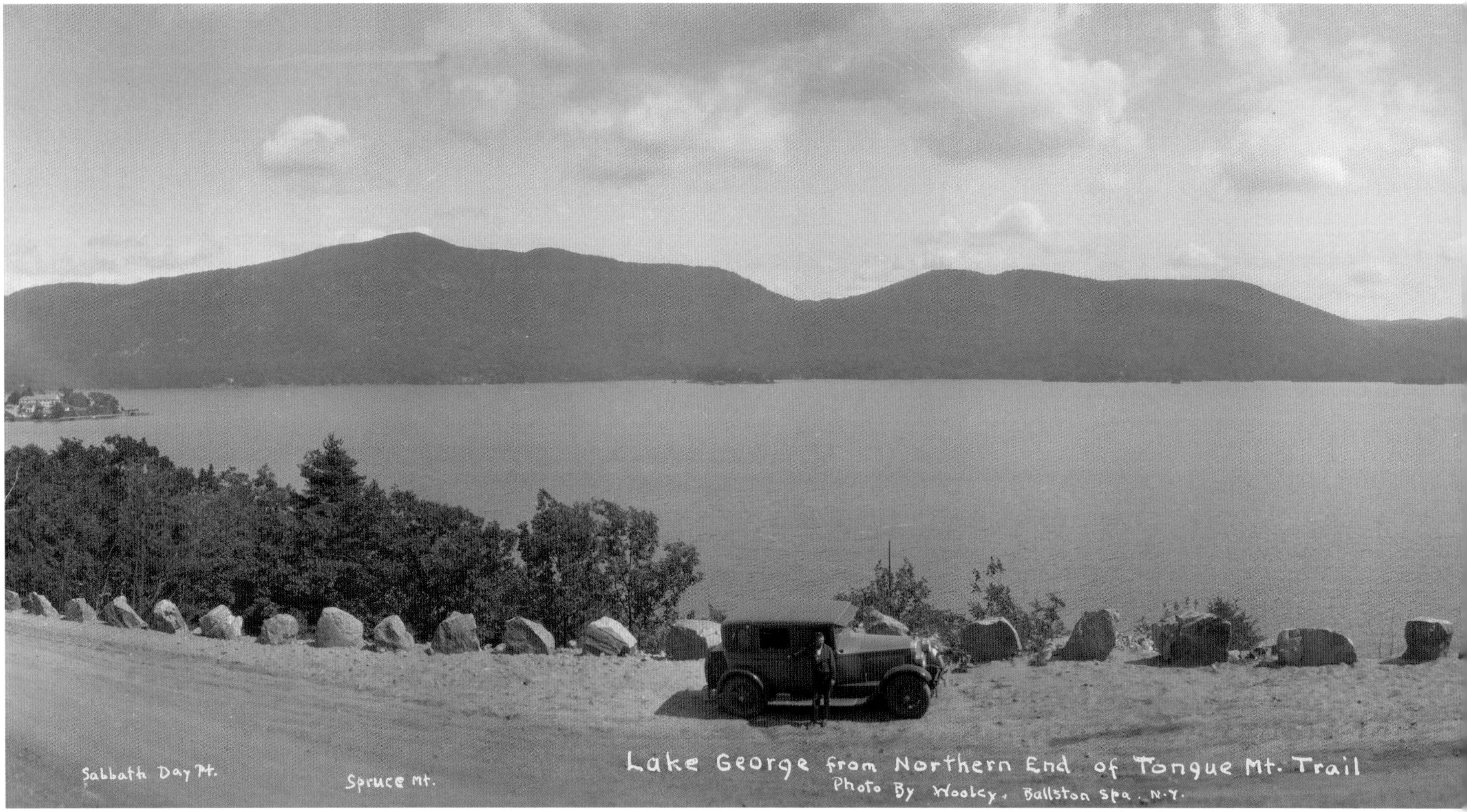

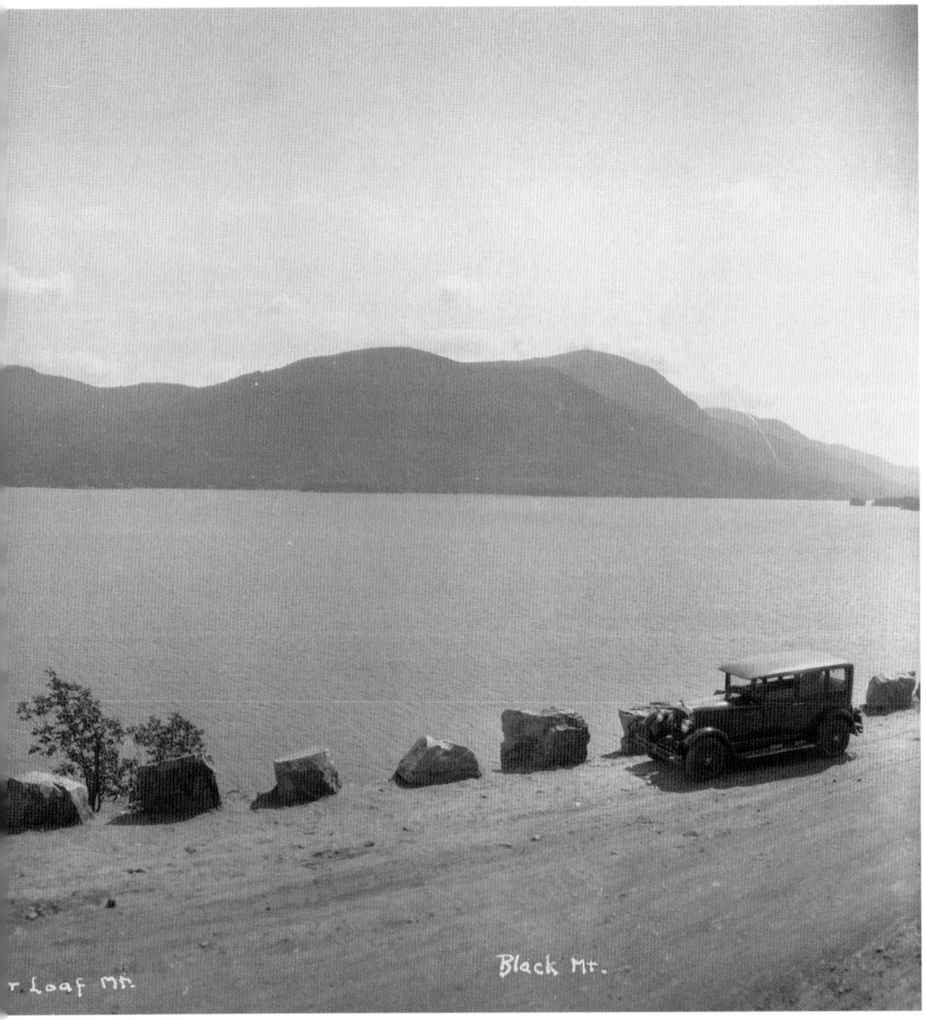

G3.1. *Lake George from Northern End of Tongue Mt. Trail*

TWIN MOUNTAINS
From Sabbath Day Pt. Lake George

G3.2. *Twin Mountains from Sabbath Day Pt. Lake George*

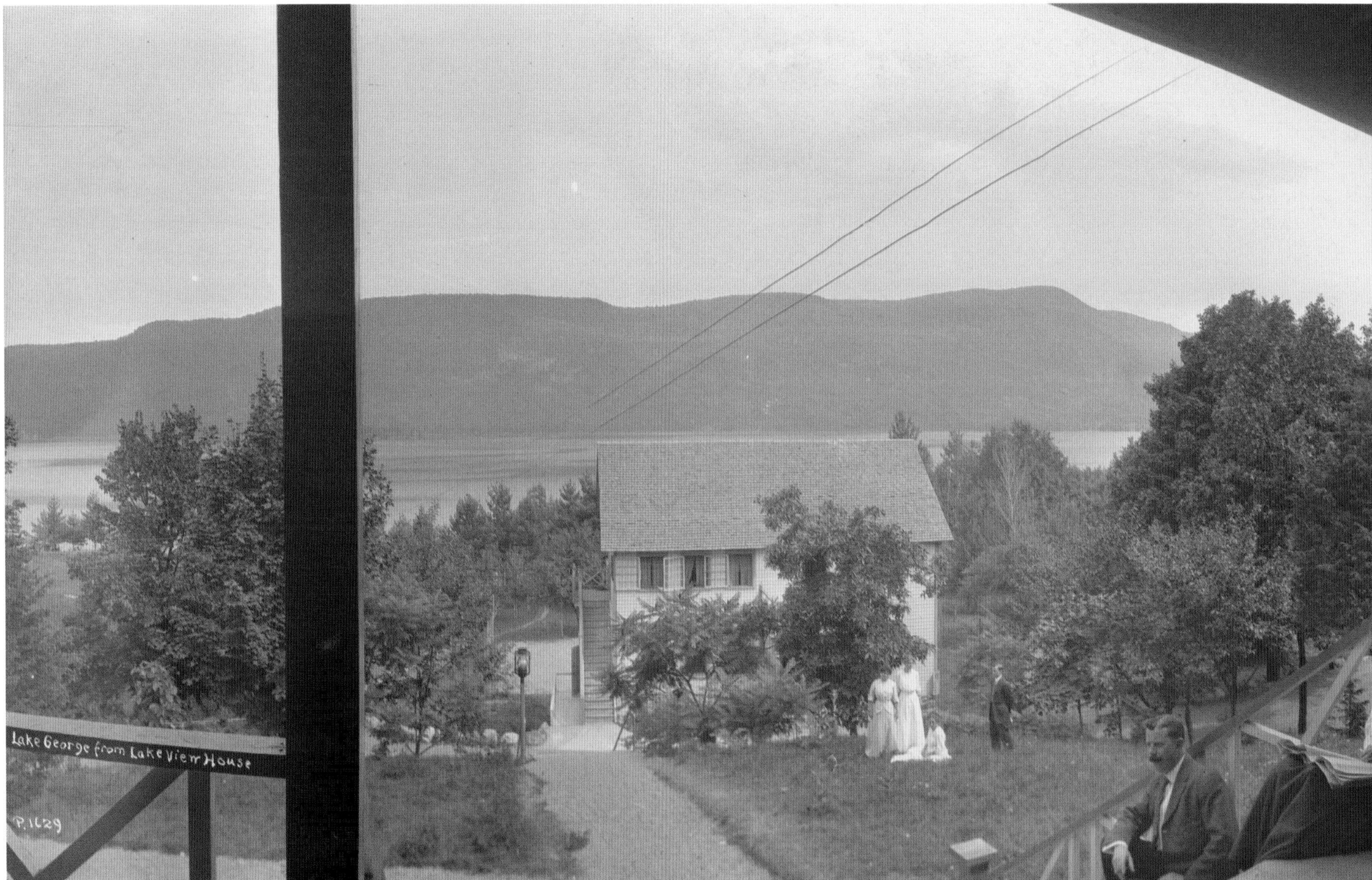
Lake George from Lake View House
P.1629

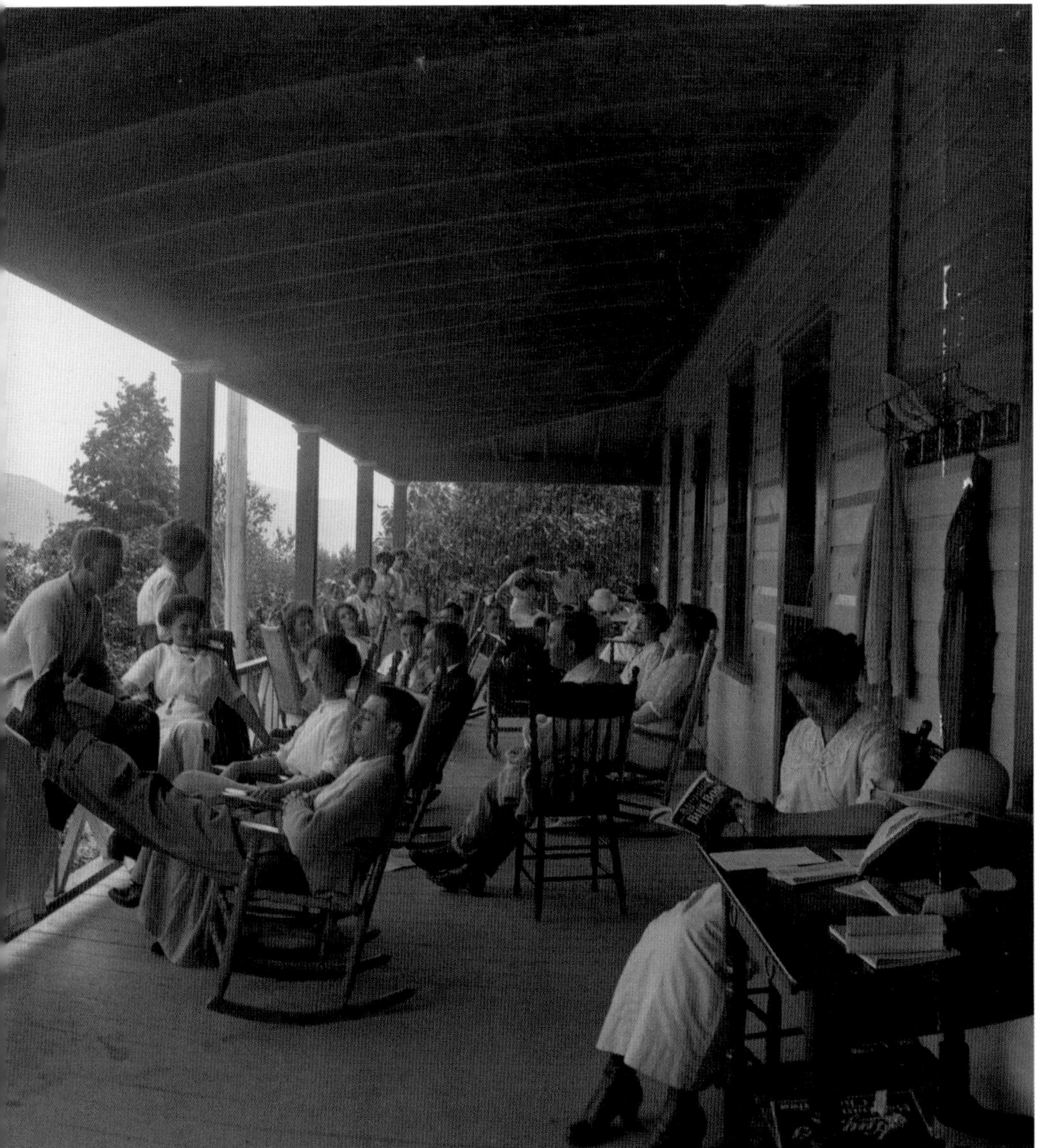

G3.3. *Lakeview House Uncas*

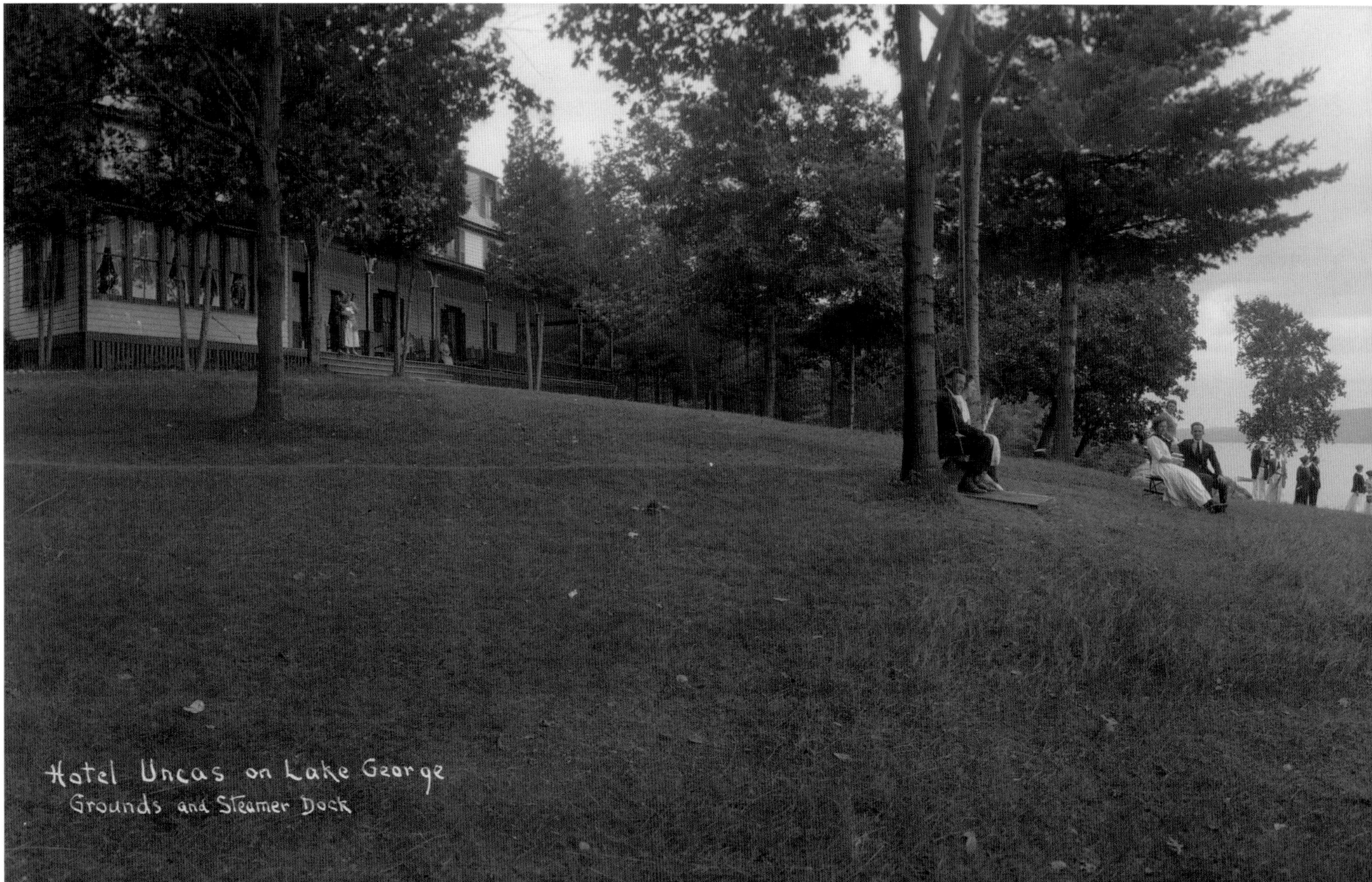
Hotel Uncas on Lake George
Grounds and Steamer Dock

G3.4. *Hotel Uncas on Lake George Grounds and Steamer Dock*

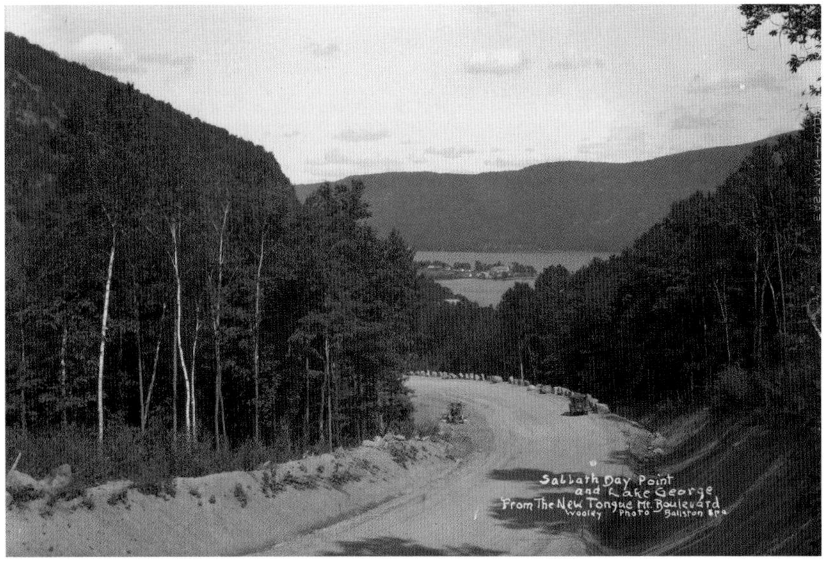

G3.5. *Sabbath Day Point and Lake George From The New Tongue Mt Boulevard*

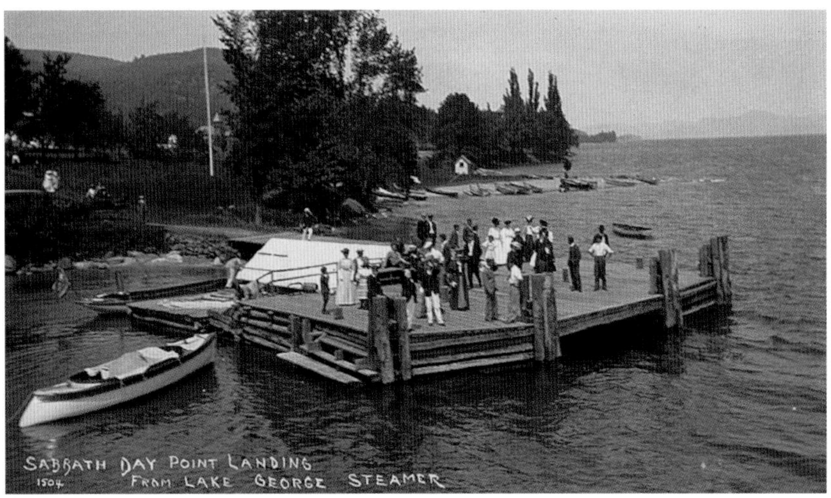

G3.6. *Sabbath Day Point Landing From Lake George Steamer*

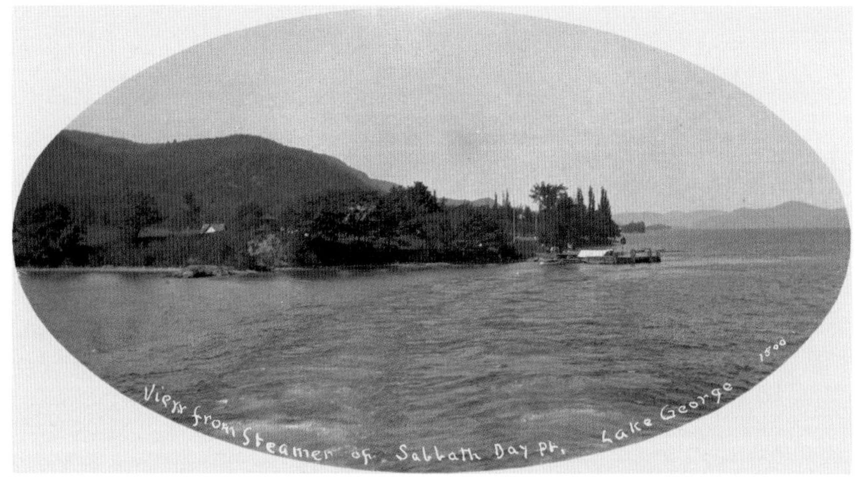

G3.7. *View from Steamer of Sabbath Day Pt. Lake George*

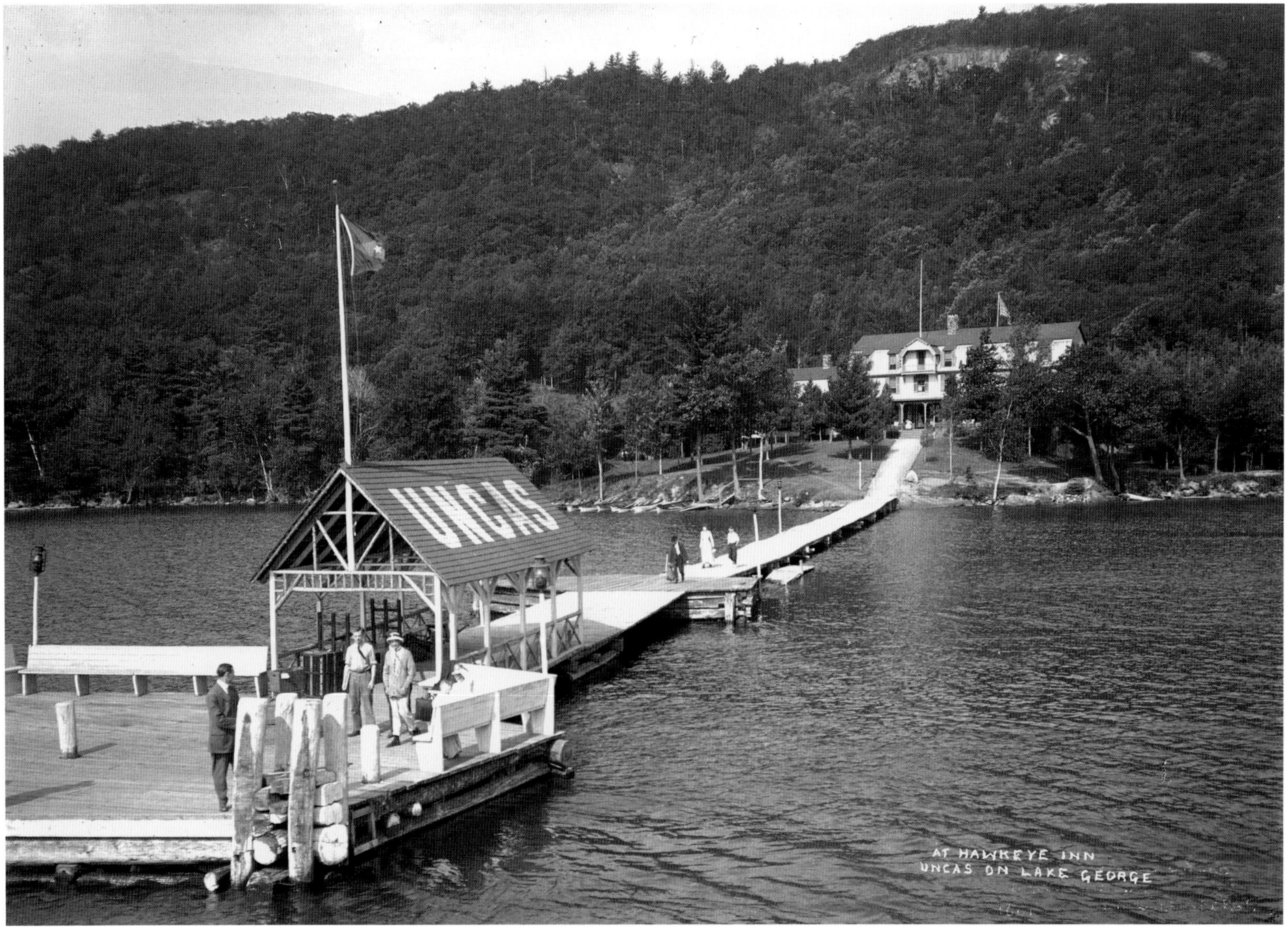

G3.8. *At Hawkeye Inn Uncas on Lake George*

Silver Bay ❧

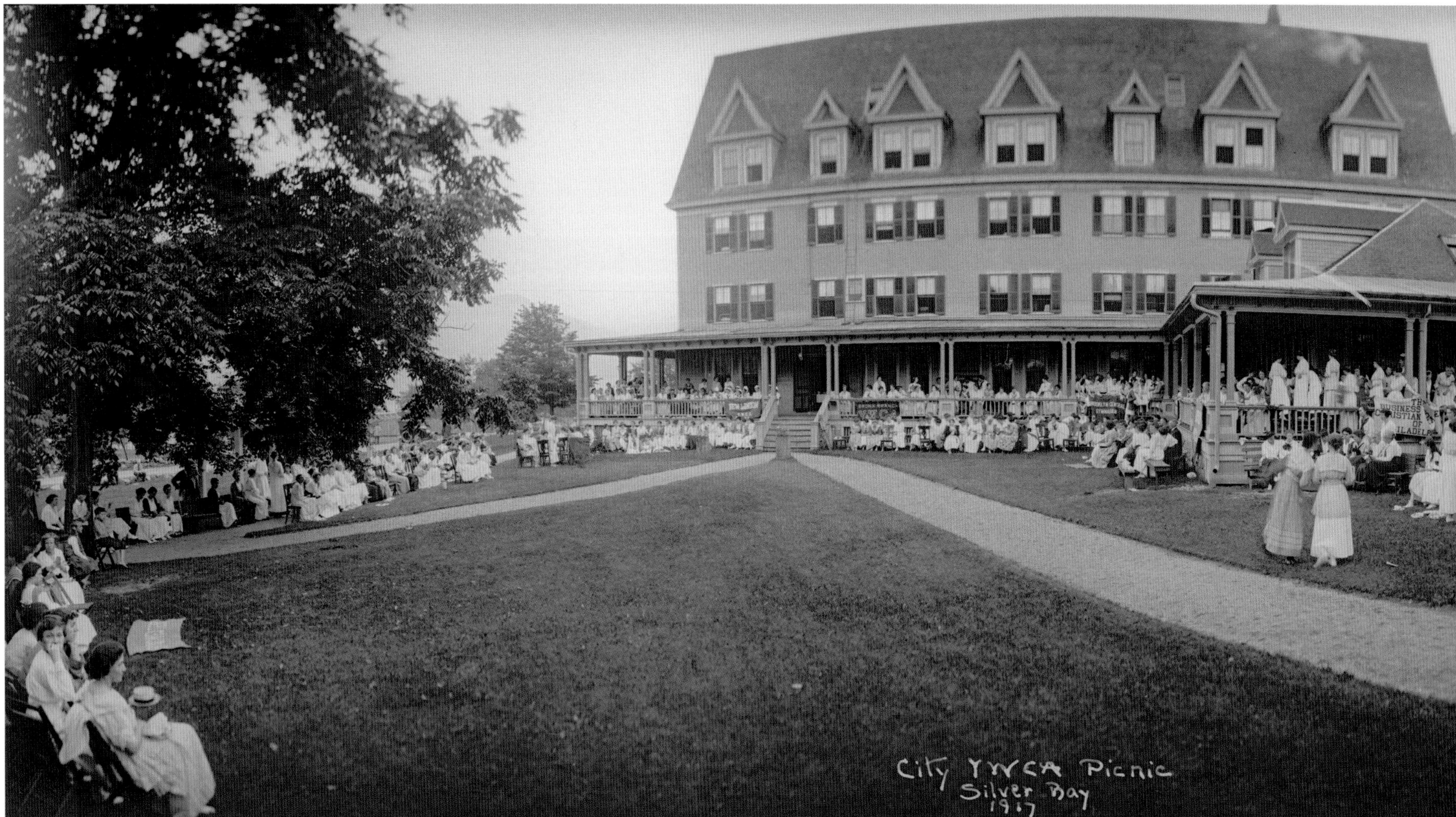

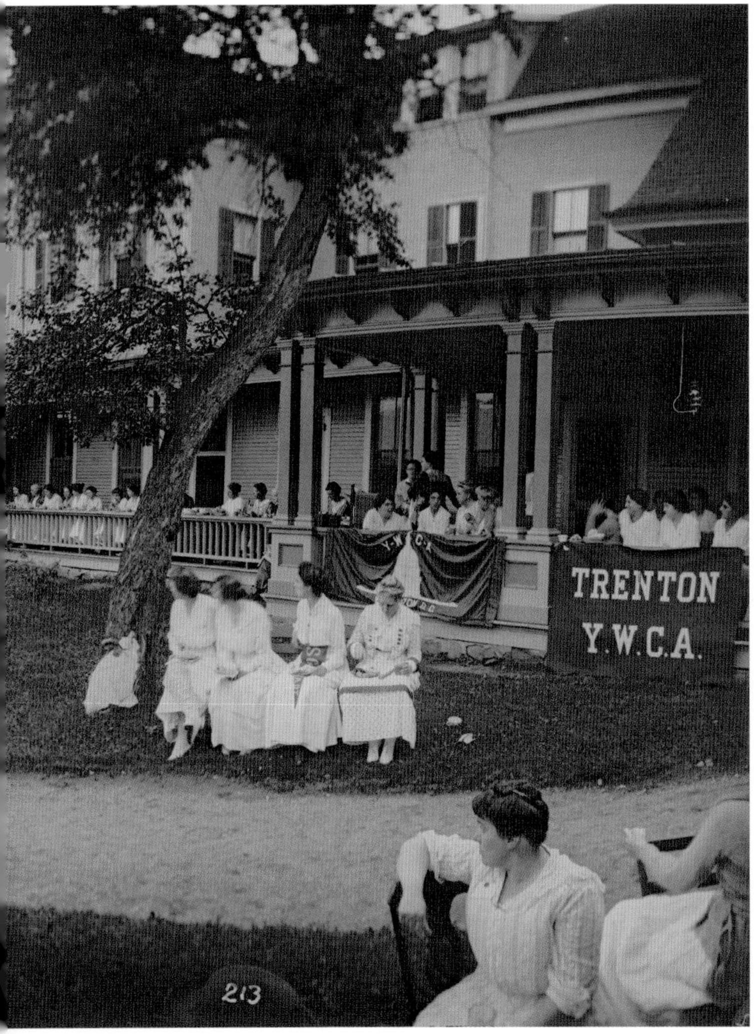

G4.1. *City YWCA Picnic, Silver Bay 1917*

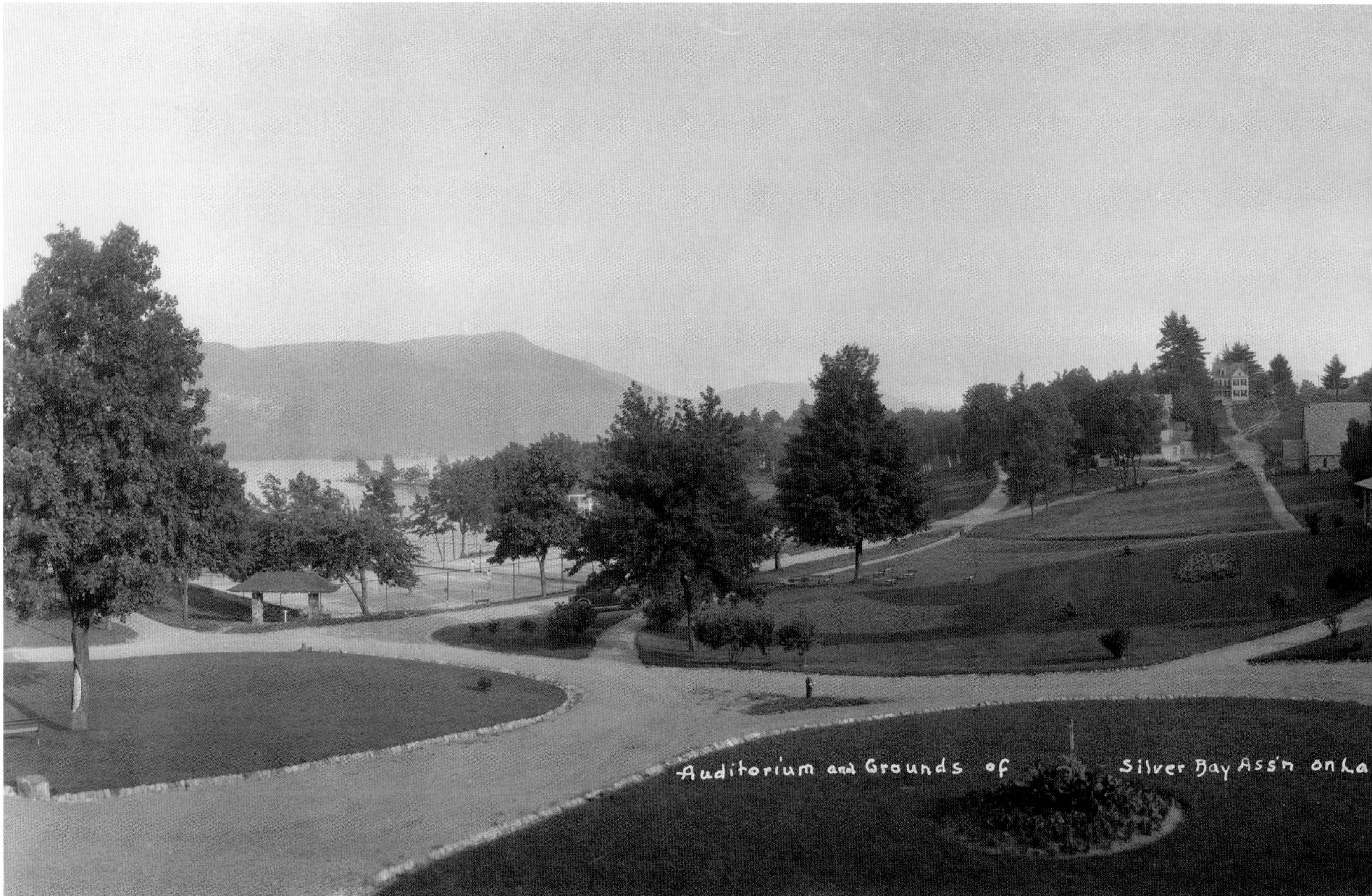
Auditorium and Grounds of Silver Bay Ass'n on Lak

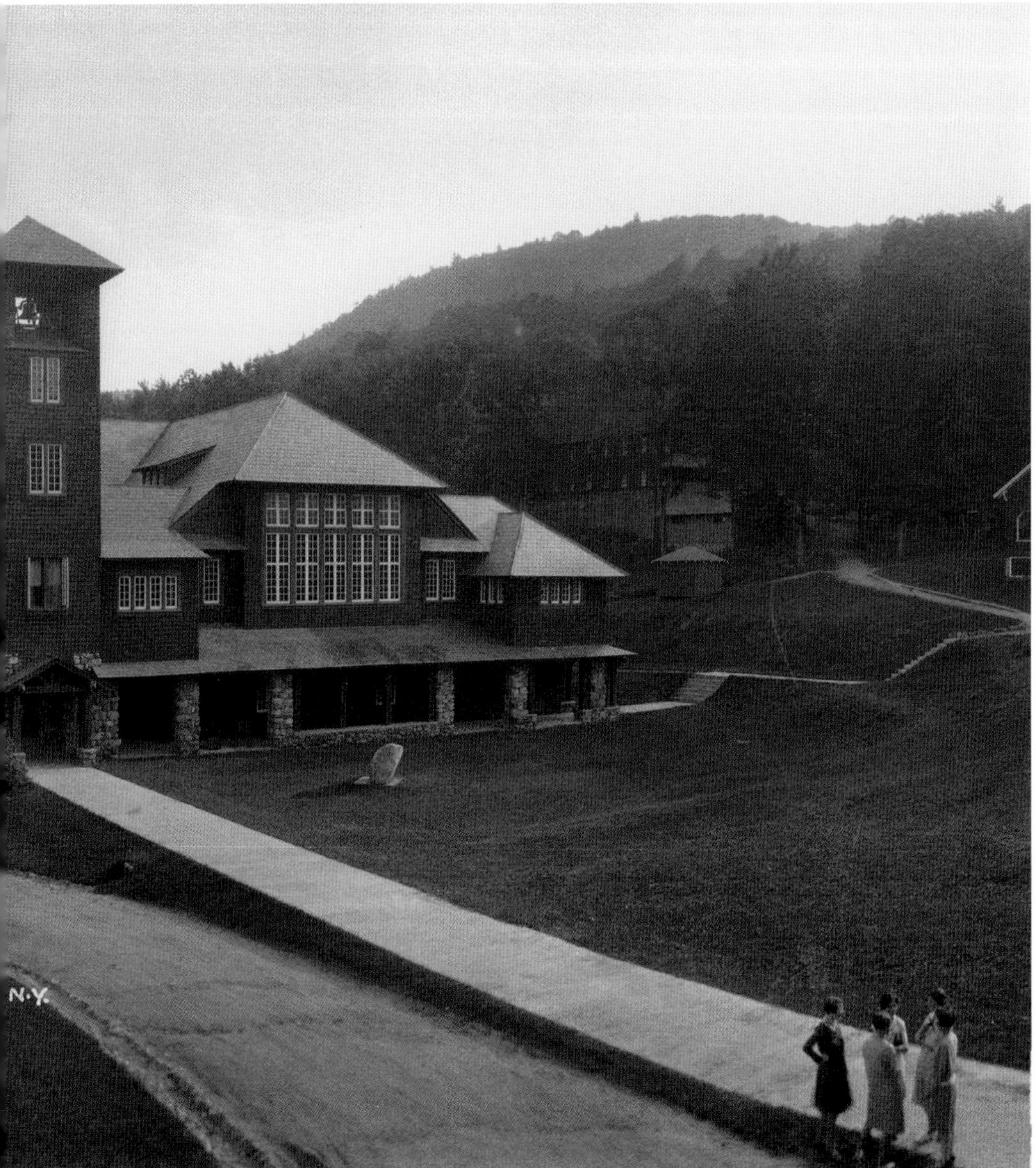

G4.2. *Auditorium and Grounds of Silver Bay Ass'n on Lake George N.Y.*

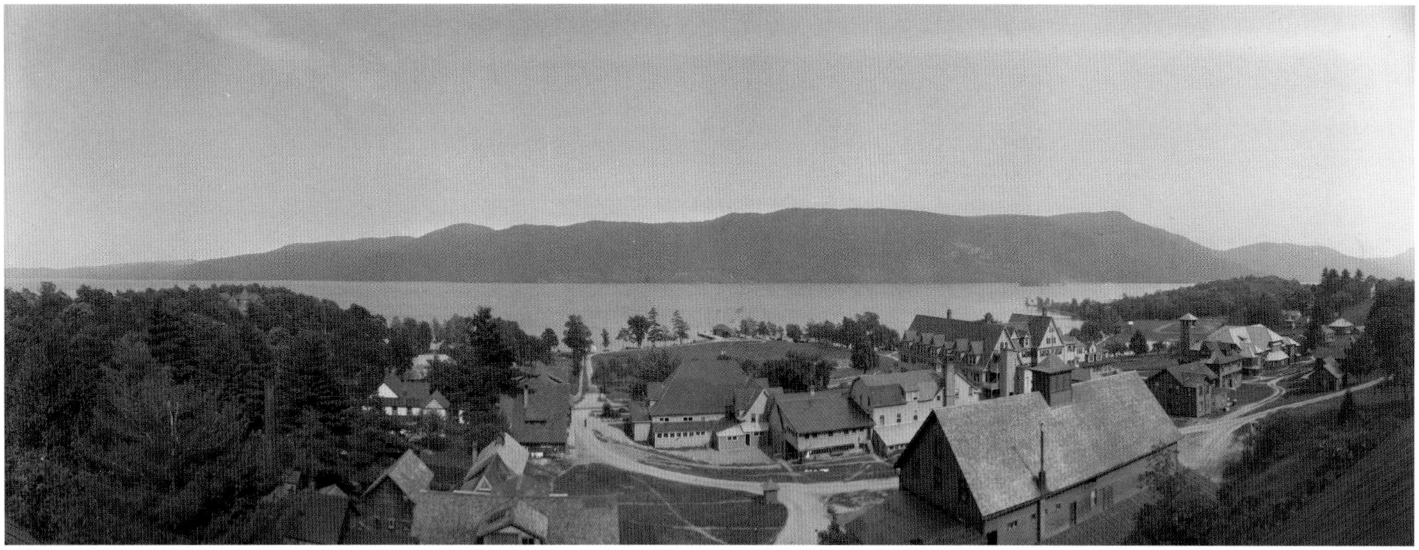

G4.3. *Silver Bay, Lake George*

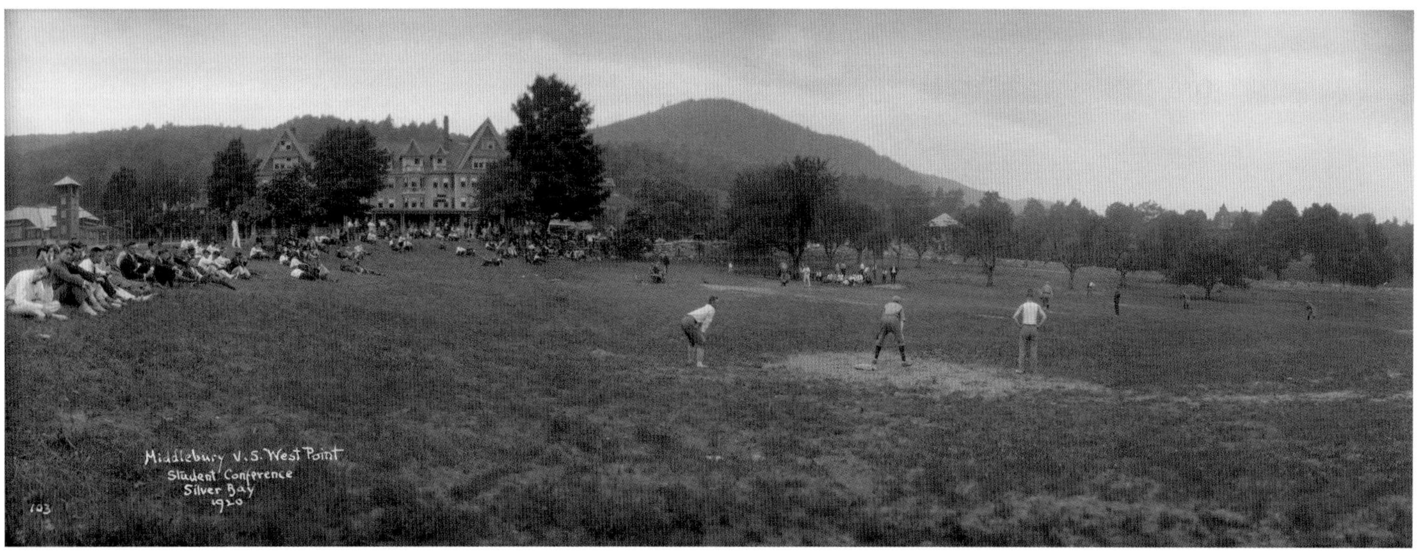

G4.4. *Middlebury v.s. West Point Student Conference Silver Bay 1920*

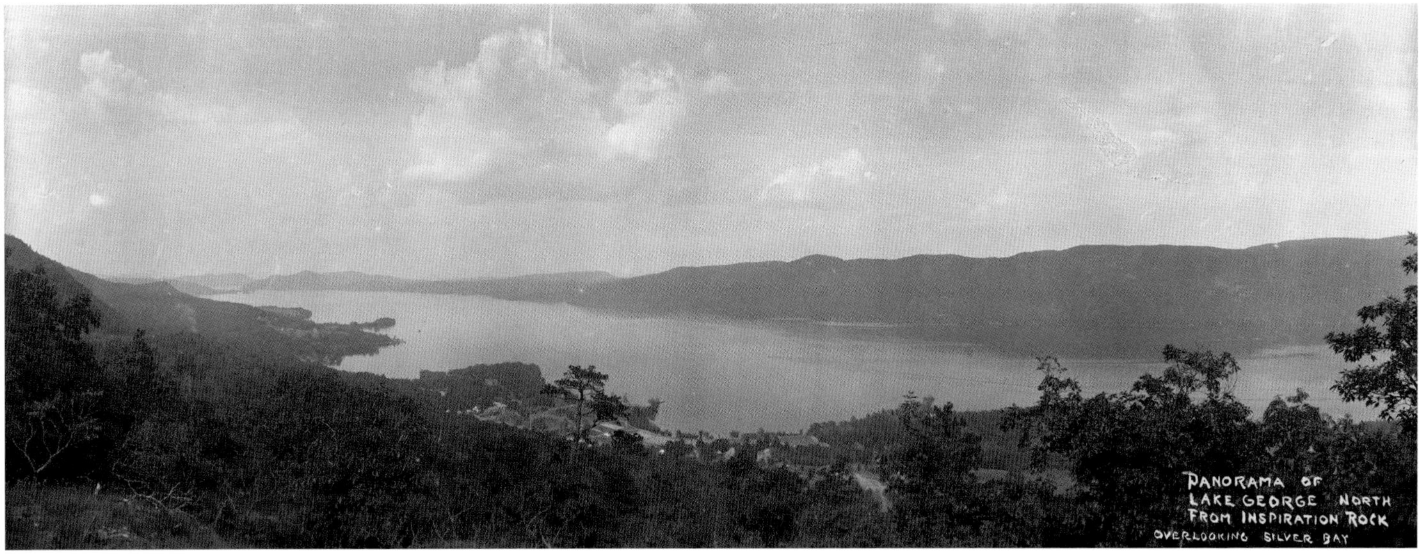

G4.5. *Panorama of Lake George North From Inspiration Rock Overlooking Silver Bay*

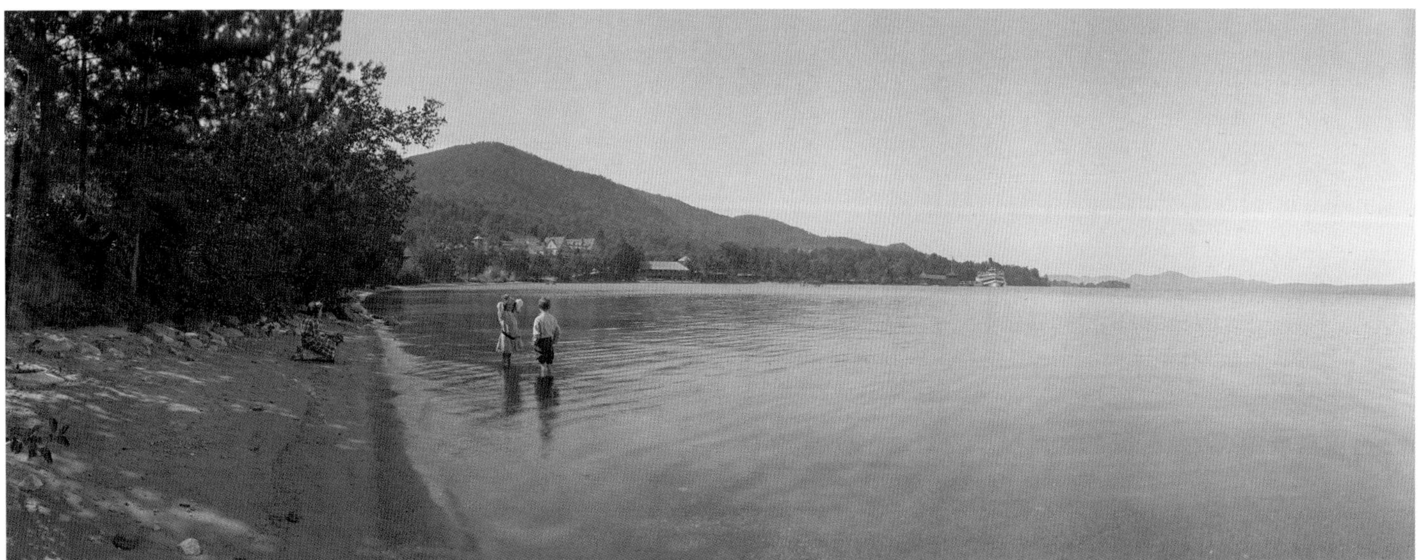

G4.6. *Children Wading in Lake George*

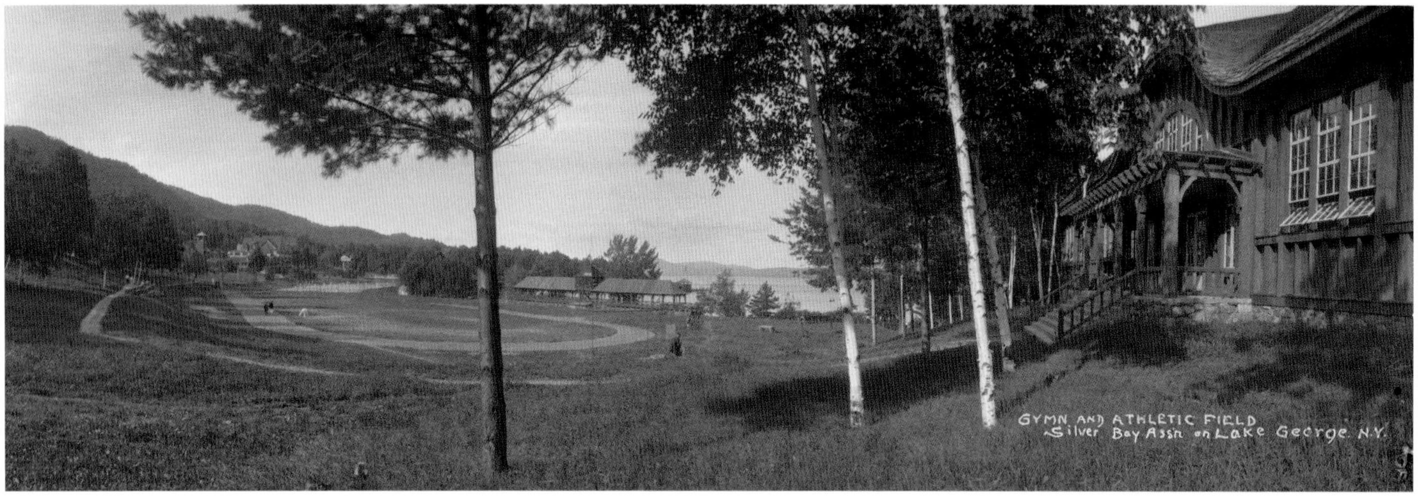

G4.7. *Gymn and Athletic Field Silver Bay Ass'n on Lake George N.Y.*

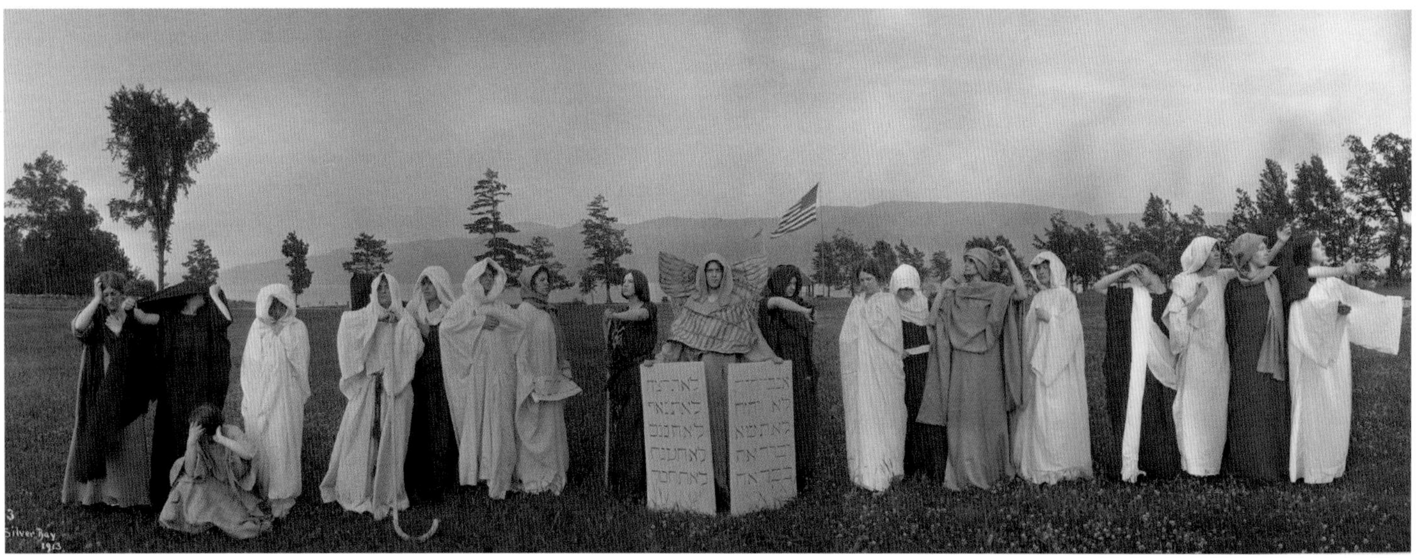

G4.8. *Silver Bay 1913*

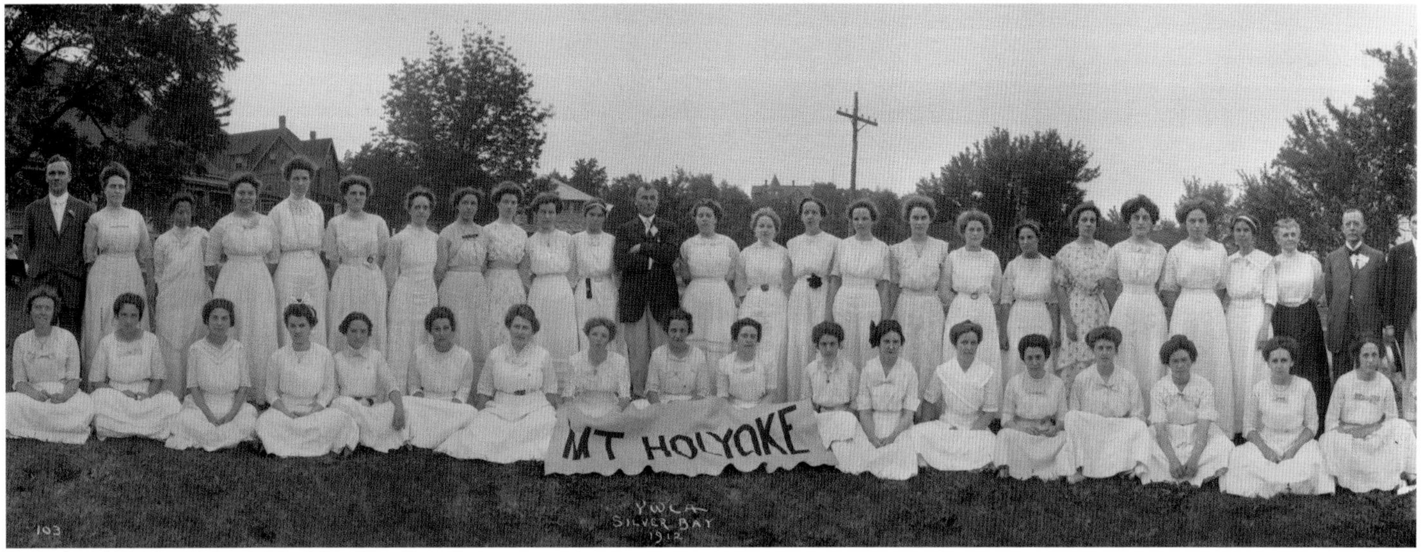

G4.9. *YWCA Silver Bay 1912*

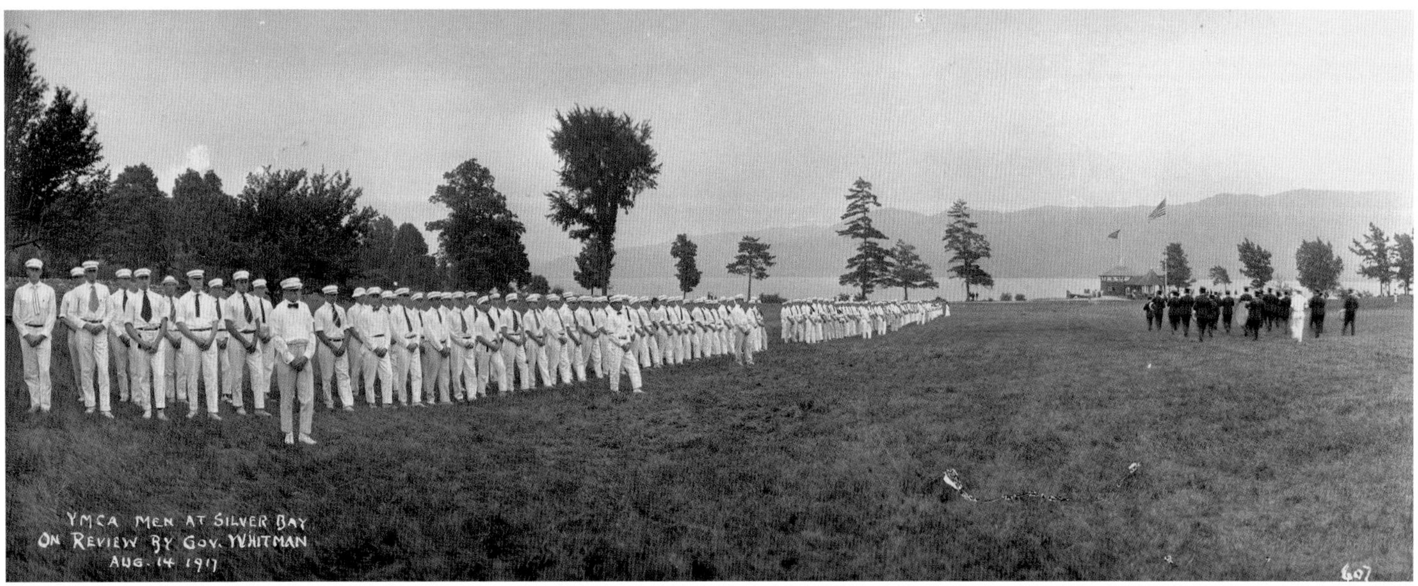

G4.10. *YMCA Men at Silver Bay on Review by Gov. Whitman Aug. 14 1917*

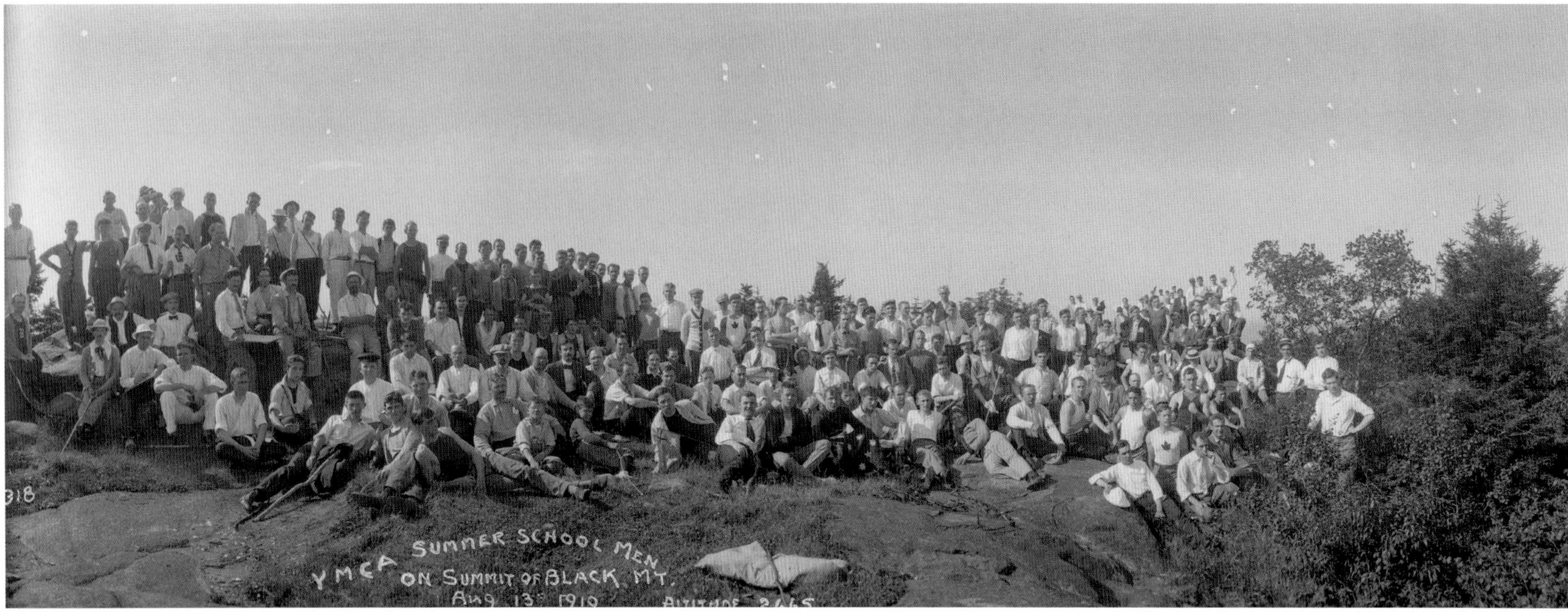

G4.11. *YMCA Summer School Men on Summit of Black Mt. Aug. 13 1910 Altitude 2665*

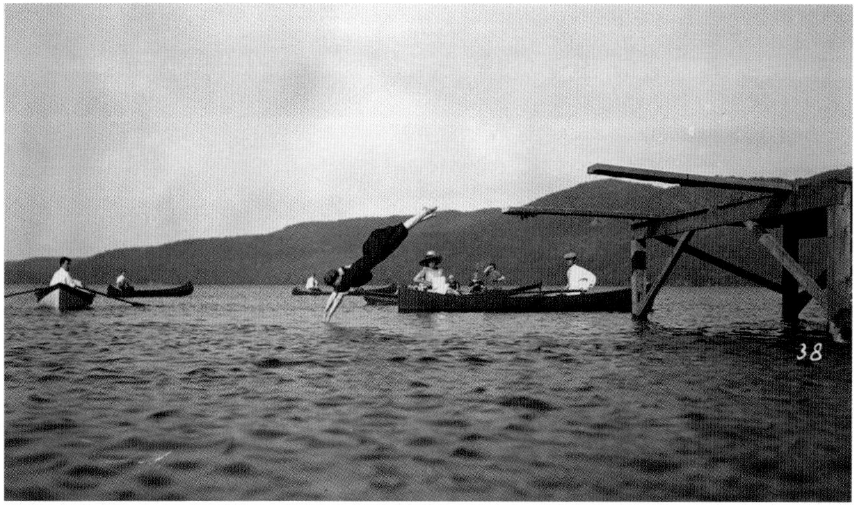

G4.12. *Swimmers at Silver Bay*

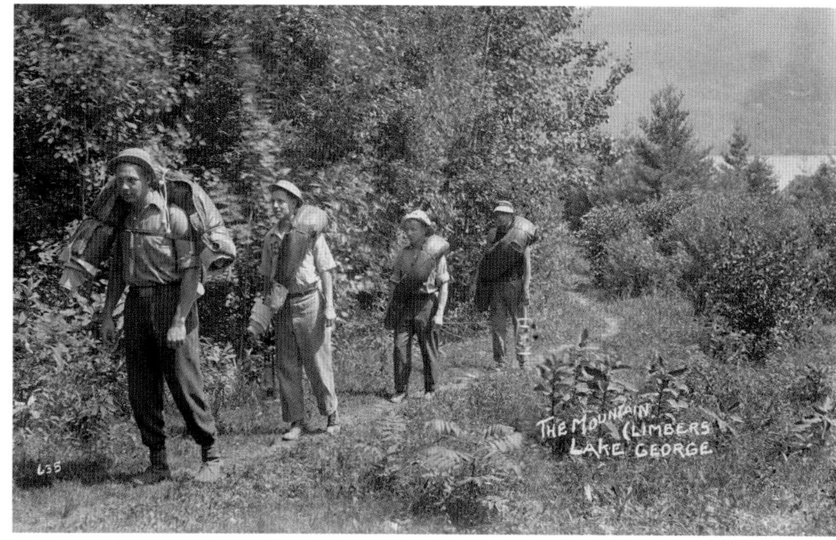

G4.14. *The Mountain Climbers Lake George*

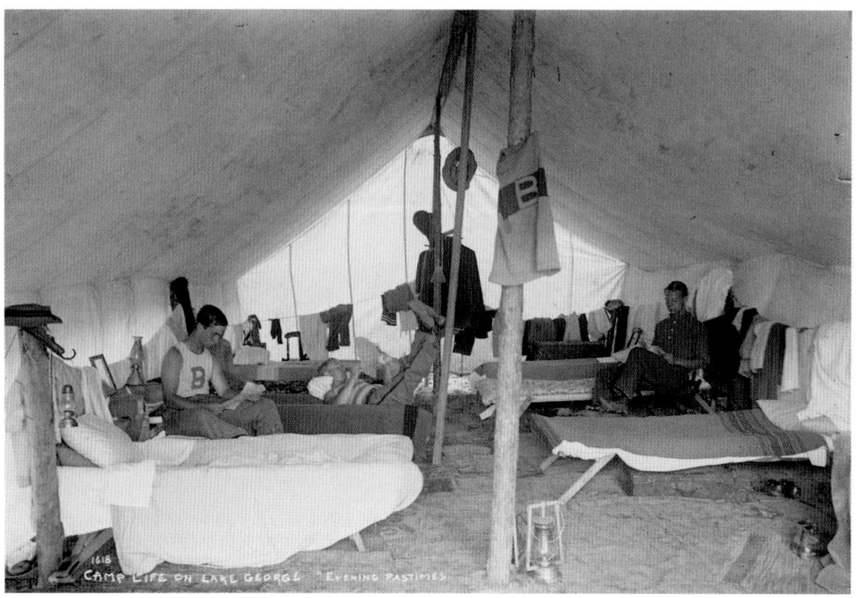

G4.13. *Camp Life on Lake George "Evening Pastimes'*

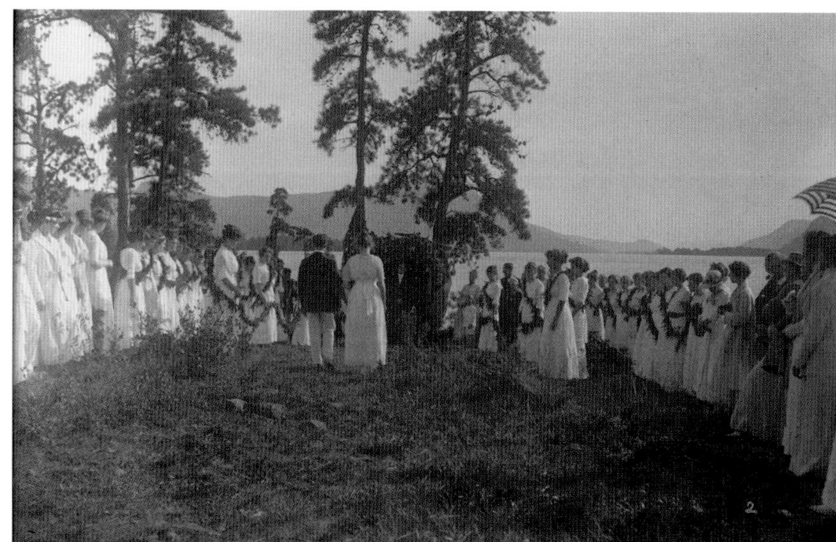

G4.15. *Wedding at Silver Bay*

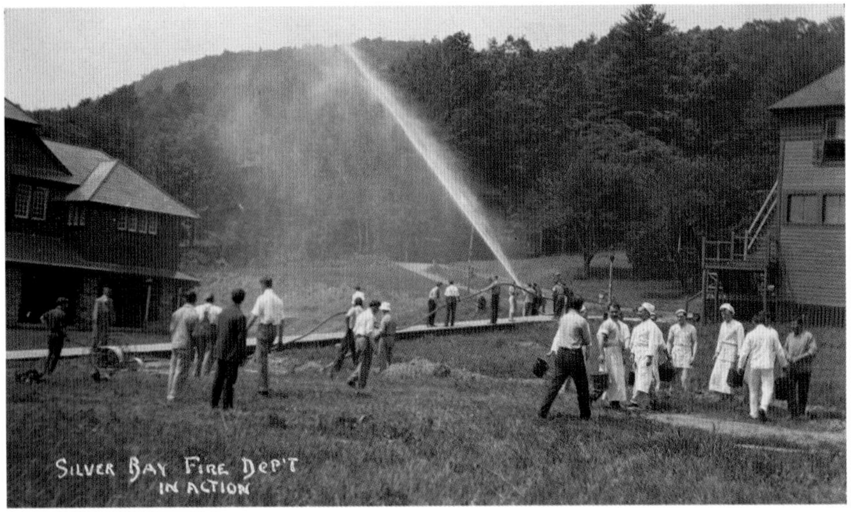

G4.16. *Silver Bay Fire Dep't in Action*

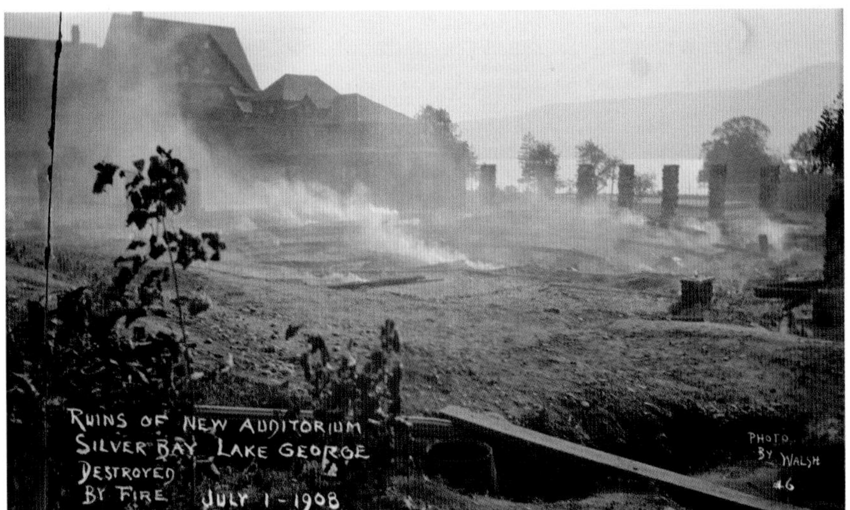

G4.17. *Ruins of New Auditorium Silver Bay Lake George Destroyed by Fire July 1-1908*

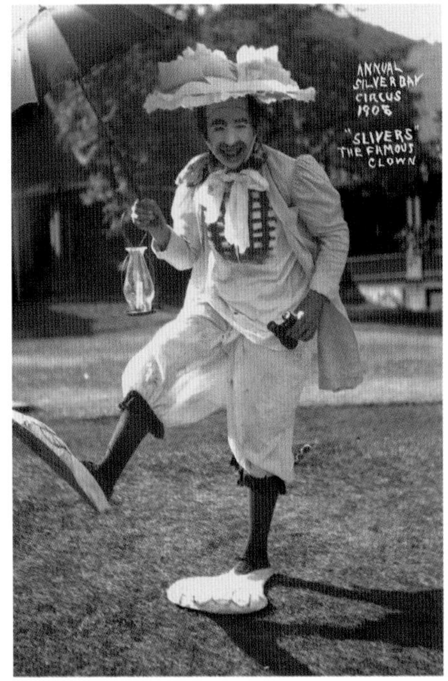

G4.18. *Annual Silver Bay Circus 1905 "Slivers" the Famous Clown*

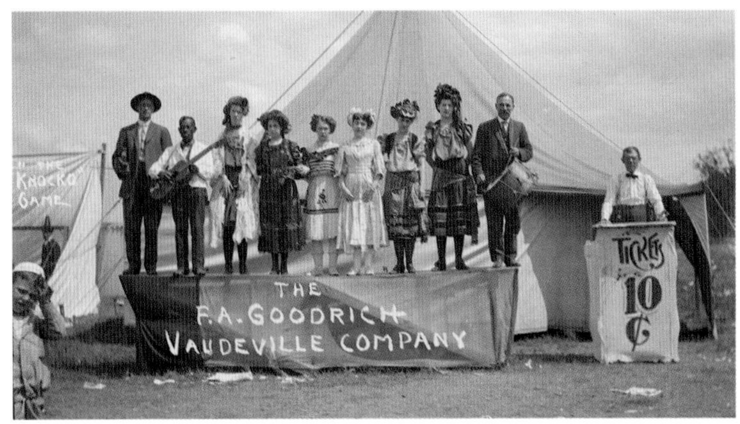

G4.19. *The "Knocko" Game The F.A. Goodrich Vaudeville Company*

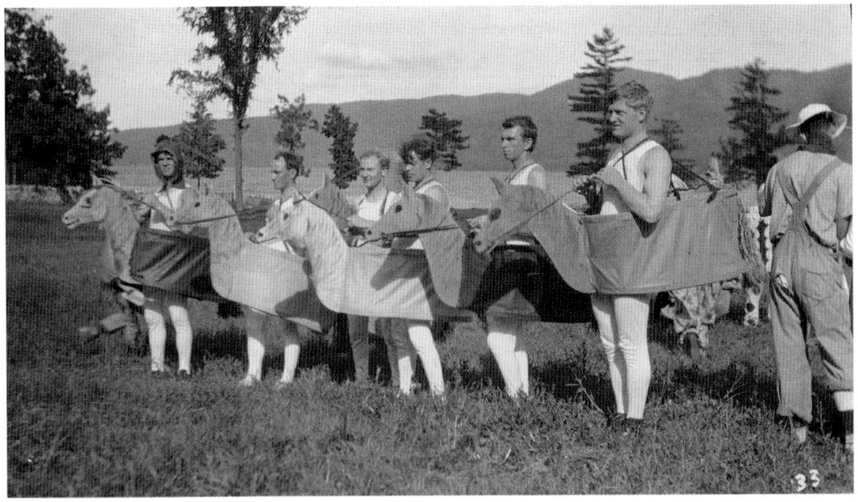

G4.20. *Silver Bay Circus*

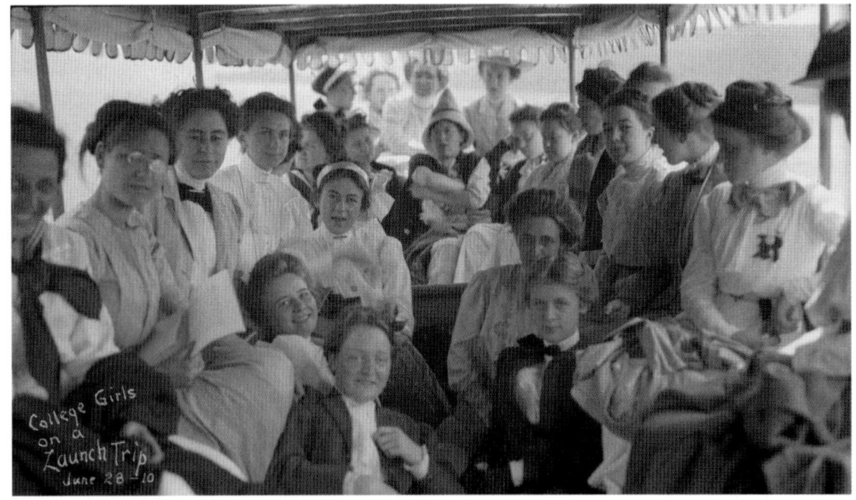

G4.22. *College Girls on a Launch Trip June 29–10*

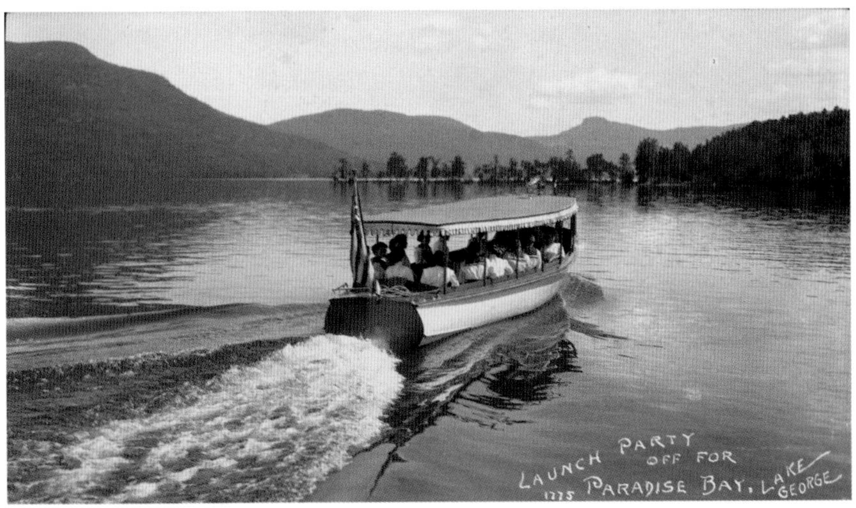

G4.21. *Launch Party Off For Paradise Bay, Lake George*

Hague

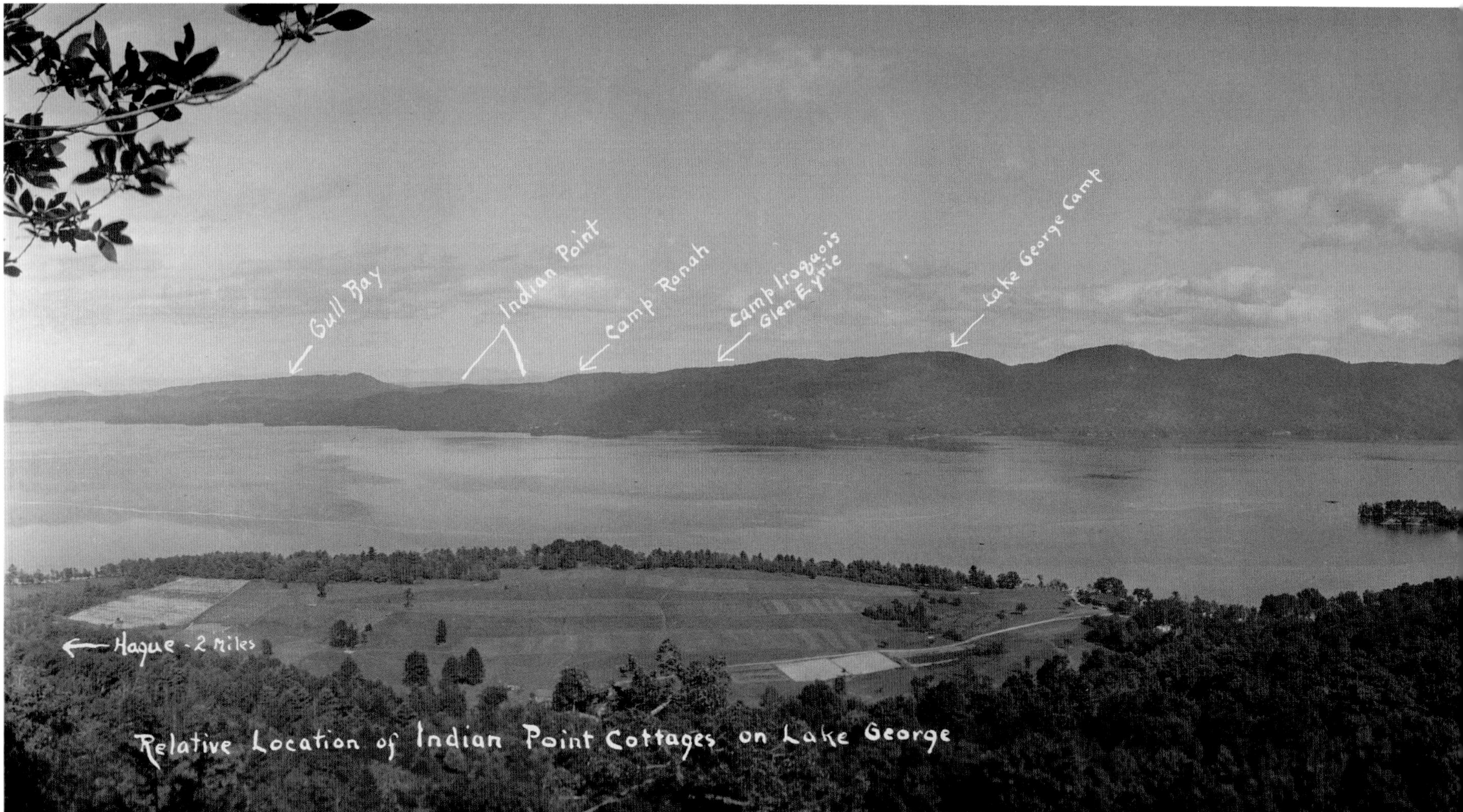

Gull Bay
Indian Point
Camp Ronah
Camp Iroquois
Glen Eyrie
Lake George Camp
← Hague - 2 Miles
Relative Location of Indian Point Cottages on Lake George

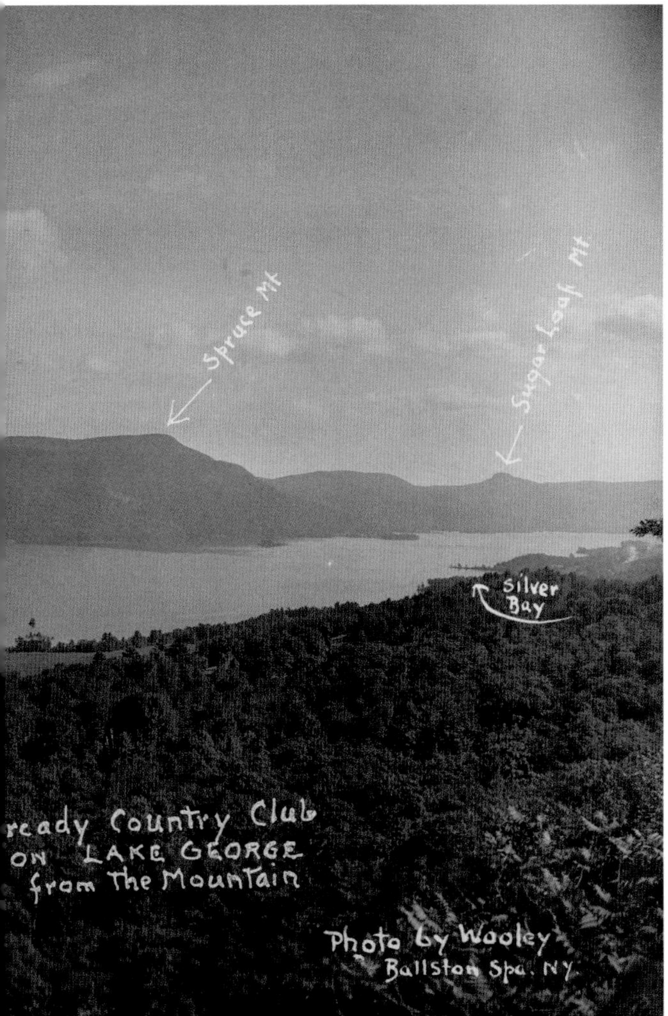

G5.1. *Relative Location of Indian Point Cottages on Lake George Arcady Country Club on Lake George from The Mountain*

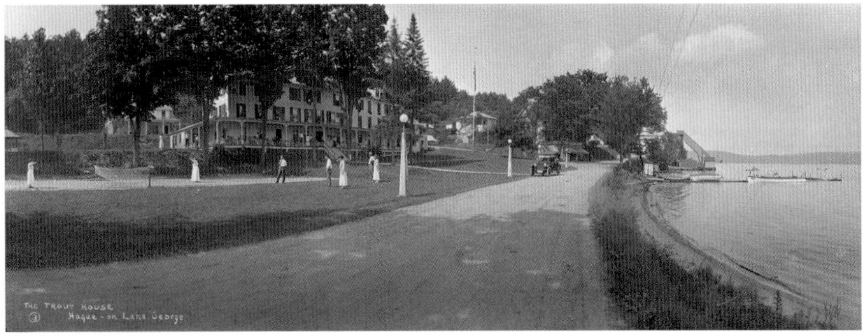

G5.2. *The Trout House Hague on Lake George*

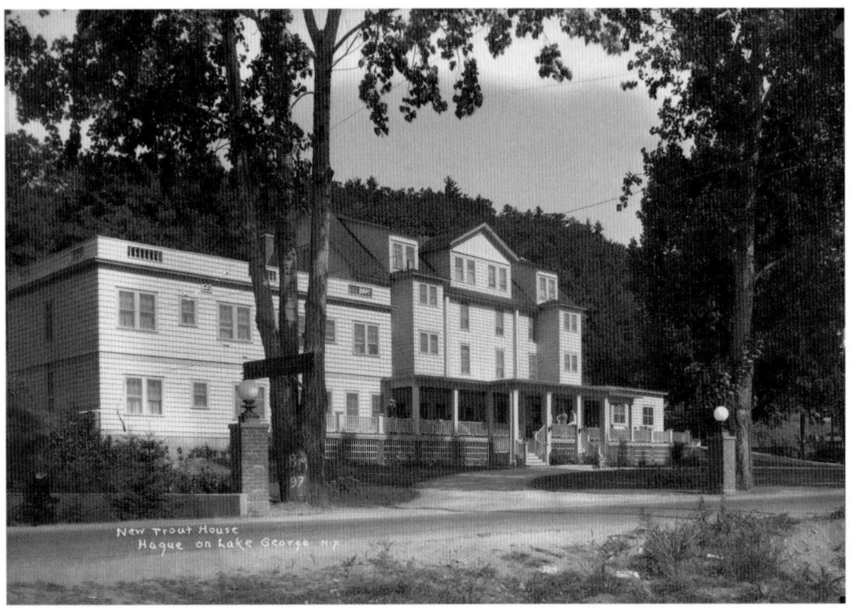

G5.3. *New Trout House Hague on Lake George*

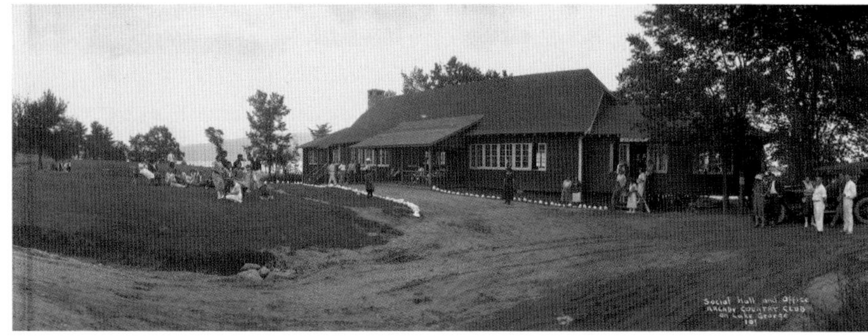

G5.4. *Social Hall and Office Arcady Country Club on Lake George*

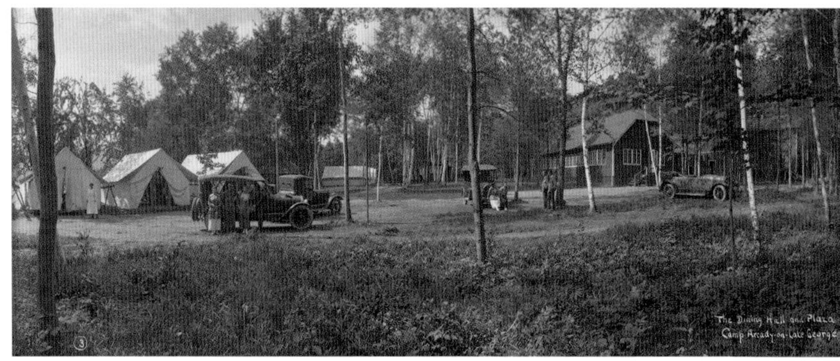

G5.5. *The Dining and Plaza Camp Arcady-on-Lake George*

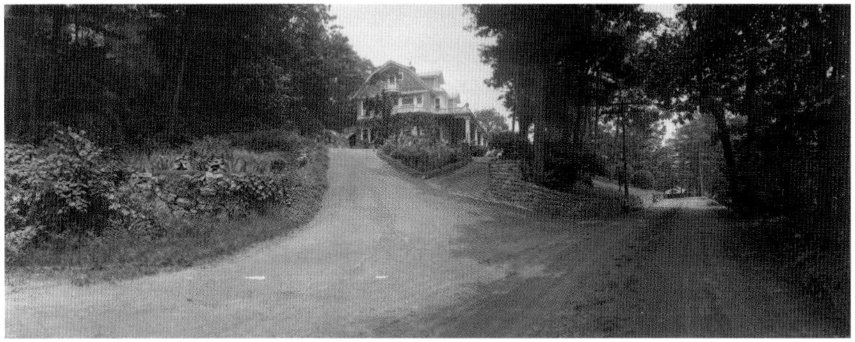

G5.6. *The Ruhah House*, Rt. 9N, Hague, NY

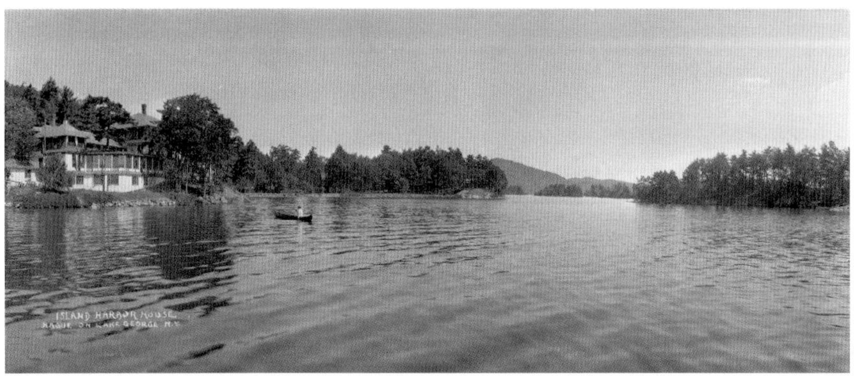

G5.7. *Island Harbor House Hague on Lake George N.Y.*

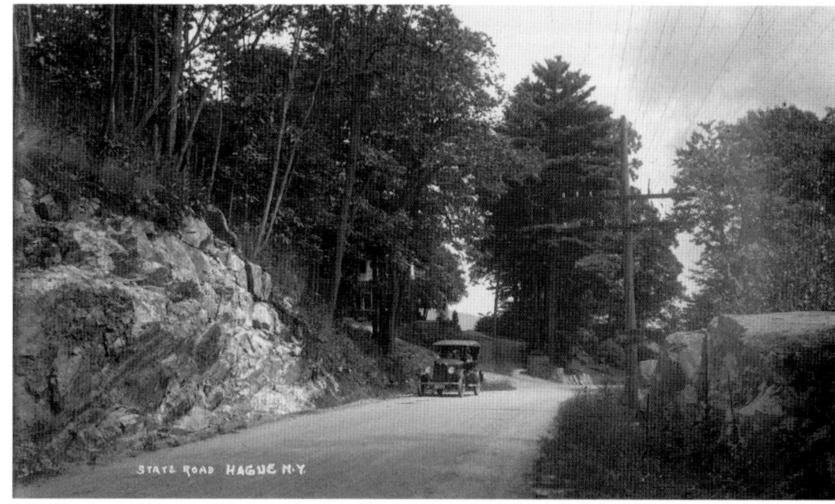

G5.8. *State Road Hague N.Y.*

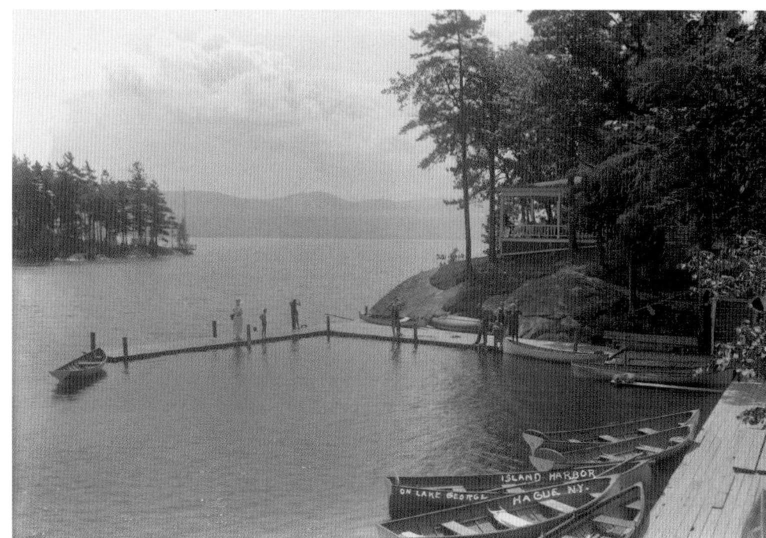

G5.9. *Island Harbor on Lake George Hague N.Y.*

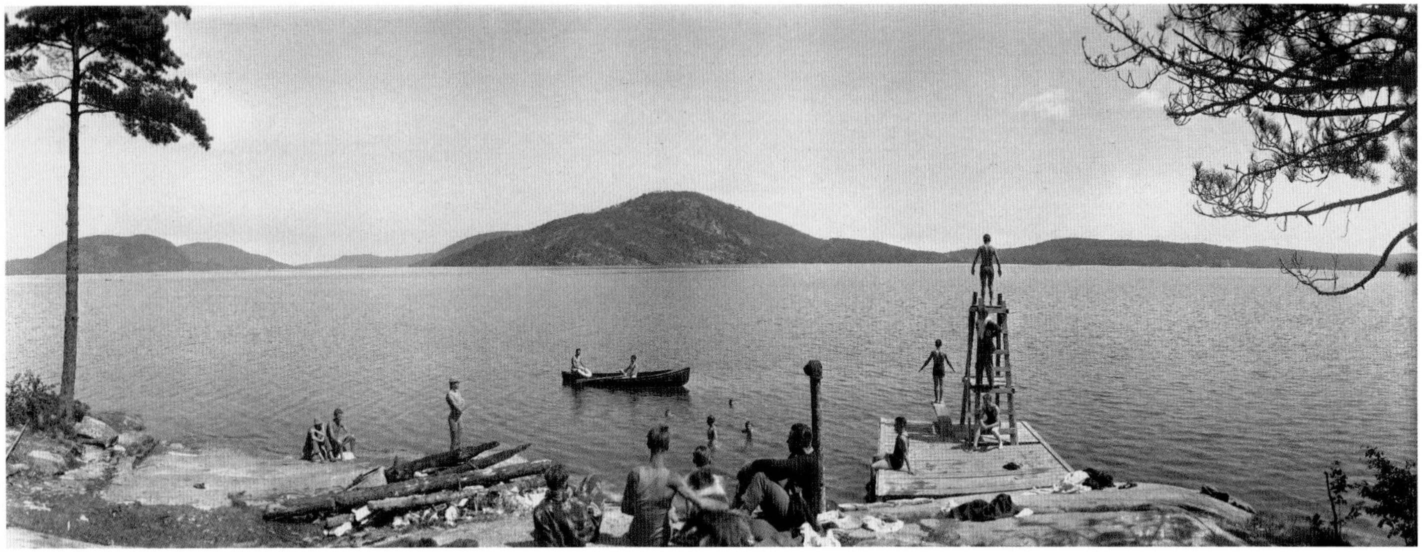

G5.10. *Swimmers and Boaters on Northern Lake George in Hague, NY, across from Anthony's Nose and Glenburnie*

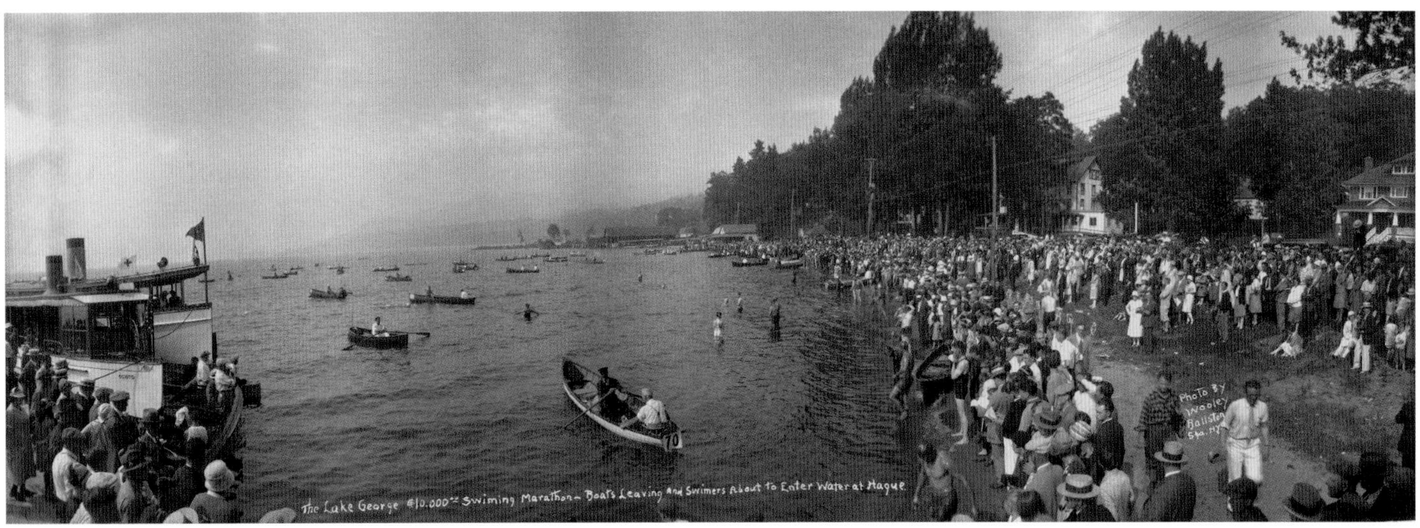

G5.11. *The Lake George $10,000.00 Swimming Marathon—Boats Leaving and Swimmers About to Enter Water at Hague*

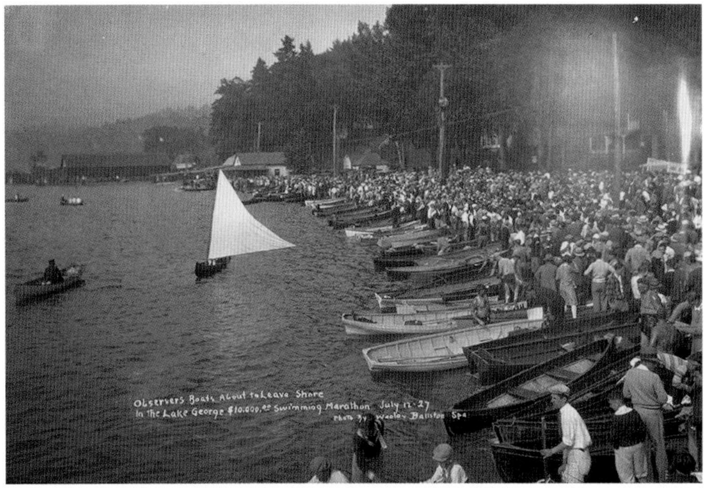

G5.12. *Observers Boats About to Leave Shore in the Lake George $10,000.00 Swimming Marathon July 12–27*

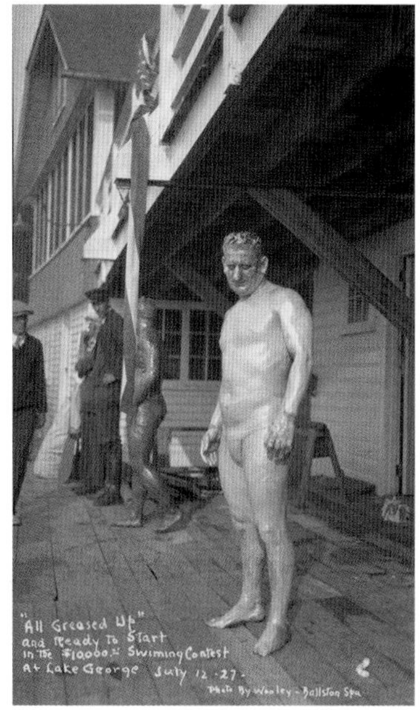

G5.14. *"All Greased Up" and Ready to Start in the $10,000.00 Swimming Contest At Lake George July 12–27*

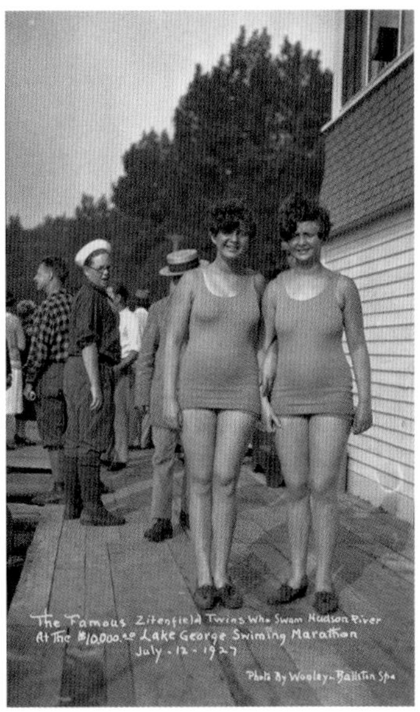

G5.13. *The Famous Zitenfield Twins Who Swam Hudson River At The $10,000.00 Lake George Swiming Marathon July-12-1927*

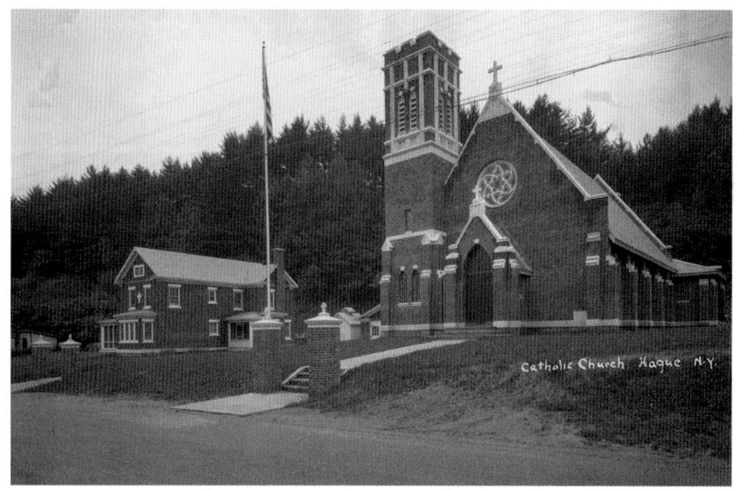

G5.15. *Catholic Church Hague N.Y.*

Ticonderoga

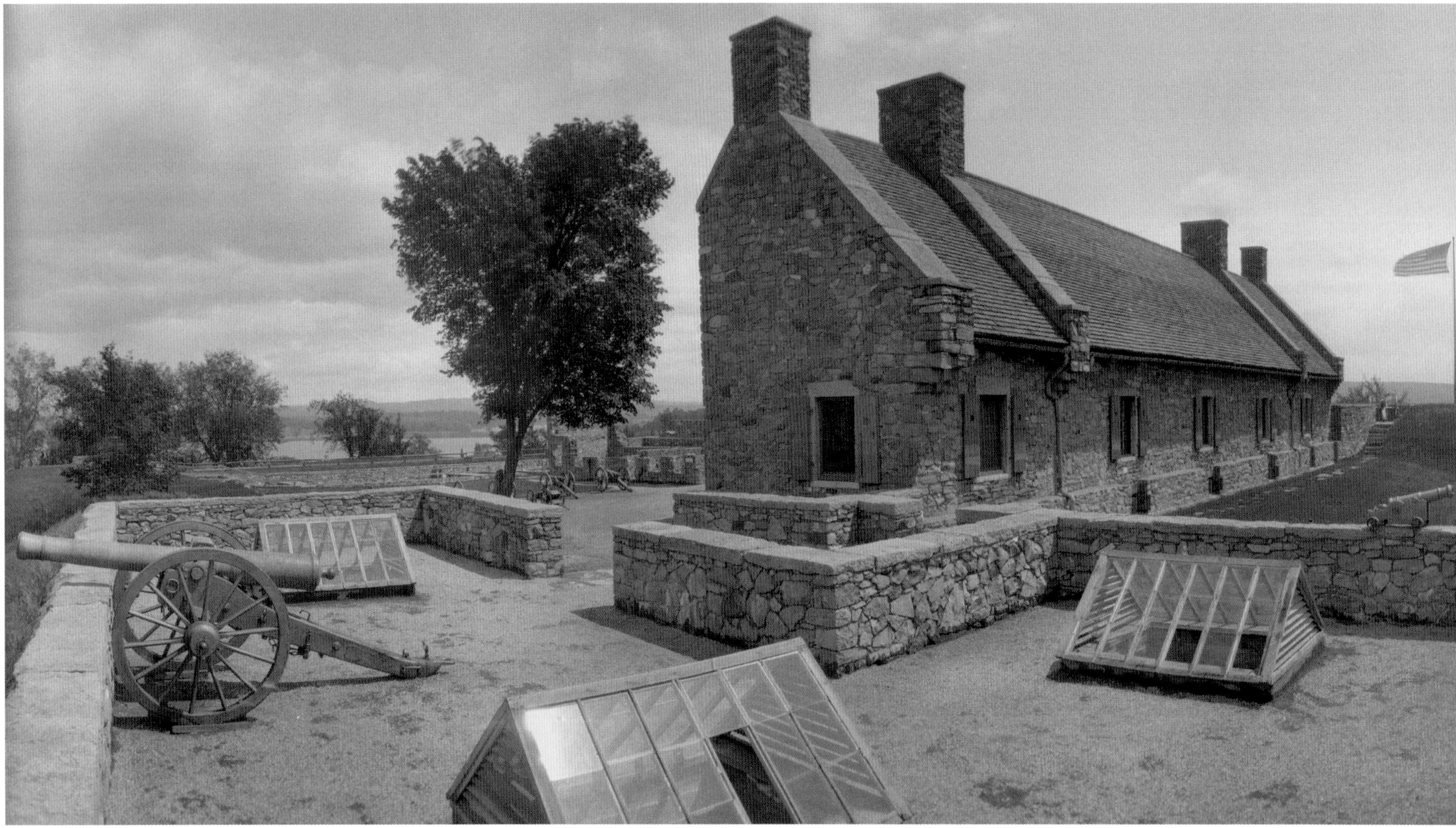

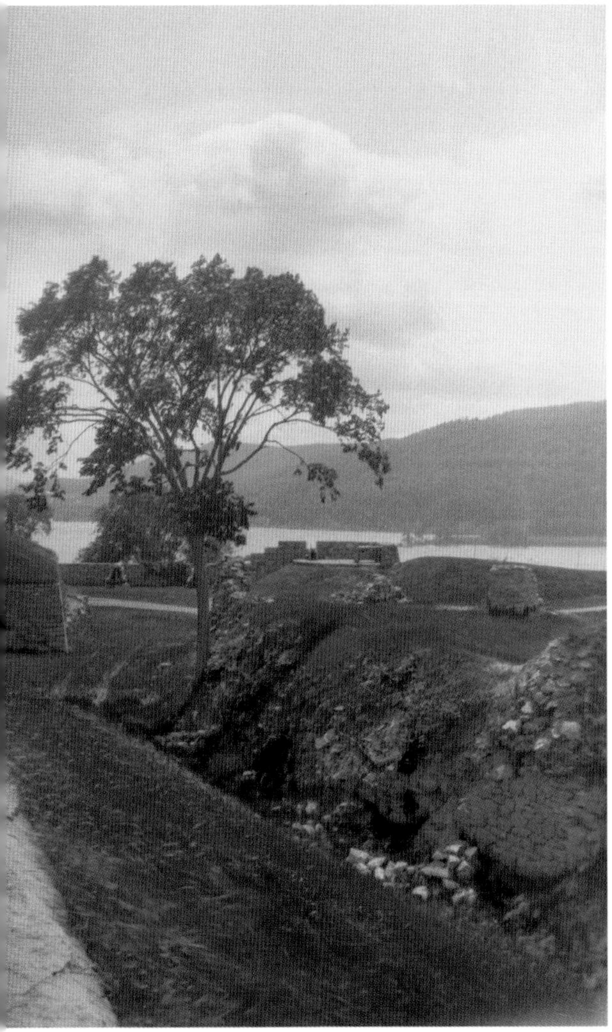

G6.1. *Fort Ticonderoga*

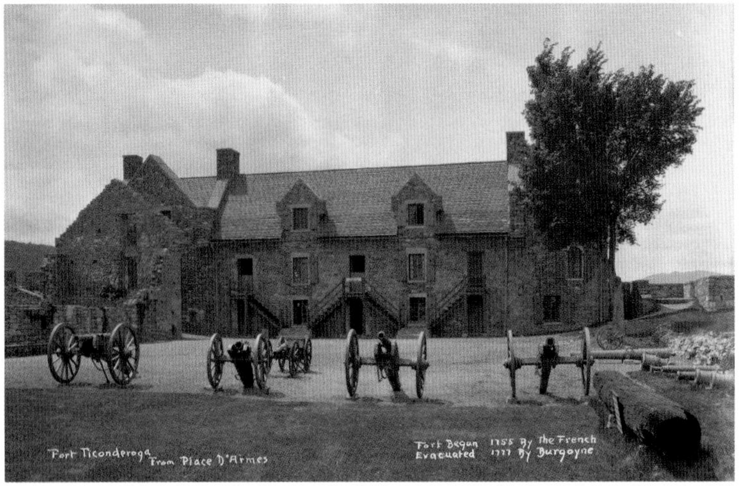

G6.2. *Fort Ticonderoga from Place D'Armes Fort Began 1755 by the French Evacuated 1777 by Burgoyne*

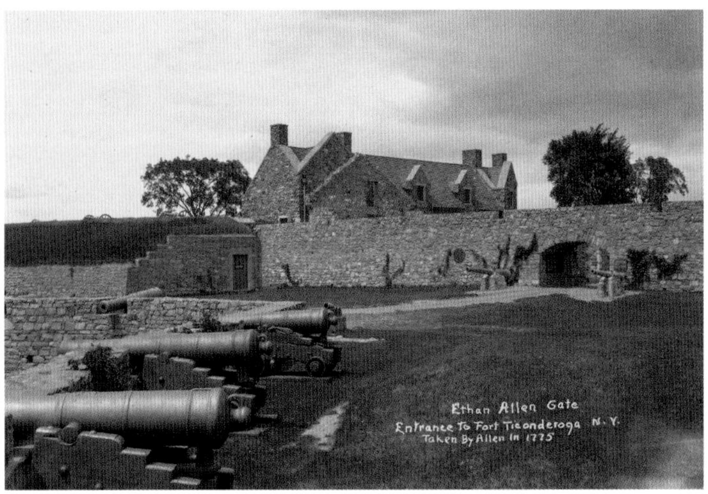

G6.3. *Ethan Allen Gate Entrance to Fort Ticonderoga N.Y. Taken by Allen in 1775*

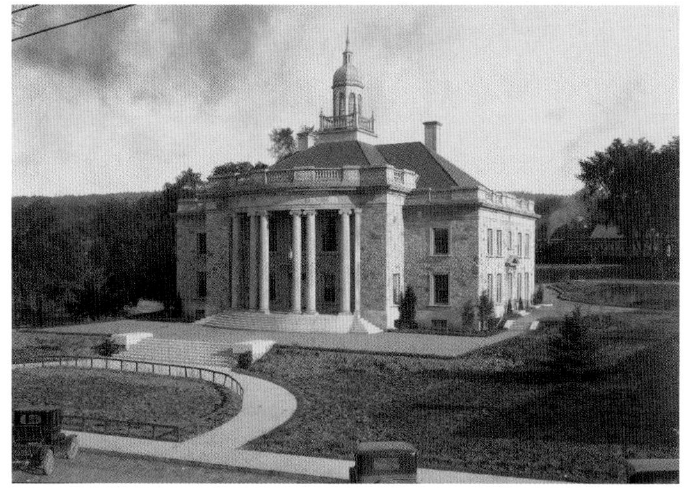

G6.4. *Ticonderoga Community Building*

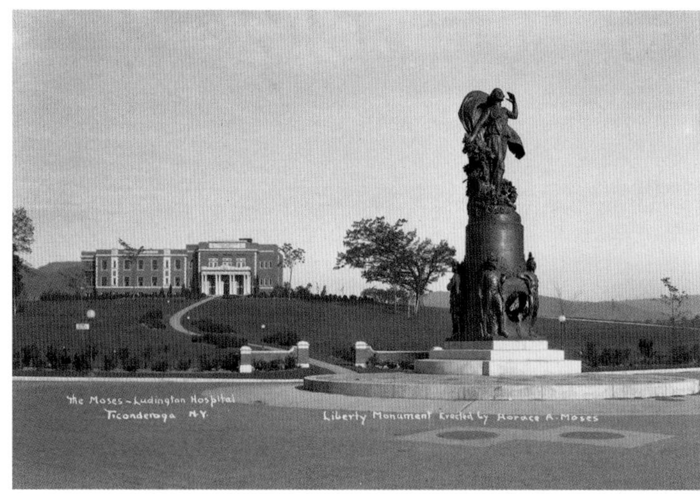

G6.5. *The Moses-Ludington Hospital Ticonderoga, N.Y. Liberty Monument Erected by Horace A. Moses*

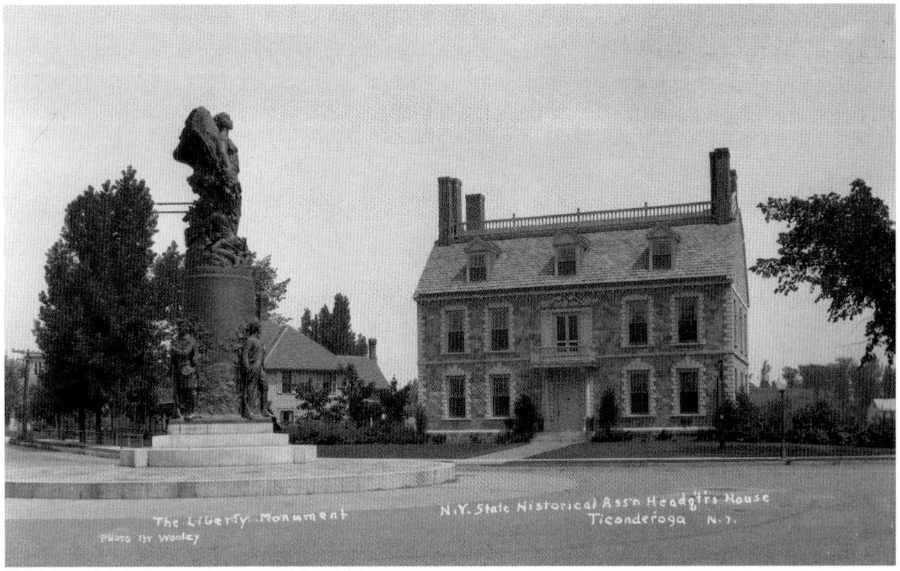

G6.6. *The Liberty Monument N.Y. State Historical Ass'n Headq't'rs House Ticonderoga, N.Y.*

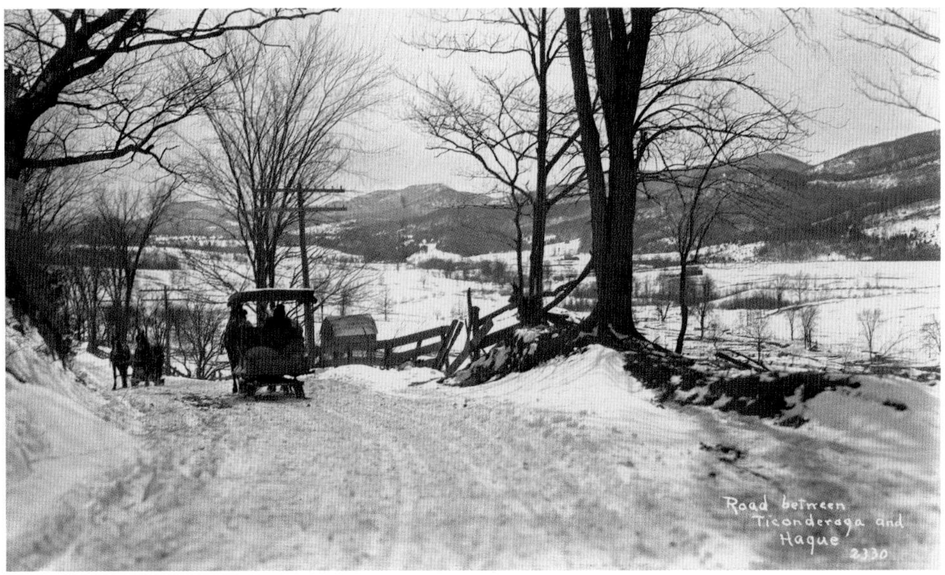

G6.7. *Road between Ticonderoga and Hague*

Plattsburgh

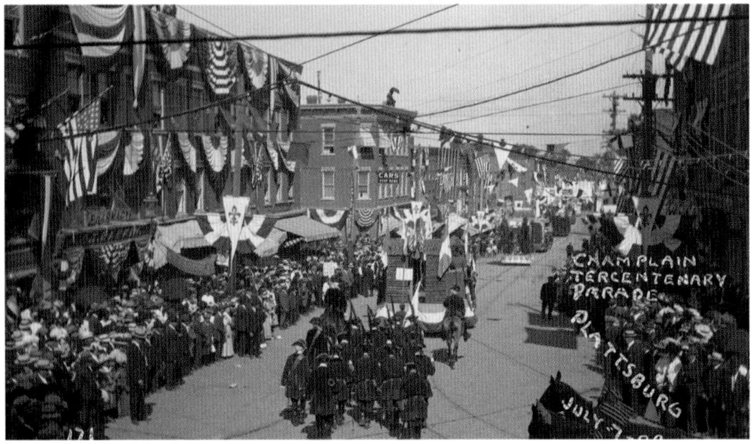

G7.1. *Champlain Tercentenary Parade Plattsburg July 7–09*

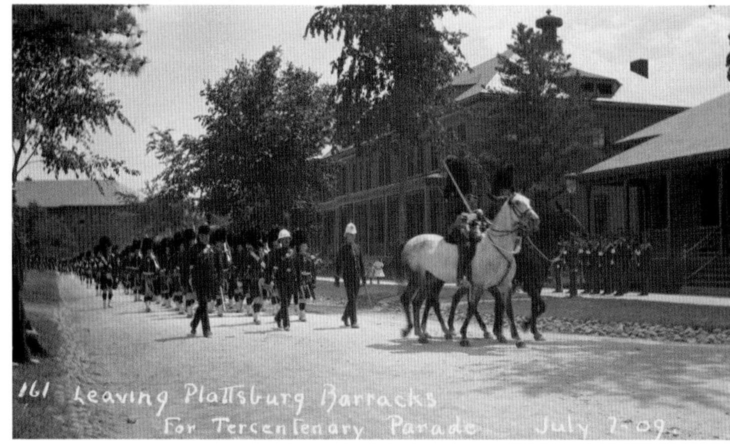

G7.3. *Leaving Plattsburg Barracks For Tercentenary Parade July 7–09*

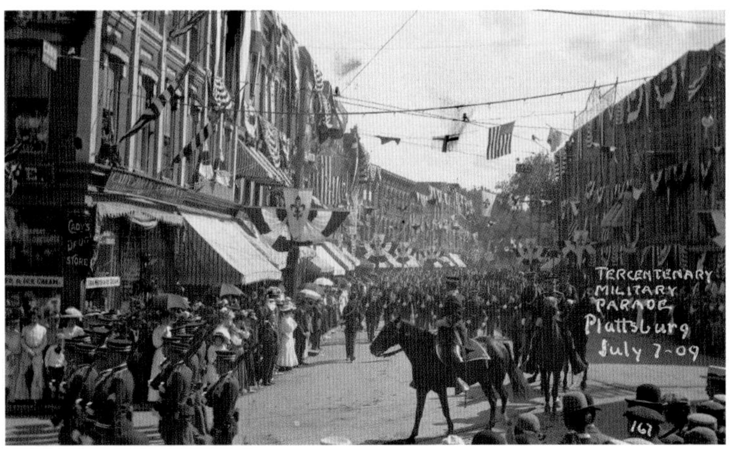

G7.2. *Tercentenary Military Parade Plattsburg July 7–09*

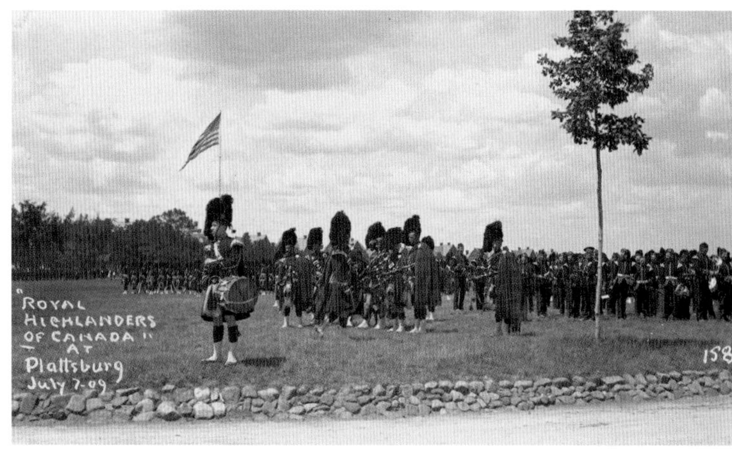

G7.4. *Royal Highlanders of Canada at Plattsburg July 7–09*

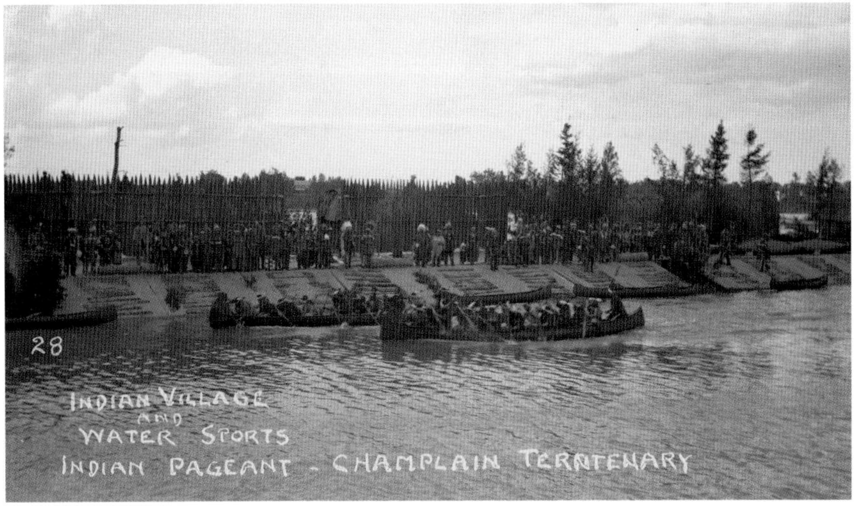

G7.5. *Indian Village and Water Sports Indian Pageant—Champlain Tercentenary*

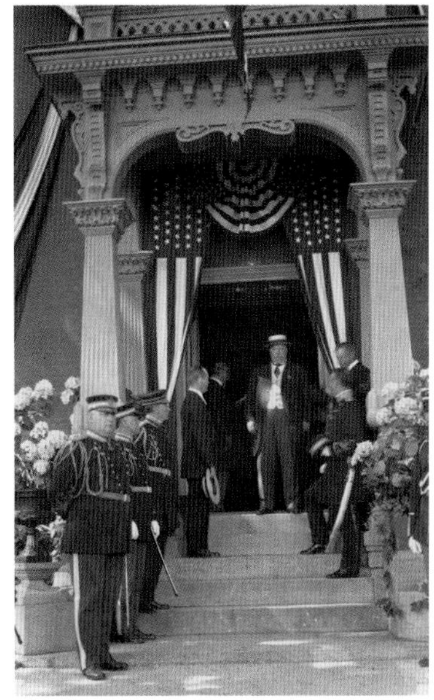

G7.7. *President Taft at Lake Champlain Tercentenary Parade*

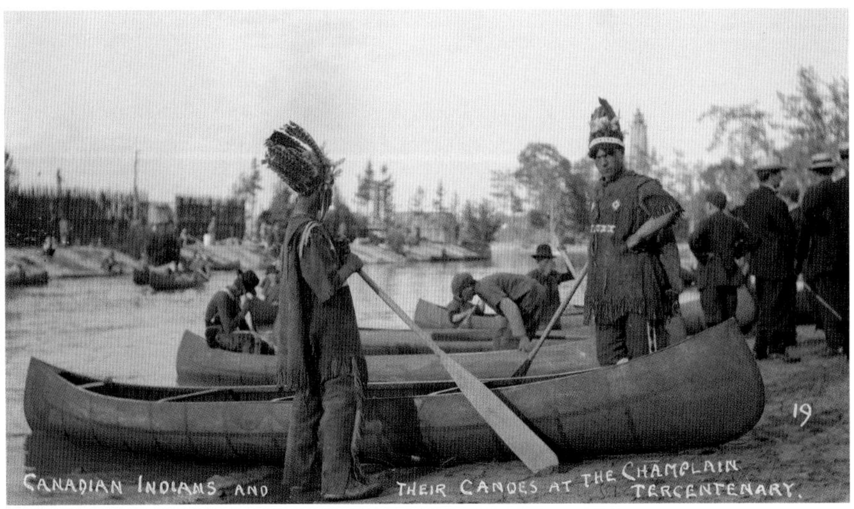

G7.6. *Canadian Indians and Their Canoes at the Champlain Tercentenary*

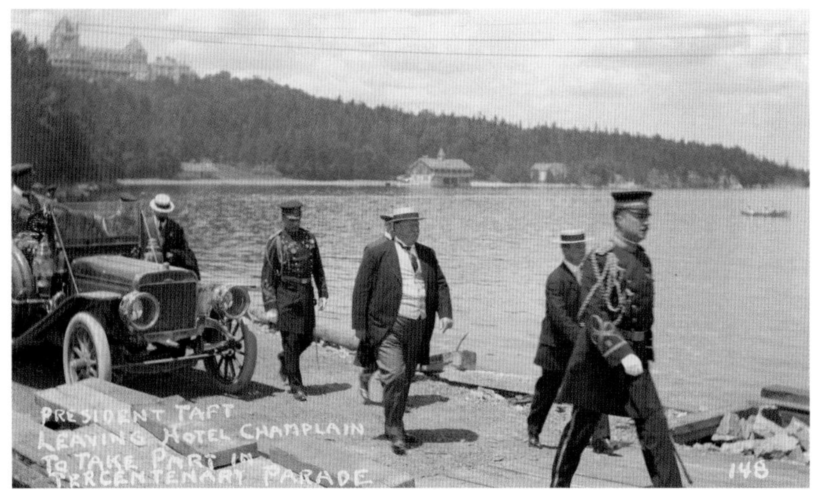

G7.8. *President Taft Leaving Hotel Champlain to Take Part in Tercentenary Parade*

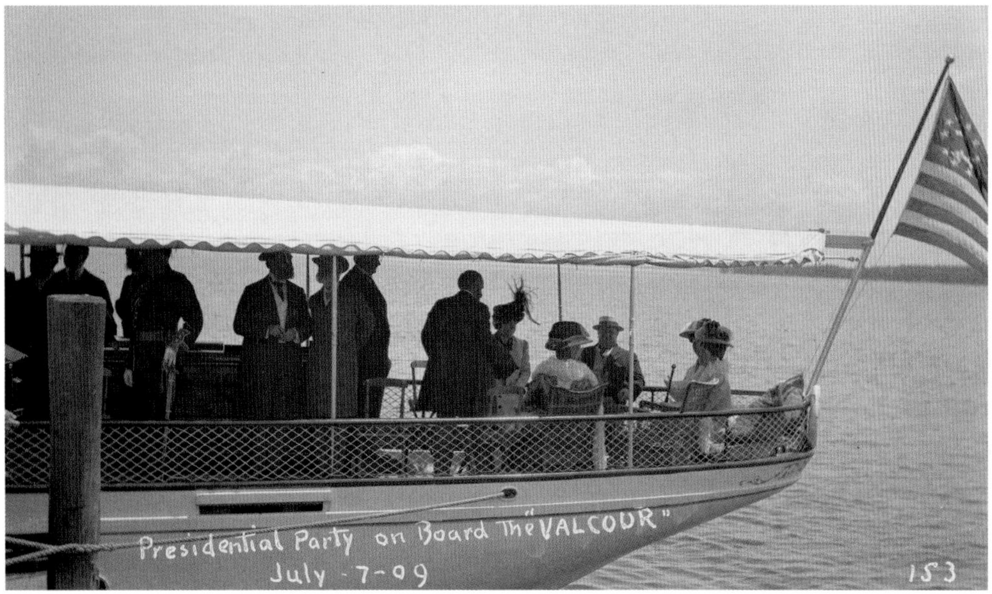

G7.9. *Presidential Party on Board The "Valcour" July 7–09*

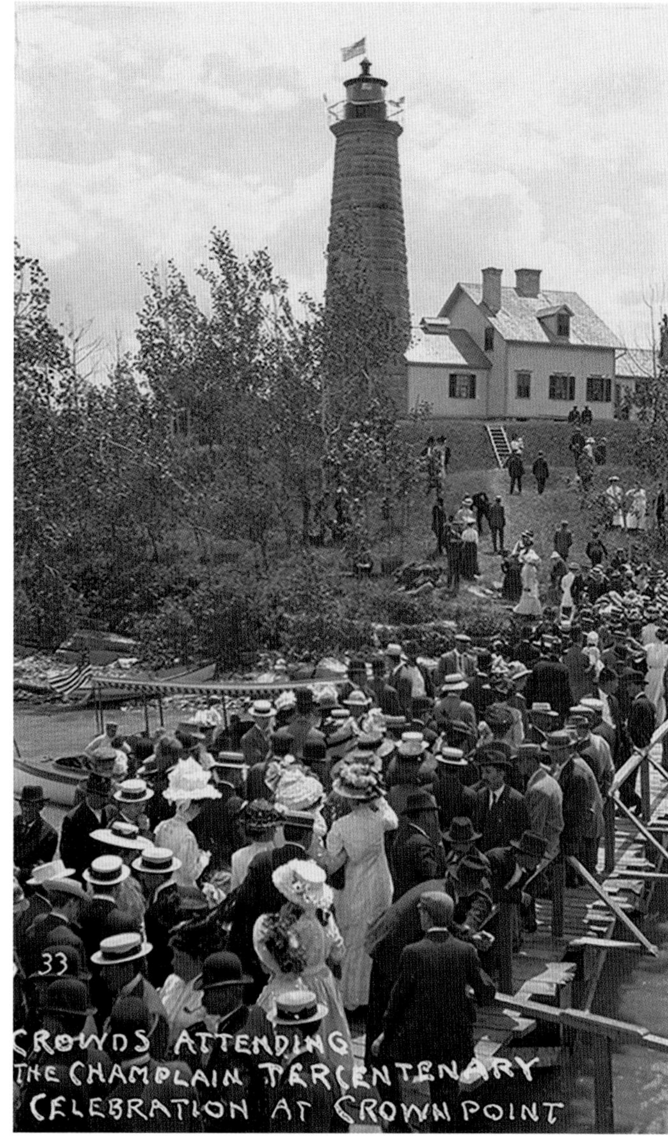

G7.10. *Crowds Attending the Champlain Tercentenary Celebration at Crown Point*

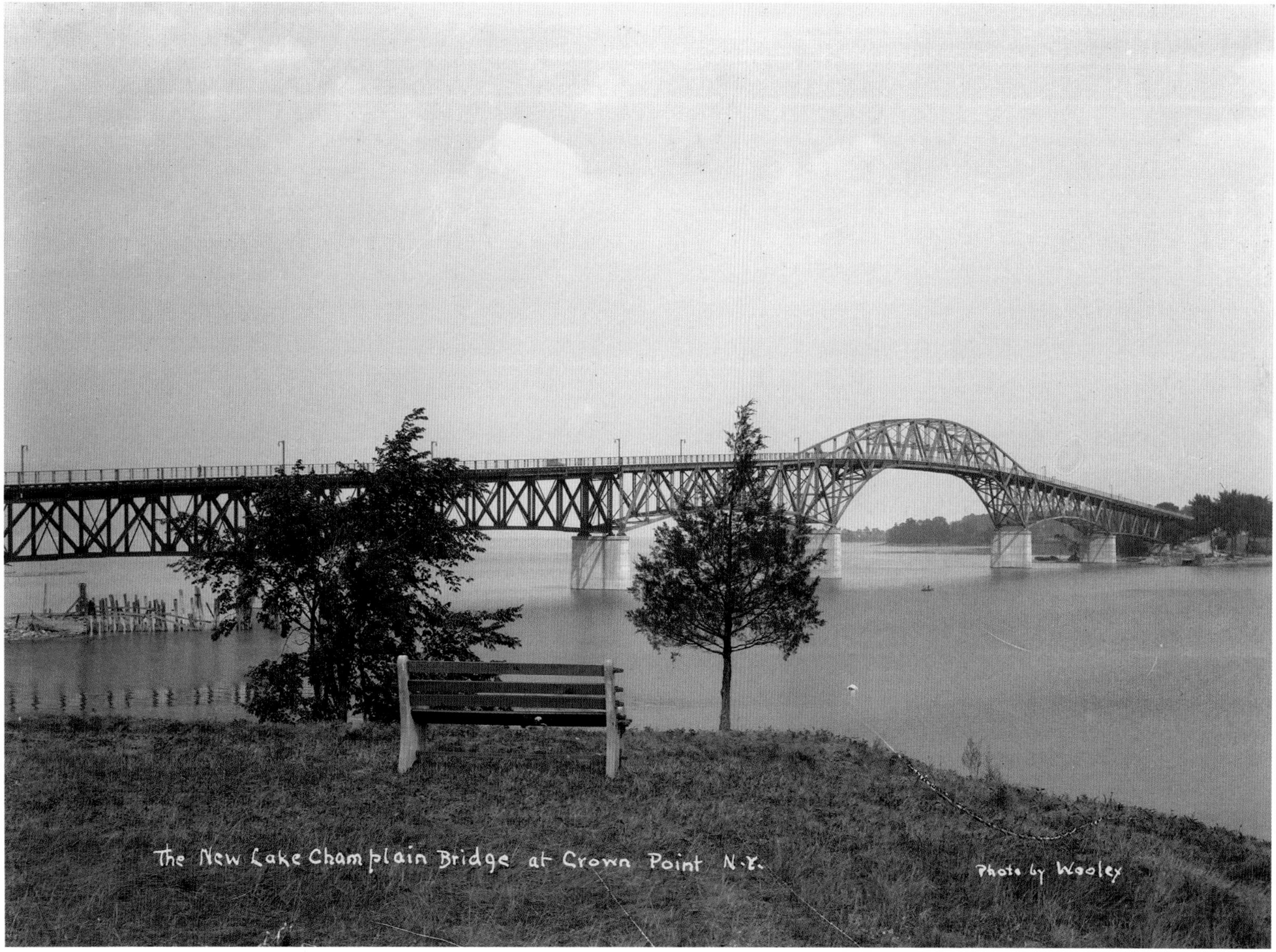

G7.11. *The New Lake Champlain Bridge at Crown Point N.Y.*

Glenburnie

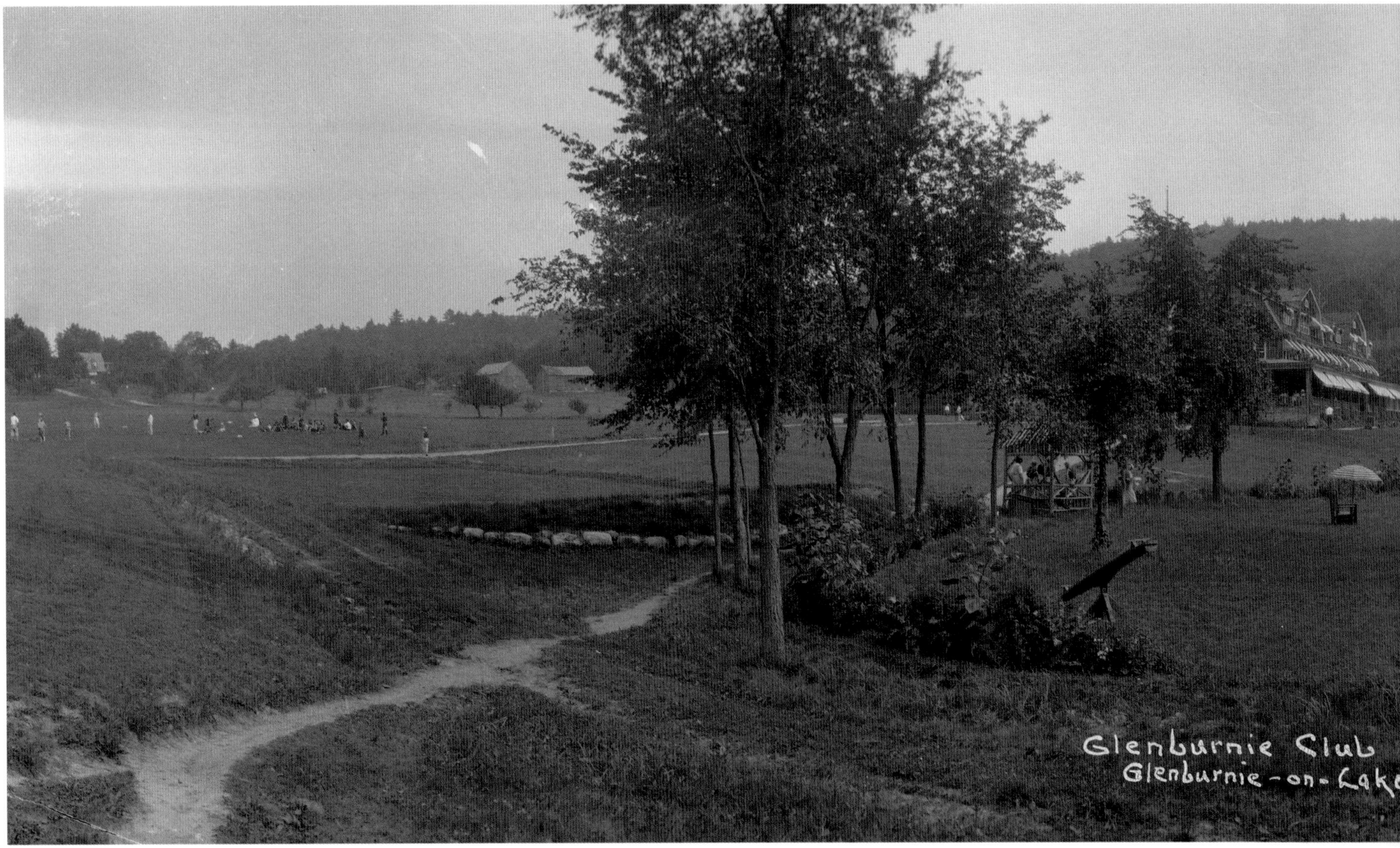

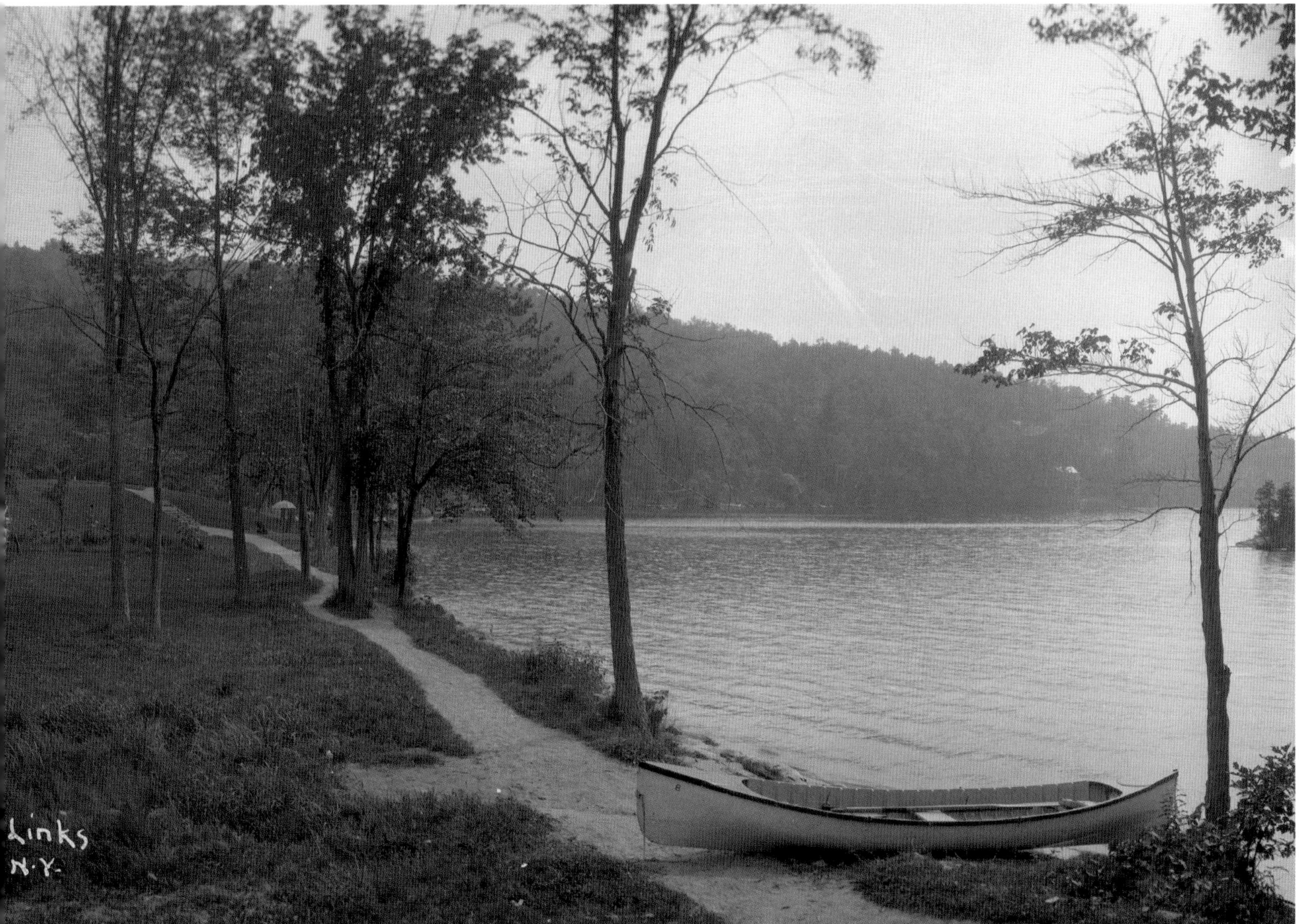

G8.1. *Glenburnie Club and Golf Links Glenburnie-on-Lake George N.Y.*

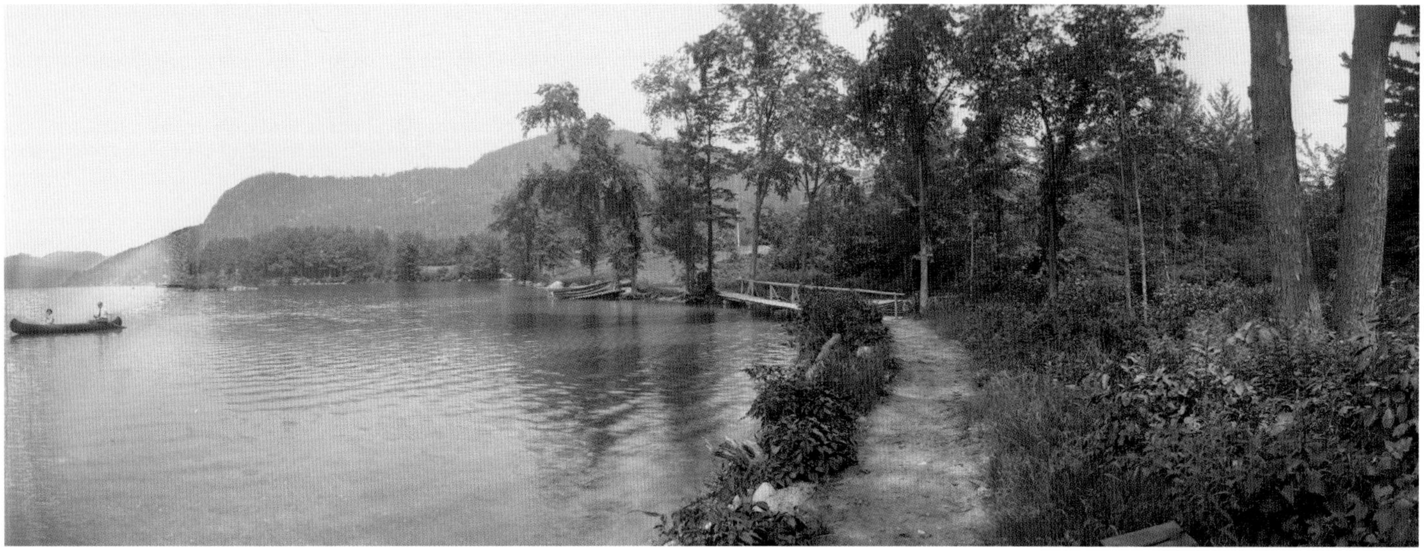

G8.2. *Glenburnie, Blair's Bay, Anthony's Nose, Lake George*

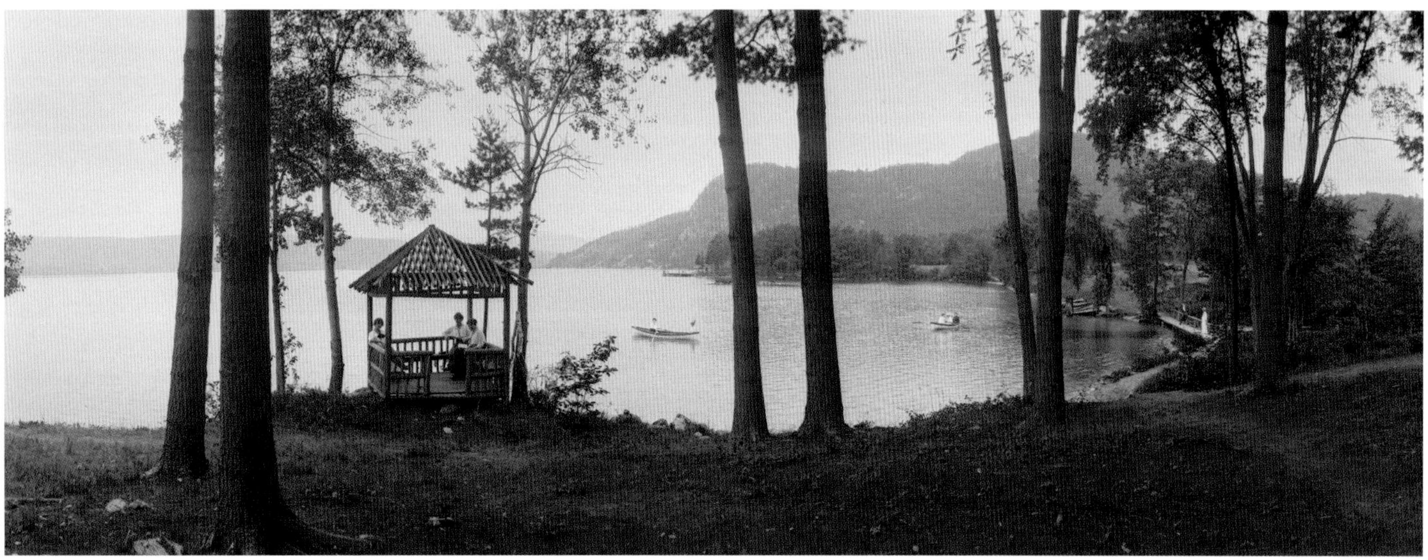

G8.3. *Blair's Bay, Glenburnie, Anthony's Nose in Background*

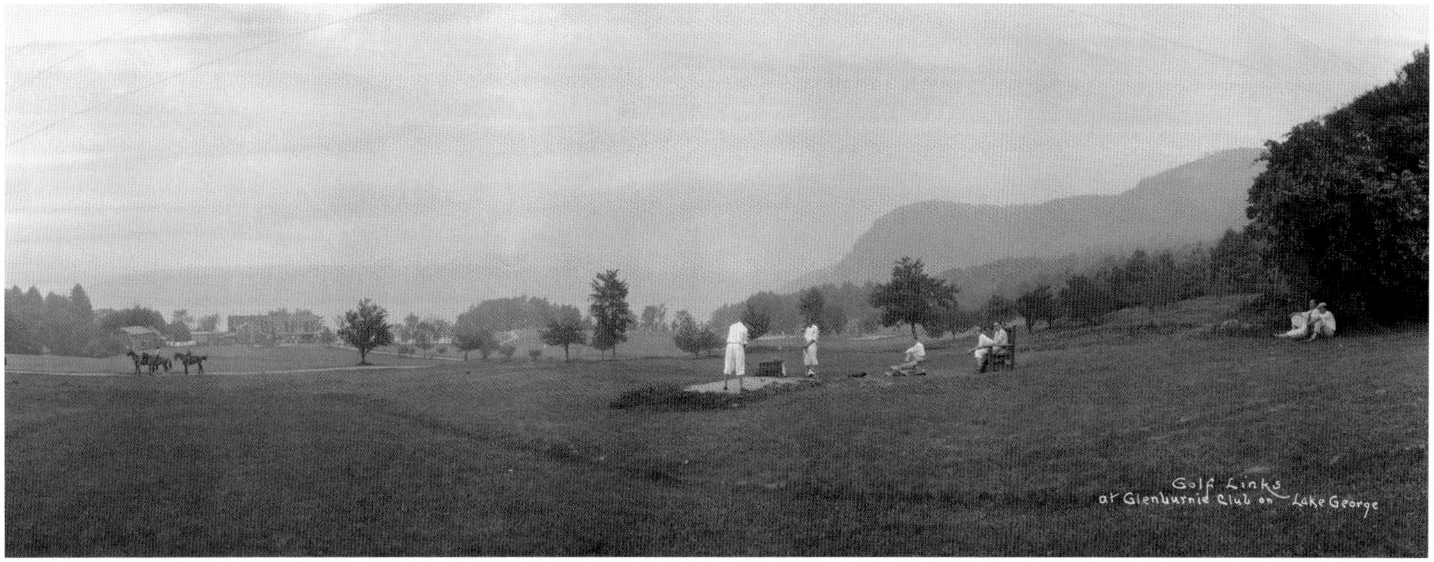

G8.4. *Beautiful Golf Links at Glenburnie Club on Lake George N.Y.*

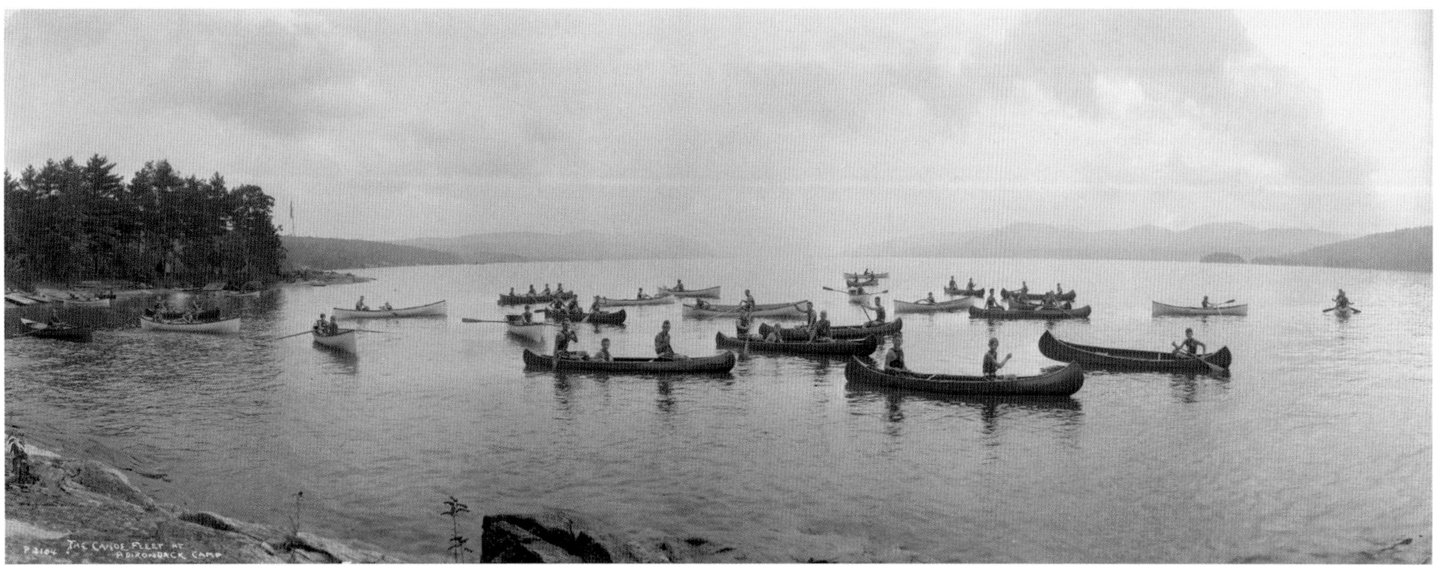

G8.5. *The Canoe Fleet at Adirondack Camp*

Lake George Eastern Shore ❧

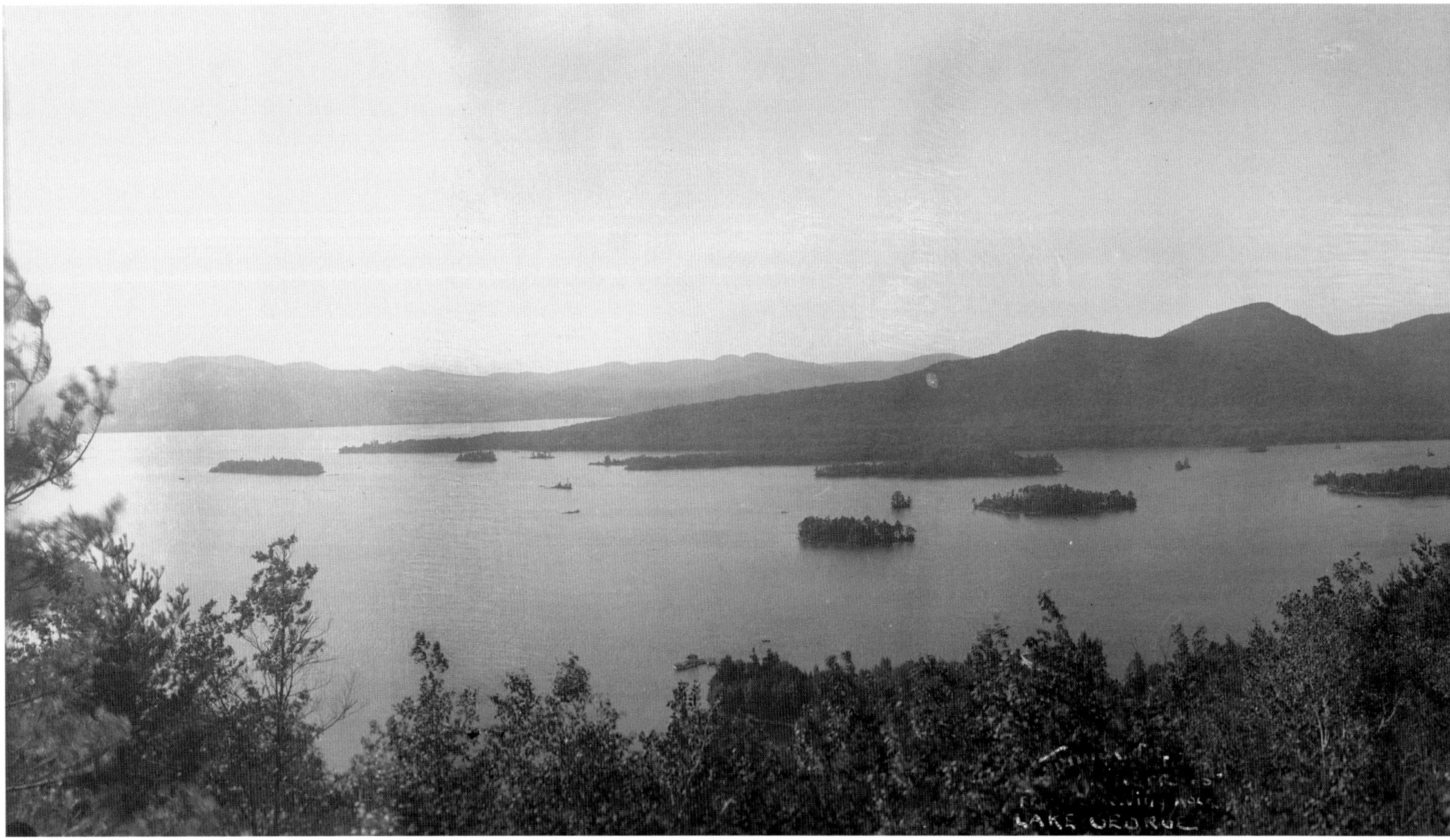

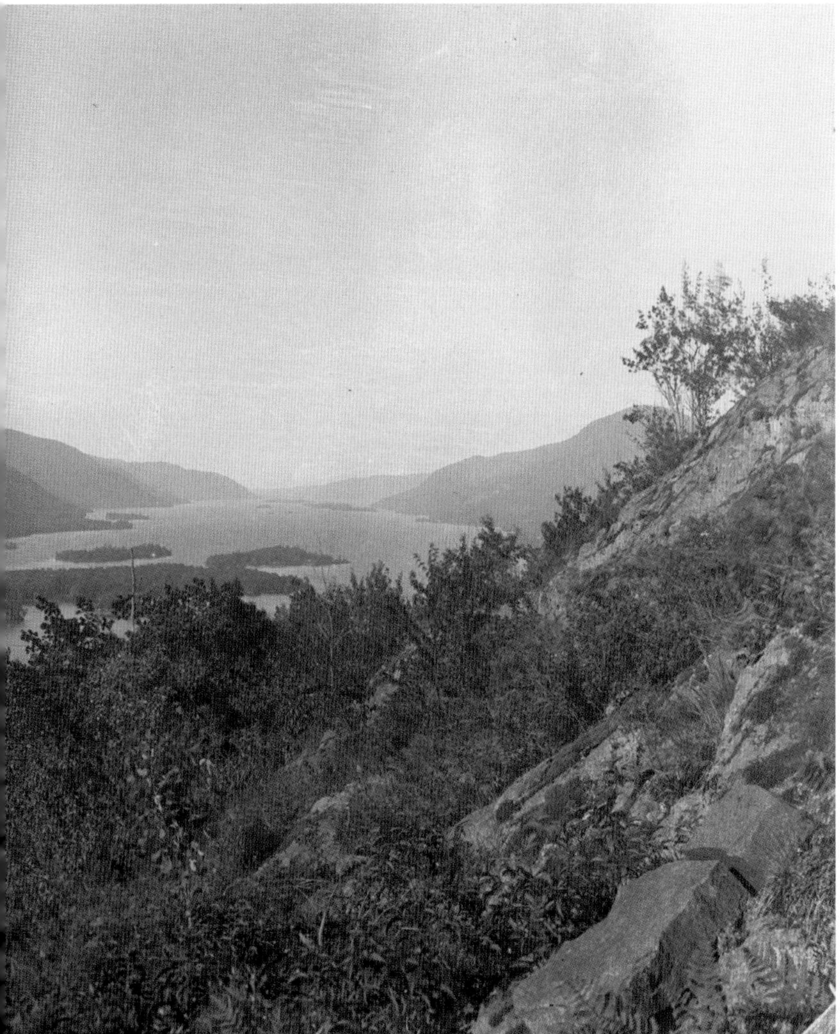

G9.1. *The Narrows and Hundred Islands Lake George N.Y.*

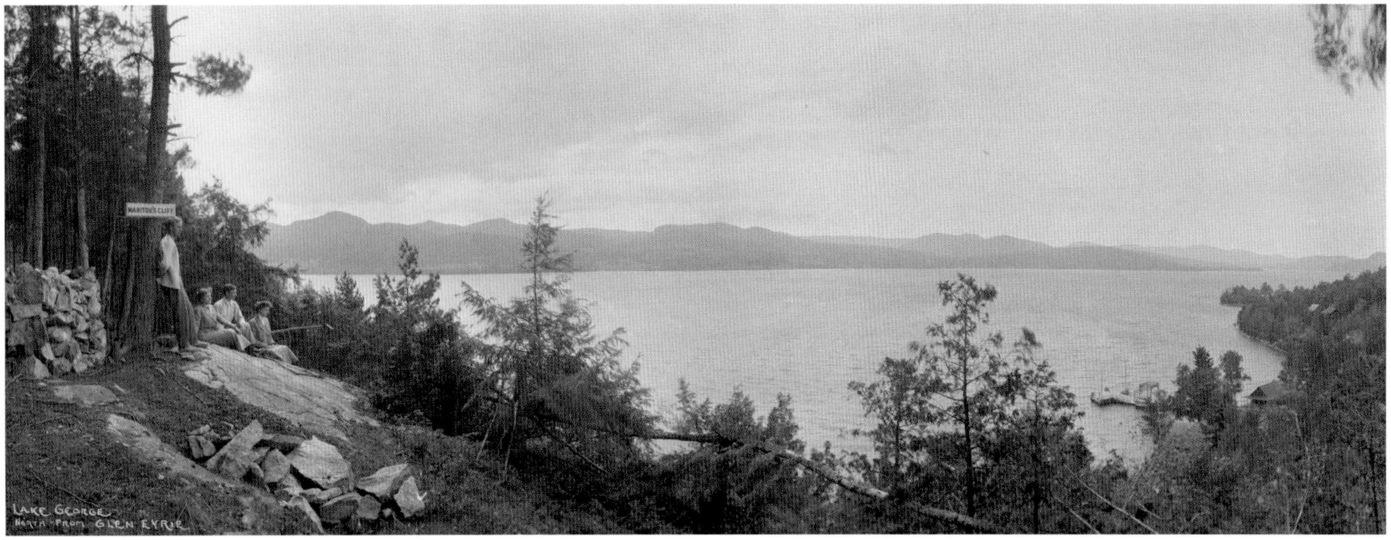

G9.2. *Lake George North from Glen Eyrie*

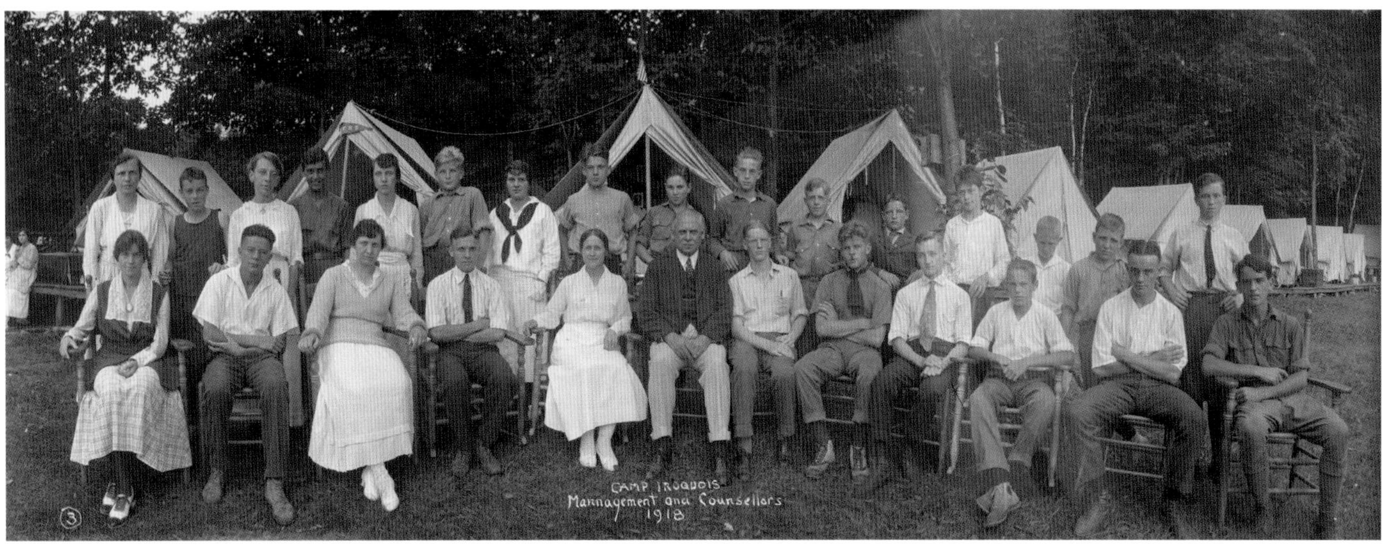

G9.3. *Camp Iroquois Management and Counsellors 1918*

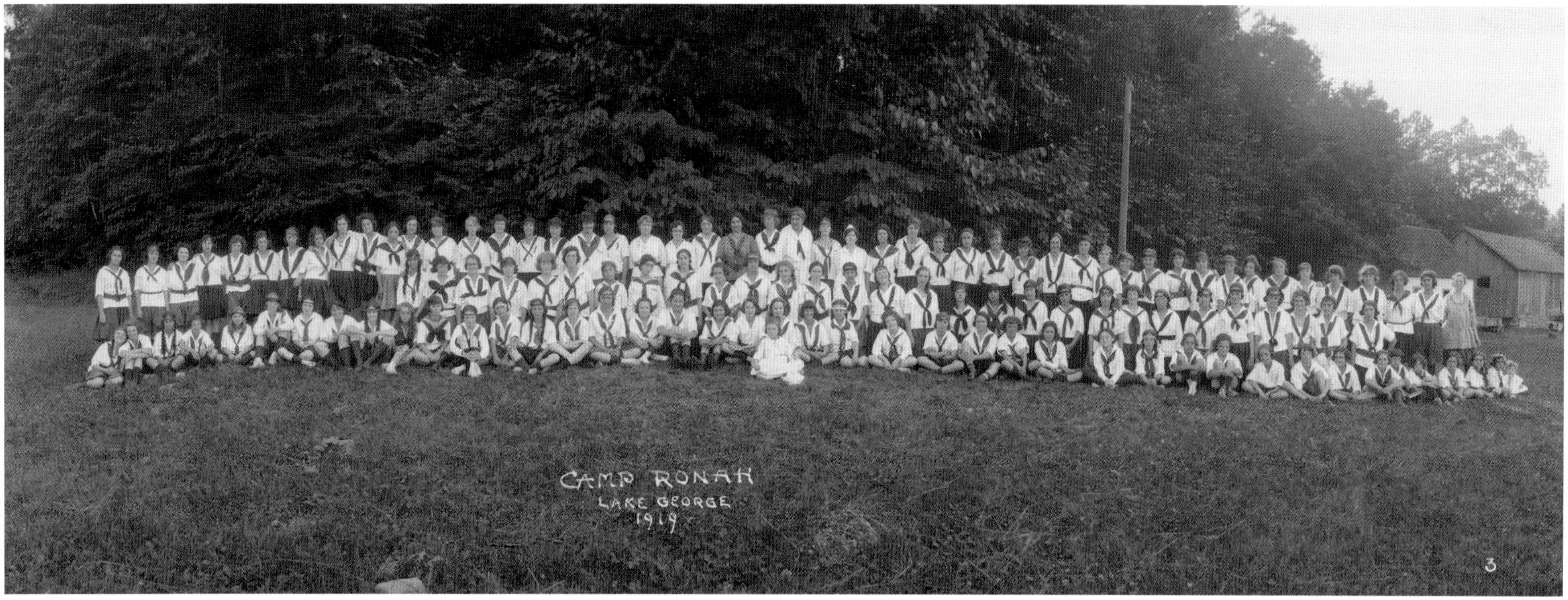

G9.4. *Camp Ronah Lake George 1919*

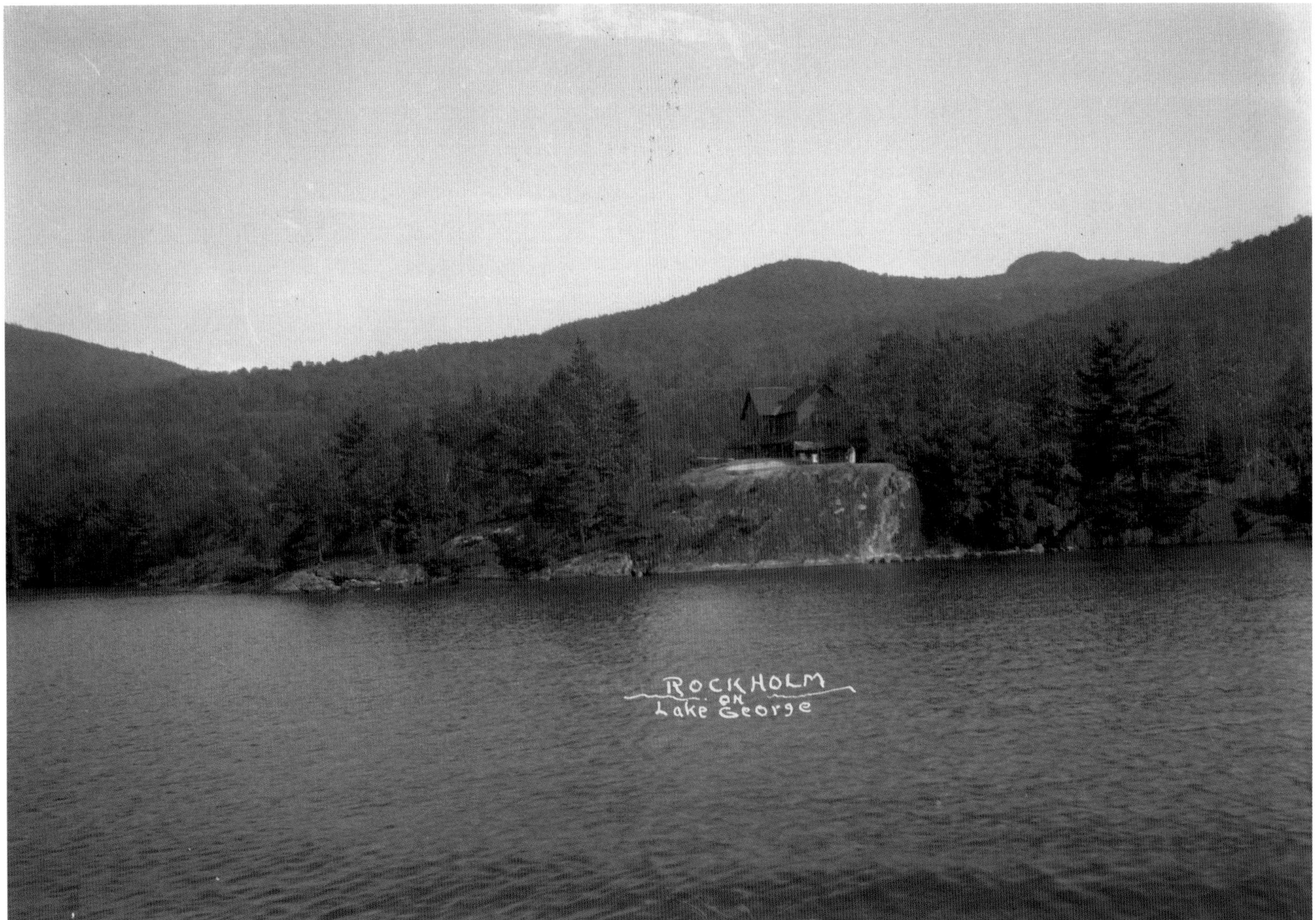

G9.5. *Rockholm on Lake George.* Currently property of DeMuro family.

Notes ❧ Bibliography ❧ Contributors ❧ Index

Notes

Foreword

1. Robert Bogdan and Todd Weseloh, *Real Photo Postcard Guide: The People's Photography* (Syracuse, NY: Syracuse University Press, 2006).

2. Robert Bogdan, *Exposing the Wilderness: Early-Twentieth-Century Adirondack Postcard Photographers* (Syracuse, NY: Syracuse University Press, 1999); David Freund, *Penny Publishing: Photographic Postcards of Central N.Y. 1905–1920* (Syracuse, NY: Light Works, 1983).

3. John Szarkowski, *Alfred Stieglitz at Lake George* (New York: Museum of Modern Art, 1995).

Seeing through the Lens: Photographing Adirondack Life and Landscape

1. John Szarkowski, *The Photographer's Eye* (New York: Museum of Modern Art, 1966), n.p.

2. Weston J. Naef, *Era of Exploration: The Rise of Landscape Photography in the American West, 1860–1885* (New York: Albright-Knox Art Gallery and The Metropolitan Museum of Art, 1975), 57. See pages 12–15 and 57–61 for further discussion of art and science and page 52 for discussion of Ruskin.

3. See Elizabeth Lindquist-Cock, *The Influence of Photography on American Landscape Painting, 1839–1880* (New York: Institute of Fine Arts, New York University, 1967).

4. See Beaumont Newhall, *The History of Photography from 1839 to the Present Day*, (New York: Museum of Modern Art and George Eastman House, 1964), 97–109, for a discussion of photograph as art.

5. See Naef, *Era of Exploration*, and Newhall, *The History of Photography*, for history of photography.

6. Philip Gefter, "A Royal Passion: Queen Victoria and Photography," *New York Times*, April 14, 2014, New York edition.

7. See Keith F. Davis, *The Origins of American Photography, 1839–1885: From Daguerreotype to Dry-Plate* (Kansas City: Nelson-Atkins Museum of Art, 2007).

8. Scott Stevens, "Fixed by a Sunbeam: Daguerreotype Portraiture in New York State," *Heritage: The Magazine of the New York State Historical Association*, March 1989.

9. Newhall, *The History of Photography*, 47–57.

10. For a description of Philosopher's Camp and its participants, see Alfred L. Donaldson, *A History of the Adirondacks* (Harrison, NY: Harbor Hill Books, 1977).

11. E. T. Cook and Alexander Wedderburn, eds., *The Works of John Ruskin*, 39 vols. (George Allen, 1903–12). This is the standard scholarly edition of Ruskin's work, known as the Library Edition, and sometimes called simply Cook and Wedderburn. For the influence of Ruskin's social and political thought, see Gill Cockram, *Ruskin and Social Reform: Ethics and Economics in the Victorian Age* (I. B. Tauris, 2007) and Stuart Eagles, *After Ruskin: The Social and Political Legacies of a Victorian Prophet, 1870–1920* (Oxford University Press, 2011). See Dinah Birch, ed., *Ruskin and the Dawn of the Modern* (Oxford University Press, 1999) for the influence of his art theories.

12. *Photographic Studies Part I. The Forest. Adirondac Woods* is in the library collection of Adirondack Experience: The Museum on Blue Mountain Lake.

13. For a discussion of Stillman's art and photography, see Linda S. Ferber, "'The Clearest Lens': William J. Stillman and American Landscape Painting," in *Poetic Localities: Photographs of William J. Stillman*, ed. Anne Ehrnenkranz (New York: Aperture in association with the International Center of Photography, 1988), 91–103.

14. Naef, *Era of Exploration*, 14.

15. See Adirondack Experience curatorial files on Adirondack photographers for Bierstadt.

16. Naef, *Era of Exploration*, 22–28.

17. See Estelle Jussim and Elizabeth Lindquist-Cook, *Landscape as Photograph* (New Haven and London: Yale University Press, 1985) for an excellent critical discussion of the philosophical interpretations and meanings of landscape photography.

18. Naef, *Era of Exploration*, 70–76.

19. Seneca Ray Stoddard, *Catalogue of Photographs of New York Scenery*, (Glens Falls: S. R. Stoddard, 1877), 13.

20. Virginia Burdick, "William Henry Jackson, 1843–1942, Pioneer Photographer, Artist, Traveler," *The Antiquarian* 9, no. 1 (Fall 1993), 21–25.

21. John Szarkowski, *Alfred Stieglitz at Lake George*, 9–30.

22. Alfred Stieglitz, *Amateur Phot.*, Sept. 19, 1923, 255, as quoted in Newhall.

23. Szarkowski, *Alfred Stieglitz at Lake George*, 348.

24. Erica D. Passantino, ed., *The Eye of Duncan Phillips*, (Washington, DC: The Phillips Collection, 1999), 378.

25. See Robert MacKay, *America by the Yard: Cirkut Camera Images from the Early Twentieth Century* (New York: W. W. Norton, 2006) for the history and technology of panoramic photography. See also Bill McBride, "Panoramic Cameras 1843–1994 Timeline" (www.panoramicphoto.com/timeline.htm).

26. See Newhall, *The History of Photography*, 89, and Davis, *The Origins of American Photography*, 267–68. See also Douglas Collins, *The Story of Kodak* (New York: Harry N. Abrams, 1990), 42–88, for a history of George Eastman and the Eastman Kodak Company.

27. See Robert Bogdan, *Exposing the Wilderness: Early-Twentieth-Century Adirondack Postcard Photographers* (Syracuse, NY: Syracuse University Press, 1999) for a definitive discussion.

28. See Bogdan, *Exposing the Wilderness*, chapter 5 for more information.

29. See Bogdan, chapter 3 for more information.

30. See Bogdan, chapter 2 for more information.

31. Peggy O'Brien, "J. Walton Pursell, Photographer 1877–1964," *Adirondack Life*, July 1984, 16–19.

32. Elizabeth Folwell, "Straight Shooter, Katherine Elizabeth McClellan was the North Country's First Camerawoman," *Adirondack Life*, July/August 1993, 43–47.

33. Bogdan, *Exposing the Wilderness*, 178.

34. John J. Duquette, "William Kollecker, Photo-historian of the North Country," *Adirondack Daily Enterprise*, December 5, 1992, 2; Bogdan, 128–33.

35. Beverly Reid, "Note on Lake Placid Photographers," *Lake Placid-North Elba Historical Society Newsletter*, December 2012, 1; 4.

36. Lohr McKinstry, "The Shooting Sexton Sisters," *Adirondack Life*, October 1997, 30–32.

37. A major repository of Adirondack regional photography is available at Adirondack Experience: The Museum on Blue Mountain Lake. The collection numbers over 70,000 images.

Jesse S. Wooley: American Photographer

1. 1875 New York State Census, Town of Wilton, County of Saratoga, p. 15. The census taker also recorded a sister, Hattie, aged nine months, and a live-in servant, twenty years old. The presence of a young woman helping with housework does not necessarily indicate wealth or any level of prosperity; it was common for young women to leave their families and board with a neighboring family before marriage.

2. Biographical information on Wooley is scant. The first attempt (other than obituaries) to put together the details of his life was undertaken by Bernhard C. Puckhaber and Annabelle H. MacMillin in a brief but useful article for *Grist Mill*, the occasional journal of the Brookside Museum of the Saratoga County Historical Society. Another source, tantalizing and cryptic, is an undated three-page typescript "Jesse Sumner Wooley (taken from his own personal diary)," in the Eugene Provenzo collection, 1978–94, Richter Library, University of Miami Special Collections (cited below as Provenzo typescript). Eugene Provenzo helped to create a website about Wooley's photographic work in Florida (http://www.library.miami.edu/specialcollections/collections/wooley/J_S_Wooley/j_s_wooley.html). I examined this website in 2012 but discovered that by October 2017 it had been taken down. I could not establish how he acquired this document, but evidence on the website suggests it was from contacts in Ballston Spa, perhaps from either Puckhaber or MacMillin, who mention the diary in a note following their article in *Grist Mill*. The diary itself has vanished. Unless indicated otherwise, the outline of Wooley's life presented here begins with and relies heavily on Bernhard C. Puckhaber and Annabelle H. MacMillin, "J. S. Wooley, Pioneer

Photographer," *Grist Mill* 12 (Winter 1978): n.p. The chapter on Wooley in Robert Bogdan, *Exposing the Wilderness: Early-Twentieth-Century Adirondack Postcard Photographers* (Syracuse, NY: Syracuse University Press, 1999), 166–98, depends largely on Puckhaber and MacMillin, with significant and useful additional research.

3. See Richard H. Gassan, *The Birth of American Tourism: New York, the Hudson Valley, and American Culture, 1790–1830* (Amherst: University of Massachusetts Press, 2008), 88.

4. Bogdan, *Exposing the Wilderness*, 169.

5. Ulysses Prentiss Hedrick, *History of Agriculture in the State of New York* (Albany: New York State Agricultural Society, 1933), 433–43; David Stradling, *The Nature of New York: An Environmental History of the Empire State* (Ithaca, NY: Cornell University Press, 2010), 64.

6. Puckhaber and MacMillin, "J. S. Wooley," n.p.; Provenzo typescript.

7. Puckhaber and MacMillin, "J. S. Wooley," n.p.

8. Gassan, *The Birth of American Tourism*, 10–11, 27.

9. Edward F. Grose, *Centennial History of the Village of Ballston Spa* (Ballston Spa, NY: Ballston Journal, 1907), 57–58.

10. Gassan, *The Birth of American Tourism*, 88.

11. Grose, *Centennial History*, 97–122.

12. Unless otherwise noted, all the information in this section is based on Puckhaber and MacMillin.

13. E.g., *Ballston Journal*, Jan 6, 1894. See also *Ballston Journal*, Feb. 4, 1893.

14. *Ballston Journal*, April 5, 1902: "J. S. Wooley left this morning for Hoosick Falls to make negatives of scenes of accidents on the B. & M. for the use of T. F. Hamilton, attorney for the line;" *Ballston Journal*, May 3, 1902: "J. S. Wooley went to Mechanicville today to take photographs of the scene of Saturday afternoon's trolley accident for the district attorney;" *Ballston Journal*, June 1, 1901: "J. S. Wooley went to Troy this morning to testify in a case connected with the Boston and Maine R. R."

15. This bicycle trip led to an album, "With Bike and Kodak: A Trip from Ballston Spa to Orange, Mass on a Wheel, 1898," now in a private collection. Given Wooley's obvious love of travel, it seems reasonable to assume that this was but one of many such expeditions.

16. The title for the collection of photographs from this trip is "A Fourth of July Bike Trip through the Adirondacks by Haley, Roods and Wooley." They follow immediately the final photograph from the Orange, Massachusetts, expedition, an image titled "Orange, Mass, End of Bike Trip."

17. The authors of the chapters in this book have devoted considerable effort to estimating the total volume of Wooley's work. The collection at Brookside houses thousands of images, mostly glass slides for his travel lectures, some of which are not Wooley's but were apparently purchased from commercial venders to supplement his travel photographs. Other thousands are known to be in private collections. Most of his studio work has disappeared. Wooley postcards frequently appear on online auction sites like eBay. Given Wooley's obvious fascination with cameras and the technology of photography, it seems safe to say that his lifetime of work constitutes tens of thousands of images.

18. Obituary in the *Saratogian*, April 29, 1943.

19. Collins, *The Story of Kodak*, 97–98. As a Kodak retail representative, Wooley would have access to cheaper paper, chemicals, and other supplies, in addition to discounted prices on photographic hardware.

20. Bogdan, *Exposing the Wilderness*, 175.

21. *Ballston Journal*, May 6, 1943.

22. Puckhaber and MacMillin, "J. S. Wooley," n.p.

23. Jeanne Winston Adler, *Early Days in the Adirondacks: The Photographs of Seneca Ray Stoddard* (New York: Harry N. Abrams, 1997), 31–32, 102.

24. Adler, *Early Days in the Adirondacks*, 60–61; Jeffrey L. Horrell, *Seneca Ray Stoddard: Transforming the Adirondack Wilderness in Text and Image* (Syracuse, NY: Syracuse University Press, 1999), 43.

25. Collins, *The Story of Kodak*, 37.

26. Adler, *Early Days in the Adirondacks*, 28; William Crowley, *Seneca Ray Stoddard: Adirondack Illustrator* (Blue Mountain Lake, NY: Adirondack Museum, 1982), 11.

27. Bogdan, *Exposing the Wilderness*, 173–75; Crowley, *Seneca Ray Stoddard*, 3; Horrell, *Seneca Ray Stoddard*, 46–47.

28. John Wilmerding, *American Light: The Luminist Movement, 1850–75* (Princeton, NJ: Princeton University Press, 1989), 143. See also Wilmerding's

foreword to Adler, *Early Days in the Adirondacks*, 21–23, and Horrell, *Seneca Ray Stoddard*, 110–11.

29. Adler, *Early Days in the Adirondacks*, 28; Horrell, *Seneca Ray Stoddard*, 47.

30. Puckhaber and MacMillin, "J. S. Wooley," n.p.

31. Jennifer Ley, "Jesse Sumner Wooley and the Chicago World's Fair, 1893," *Grist Mill* 26 (December 1997): 1–6.

32. Puckhaber and MacMillin, "J. S. Wooley," n.p.; Bogdan, *Exposing the Wilderness*, 173–77.

33. Puckhaber and MacMillin, n.p.

34. Steven Dotterer and Galen Cranz, "The Picture Postcard: Its Development and Role in American Urbanization," *Journal of American Culture* 5 (1986): 44. See also Bogdan and Weseloh, *Real Photo Postcard Guide*, 2–5.

35. Bogdan, *Exposing the Wilderness*, 3–7; Bogdan and Weseloh, 60.

36. Howard B. Leighton, "The Days of Magic Lanterns," *Nineteenth Century* 5 (Spring 1984): 44.

37. Leighton, "Magic Lanterns," 45; Robert P. Spindler, "Windows to the American Past: Lantern Slides as Historic Evidence," *Visual Resources* 5 (1988): 2.

38. Martha A. Sandweiss, *Print the Legend: Photography and the American West* (New Haven, CT: Yale University Press, 2002), 174.

39. The Brookside Museum of the Saratoga County Historical Society houses fourteen lantern slideshows attributed to Wooley. These are "A Summer through the Adirondacks," "Ice & Snow to Flowers and Fruit," "Moonlight on the Hudson," "New York City/Washington, DC," "New England," "Mexico," "Latin America," "Germany & Ireland," "Paris and More," "Italy and the Netherlands," "Chicago World's Fair," "Military Ships," "[Unitled]," and "Switzerland & Russia." There is no evidence that Wooley traveled to Latin America (with the exception, perhaps, of Cuba) or Russia.

40. Sandweiss, *Print the Legend*, 174.

41. Howard B. Leighton, "The Lantern Slide and Art History," *History of Photography* 8 (April–June 1984): 108.

42. Leighton, "Magic Lanterns," 47.

43. Quoted in Sandweiss, *Print the Legend*, 175.

44. "All on Board for a Trip to Washington," *Ballston Journal*, clipping in Robert Bogdan's files on Wooley, dated only "April 1893."

45. "J. S. Wooley," *Ballston Spa Journal—Souvenir Edition* (1899): 22.

46. Philip G. Terrie, *Contested Terrain: A New History of Nature and People in the Adirondacks*, 2nd ed. (Syracuse, NY: Syracuse University Press, 2008), 61–82.

47. Terrie, *Contested Terrain*, 83–105.

48. For example, in box 1 of Wooley's Adirondack glass slides at Brookside Museum is a colored slide of a famous Stoddard photograph of guides playing cards next to a campfire, reproduced in Jeanne Winston Adler, *Early Days in the Adirondacks*, 54.

49. See, among many others, James Buel, *The Magic City* (New York: Arno, 1974).

50. Brookside Museum, PB 114; PB 100.

51. Collins, *The Story of Kodak*, 78.

52. Provenzo typescript.

53. The details of Wooley's several trips to Florida and his incorporation of Florida photographs in illustrated lectures was the subject of an excellent website hosted by the Special Collections library at the University of Miami. It was researched and mounted by Eugene F. Provenzo, Jr., and William E. Brown. The account here of Wooley's chronology depends on the text supplied with this website, http://www.library.miami.edu/specialcollections/collections/wooley/index.html, accessed Feb. 4, 2013, cited hereafter as Provenzo and Brown.

54. Provenzo and Brown; Floyd Rinhart and Marion Rinhart, *Victorian Florida: America's Last Frontier* (Atlanta: Peachtree Publishers, 1986), 12.

55. This and all subsequent quotations from Wooley about Florida are from Provenzo and Brown.

56. Offensive as such racism is to the modern consciousness, it is important to note how casually and unashamedly Wooley trafficked in it. Clearly, none of this would have offended his ticket-buying customers. Illustrated slide travelogues constituted a means of cultural indoctrination, even in the hands of someone as unaware of what he was doing as Wooley apparently was. Images of African Americans, displayed condescendingly, often contrasted with images of white middle-class people, advanced a dominant narrative wherein the kind of people

who bought tickets for Wooley's lectures could comfort themselves with the idea that they—middle-class whites—were the real Americans and that anyone else was either exotic or marginal. As cultural historian Shawn Michelle Smith explains, such depictions illustrate the role of "photography in the constitution and transformation of middle-class identities in the nineteenth century" and "demonstrate the role that photography played in envisioning racially codified American identities at the turn of the century." What was at stake here was the very concept of who was truly American. In the minds of Wooley and his audience, whose own American identity appeared beyond question, the American-ness of African Americans was implicitly disputed. See Shawn Michelle Smith, *American Archives: Gender, Race, and Class in Visual Culture* (Princeton, NJ: Princeton University Press, 1999), 3–10.

57. The hotel was designed by architects John Carrere and Thomas Hastings of the distinguished New York firm of McKim, Mead, and White. Now the primary building of Flagler College, it is on the National Register of Historic Places. See http://www.nps.gov/nr/travel/geo-flor/26.htm, accessed Dec. 15, 2016.

58. On the cultural work of Chautauqua, see Charlotte Canning, *The Most American Thing in America: Circuit Chautauqua as Performance* (Iowa City: University of Iowa Press, 2005).

59. *Ballston Journal*, July 3, 1897.

60. Brookside Museum, PB 120 "JSW California Tour," books one and two, undated, but, if we judge from the itinerary, probably the 1897 western trip.

61. *Ballston Journal*, July 7, 1900.

62. Horrell, *Seneca Ray Stoddard*, 45.

63. Philip G. Terrie, *Forever Wild: A Cultural History of Wilderness in the Adirondacks* (Syracuse, NY: Syracuse University Press, 1994). 22.

64. On the response of various artists to the scenic wonders of Lake George, see Erin Coe and Gwendolyn Brooks, *Painting Lake George, 1774–1900* (Syracuse, NY: Syracuse University Press, 2005).

65. William Preston Gates, *Millionaires' Row on Lake George, NY* (Bolton Landing, NY: W. P. Gates Publishing, 2008), 5.

66. Bogdan, *Exposing the Wilderness*, 184. The importance of the automobile to Wooley's body of work cannot be overstated. To an energetic, often apparently restless photographer like Wooley the expansion of accessible country afforded by a family car, even at a time when roads were primitive, must have seemed providential. See, among others, Warren Belasco, *Americans on the Road: From Autocamp to Motel, 1910–1945* (Cambridge, MA: MIT Press, 1979).

67. The best history of the Silver Bay Association is an undated, unpublished manuscript by Bruce Ronda, "History of Silver Bay," in the Silver Bay Association archives. Correspondence with Dr. Ronda, who now teaches American studies at Colorado State University, reveals it to have been written in 1984. See also Thomas Winter, *Making Men, Making Class: The YMCA and Workingmen, 1877–1920* (Chicago: University of Chicago Press, 2002), and E. Clark Worman, *The Silver Bay Story* (Silver Bay, NY: Silver Bay Association, 1952).

68. Russell P. Bellico, *Sails and Steam in the Mountains: A Maritime and Military History of Lake George and Lake Champlain* (Fleischmanns, NY: Purple Mountain Press, 1992), 292.

69. Gates, *Millionaires' Row*, 52–53.

70. Bruce Ronda, "History of Silver Bay, unpublished ms., Silver Bay Association Archives, [1984]. See also *Silver Bay Blog*, Feb. 26, 2014, http://kihm4.wordpress.com/2014/02/26/the-helen-hughes-chapel/

71. Robert MacKay, *America by the Yard*, 8–9, 14–15.

72. Sandweiss, *Print the Legend*, 2.

J. S. Wooley: Technique and Aesthetics

1. Sources for this chapter are as follows: Bill McBride, "Al-Vista Panoramic Cameras," *The Photographist: Journal of the Western Photographic Collectors Association* 78–79 (Summer/Fall 1988): 1–30, and Robert MacKay, *America by the Yard: Cirkut Camera Images from the Early Twentieth Century* (New York: W. W. Norton, 2006). I have also relied on the catalogs of the Multiscope & Film Company of Burlington, Wisconsin (1903 and 1904), and an undated price list from the same company, "Catalog and Price List No. 15."

Bibliography

Adler, Jeanne Winston. *Early Days in the Adirondacks: The Photographs of Seneca Ray Stoddard*. New York: Harry N. Abrams, 1997.

Belasco, Warren. *Americans on the Road: From Autocamp to Motel, 1910–1945*. Cambridge, MA: MIT Press, 1979.

Bellico, Russell P. *Sails and Steam in the Mountains: A Maritime and Military History of Lake George and Lake Champlain*. Fleischmanns, NY: Purple Mountain Press, 1992.

Bogdan, Robert. *Exposing the Wilderness: Early-Twentieth-Century Adirondack Postcard Photographers*. Syracuse, NY: Syracuse University Press, 1999.

Bogdan, Robert and Todd Weseloh. *Real Photo Postcard Guide: The People's Photography*. Syracuse, NY: Syracuse University Press, 2006.

Buel, James. *The Magic City*. New York: Arno, 1974.

Burdick, Virginia. "William Henry Jackson, 1843–1942, Pioneer Photographer, Artist, Traveler." *The Antiquarian* 9, no. 1 (Fall 1993).

Canning, Charlotte. *The Most American Thing in America: Circuit Chautauqua as Performance*. Iowa City: University of Iowa Press, 2005.

Coe, Erin and Gwendolyn Brooks. *Painting Lake George, 1774–1900*. Syracuse, NY: Syracuse University Press, 2005.

Collins, Douglas. *The Story of Kodak*. New York: Harry N. Abrams, 1990.

Cook, E. T. and Alexander Wedderburn, eds., *The Works of John Ruskin*, 39 vols. George Allen, 1903–12.

Davis, Keith F. *The Origins of American Photography, 1839–1885: From Daguerreotype to Dry-Plate*. Kansas City: Nelson-Atkins Museum of Art, 2007.

Donaldson, Alfred L. *A History of the Adirondacks*. Harrison, NY: Harbor Hill Books, 1977.

Dotterer, Steven and Galen Cranz. "The Picture Postcard: Its Development and Role in American Urbanization." *Journal of American Culture* 5 (1986).

Duquette, John J. "William Kollecker, Photo-historian of the North Country." *Adirondack Daily Enterprise*, December 5, 1992.

Folwell, Elizabeth. "Straight Shooter, Katherine Elizabeth McClellan was the North Country's First Camerawoman." *Adirondack Life*, July/August 1993.

Freund, David. *Penny Publishing: Photographic Postcards of Central N.Y. 1905–1920*. Syracuse, NY: Light Works, 1983.

Gassan, Richard H. *The Birth of American Tourism: New York, the Hudson Valley, and American Culture, 1790–1830*. Amherst: University of Massachusetts Press, 2008.

Gates, William Preston. *Millionaires' Row on Lake George, NY*. Bolton Landing, NY: W. P. Gates Publishing, 2008.

Grose, Edward F. *Centennial History of the Village of Ballston Spa*. Ballston Spa, NY: Ballston Journal, 1907.

Hedrick, Ulysses Prentiss. *History of Agriculture in the State of New York*. Albany: New York State Agricultural Society, 1933.

Horrell, Jeffrey L. *Seneca Ray Stoddard: Transforming the Adirondack Wilderness in Text and Image*. Syracuse: Syracuse University Press, 1999.

Jussim, Estelle and Elizabeth Lindquist-Cook. *Landscape as Photograph*. New Haven and London: Yale University Press, 1985.

Leighton, Howard B. "The Days of Magic Lanterns." *Nineteenth Century* 5 (Spring 1984): 44–47.

———. "The Lantern Slide and Art History." *History of Photography* 8 (April–June 1984): 107–18.

Ley, Jennifer. "Jesse Sumner Wooley and the Chicago World's Fair, 1893." *Grist Mill* 26 (December 1997).

Lindquist-Cock, Elizabeth. *The Influence of Photography on American Landscape Painting, 1839–1880.* New York: Institute of Fine Arts, New York University, 1967.

MacKay, Robert. *America by the Yard: Cirkut Camera Images from the Early Twentieth Century.* New York: W. W. Norton, 2006.

McKinstry, Lohr. "The Shooting Sexton Sisters." *Adirondack Life*, October 1997.

Naef, Weston J. *Era of Exploration: The Rise of Landscape Photography in the American West, 1860–1885.* New York: Albright-Knox Art Gallery and The Metropolitan Museum of Art, 1975.

Newhall, Beaumont. *The History of Photography from 1839 to the Present Day.* New York: Museum of Modern Art and George Eastman House, 196.)

O'Brien, Peggy. "J. Walton Pursell, Photographer 1877–1964." *Adirondack Life*, July 1984.

Passantino, Erica D., ed. *The Eye of Duncan Phillips.* Washington, DC: The Phillips Collection, 1999.

Puckhaber, Bernhard C. and Annabelle H. MacMillin. "J. S. Wooley, Pioneer Photographer." *Grist Mill* 12 (Winter 1978): n.p.

Rinhart, Floyd and Marion Rinhart. *Victorian Florida: America's Last Frontier.* Atlanta: Peachtree Publishers, 1986.

Ronda, Bruce. "History of Silver Bay." Unpublished ms. Silver Bay Association Archives, [1984].

Sandweiss, Martha A. *Print the Legend: Photography and the American West.* New Haven: Yale University Press, 2002.

Smith, Shawn Michelle. *American Archives: Gender, Race, and Class in Visual Culture.* Princeton, NJ: Princeton University Press, 1999.

Spindler, Robert P. "Windows to the American Past: Lantern Slides as Historic Evidence." *Visual Resources* 5 (1988): 1–15.

Stevens, Scott. "Fixed by a Sunbeam: Daguerreotype Portraiture in New York State." *Heritage: The Magazine of the New York State Historical Association*, March 1989.

Stradling, David. *The Nature of New York: An Environmental History of the Empire State.* Ithaca, NY: Cornell University Press, 2010.

Szarkowski, John. *Alfred Stieglitz at Lake George.* New York: Museum of Modern Art, 1995.

———. *The Photographer's Eye.* New York: Museum of Modern Art, 1966.

Terrie, Philip G. *Contested Terrain: A New History of Nature and People in the Adirondacks*, 2nd ed. Syracuse, NY: Syracuse University Press, 2008.

———. *Forever Wild: A Cultural History of Wilderness in the Adirondacks.* Syracuse, NY: Syracuse University Press, 1994.

Wilmerding, John. *American Light: The Luminist Movement, 1850–75.* Princeton, NJ: Princeton University Press, 1989.

Winter, Thomas. *Making Men, Making Class: The YMCA and Workingmen, 1877–1920.* Chicago: University of Chicago Press, 2002.

Worman, E. Clark. *The Silver Bay Story.* Silver Bay, NY: Silver Bay Association, 1952.

Contributors

Robert Bogdan is Distinguished Professor of Social Science and Education, Emeritus, at Syracuse University. He is the author of several books, including *Adirondack Vernacular: The Photography of Henry M. Beach.*

Matt Finley is associate dean emeritus at Dutchess Community College and former vice president of the Lake George Association's Board of Directors. A native of Bolton, on Lake George, he is a musician who has played professionally for fifty-five years and has performed and recorded with many fine jazz musicians. He currently leads Rio JAZZ and splits his time between New York's Mid-Hudson Valley and Bolton on Lake George.

Philip Terrie is professor emeritus of American culture studies and environmental studies at Bowling Green State University. He is the author of several books, including *Contested Terrain: A New History of Nature and People in the Adirondacks* and *Seeing the Forest: Reviews, Musings, and Opinions from an Adirondack Historian.*

Richard Timberlake is a professional photographer who began his career in Columbus, Ohio. He owned his own finishing business until Fuji Film USA moved him to the East Coast, where he worked with Agfa-Gevaert, General Electric Non-Destructive Testing Division, and Fuji Film Medical Imaging. He now resides in Saratoga Springs, NY, where he combines his imagining talents with a career in real estate.

Caroline M. Welsh, director emerita of Adirondack Experience: The Museum on Blue Mountain Lake (formerly the Adirondack Museum), is an art and museum consultant. An art historian, she worked at the Adirondack Museum for more than two decades in a variety of capacities. Her scholarly activities include authoring books, articles, and lectures about Adirondack art and history, and she has curated numerous exhibits.

Jamie Young is adjunct professor at Syracuse University College of Visual and Performing Arts, and at PrattMWP College of Art and Design. He is the proprietor of Jamie Young Photography, a commercial photography business based in Syracuse, NY, and has a passionate interest in restoring and using antique panoramic and other film cameras for his personal photographic work.

Index

Italic page numbers denote illustrations.